PARENTING ANXIETY

PARENTING ANXIETY

Breaking the Cycle of Worry and
Raising Resilient Kids

MEREDITH ELKINS, PhD

CROWN
NEW YORK

CROWN

An imprint of the Crown Publishing Group
A division of Penguin Random House LLC
1745 Broadway
New York, NY 10019
crownpublishing.com
penguinrandomhouse.com

CROWN and the Crown colophon are registered trademarks of Penguin Random
House LLC.

Library of Congress Cataloging-in-Publication Data is on file with the publisher.

Hardcover ISBN 978-0-593-79881-2
Ebook ISBN 978-0-593-79882-9

Editors: Amanda Cook and Libby Burton
Editorial assistant: Katie Berry
Production editor: Natalie Blachere
Text designer: Andrea Lau
Production: Jessica Heim
Copy editor: Amy J. Schneider
Proofreaders: Judy Kiviat and Michael Fedison
Indexer: Elise Hess
Publicist: Tammy Blake
Marketer: Kimberly Lew

Manufactured in the United States of America

1st Printing

First Edition

The authorized representative in the EU for product safety and compliance is
Penguin Random House Ireland, Morrison Chambers, 32 Nassau Street,
Dublin D02 YH68, Ireland, https://eu-contact.penguin.ie.

For my beloved daughter

CONTENTS

AUTHOR'S NOTE

Every person has a unique story, and protecting their privacy is a sacred trust. This is why the narratives in this book are not direct retellings of real cases. Instead, they are carefully crafted composites, woven together from years of clinical practice and personal interactions. While no single character represents a single person, each story is an authentic representation of the themes, challenges, and triumphs of addressing anxiety in kids and in parents, allowing exploration of these important issues while ensuring the privacy of my patients, colleagues, and friends.

PARENTING ANXIETY

INTRODUCTION

"I totally blew it," Heather says, sitting across from me at a local coffee shop. Heather and I have been friends since our kids met in preschool several years ago. A warm, intelligent woman in her late thirties, Heather is a married lawyer with two young children, and we instantly clicked. Heather reached out to me about a week earlier, asking for advice. Her son, Liam, has been struggling with frequent meltdowns, dissolving into angry tears in the face of any minor disappointment.

"We have been working on him doing more things independently, and he was doing a math worksheet while I was making dinner," she says. "All of a sudden, he chucked his pencil and started crying that he couldn't do it. I know I am supposed to stay calm and validate his feelings—and I did, for a while—but then he whacked his elbow on the table when I tried to help him with the worksheet, and it was game over from there. He wouldn't accept any help and nothing I suggested was good enough. Eventually the mom rage just got to me, and I completely snapped. I shouted at him, basically telling him to figure it out himself, and stormed off. But then a second later I felt like the absolute worst parent in the world."

I tell her that sounds like quite an indictment.

She rolls her eyes, but good-naturedly, and sips her coffee. "Okay, well maybe not *the worst,* but definitely not my finest parenting moment."

We've all been there, I remind her.

"I get it, but I need to do way better. I don't know what your social media feeds look like, but everything I see on mine says that I need to be calm and confident when my kids are having a tough time so that *they* can learn to be calm and confident. I'm not supposed to lose it on this eight-year-old who is just frustrated with his homework. But there have been way more big feelings recently. Like he is refusing to go to soccer, which he loved last year, because he says he is nervous, but he can't say why. His teachers even reached out to say that he has been sort of crumpling when something is hard. They say he seems afraid to try anything new."

I acknowledge how hard that must have been to hear, and she nods.

"Yeah, it's been rough. I've been thinking about it a lot, because I was a bit like this at his age, a lot of anxiety and self-doubt. Well, I mean, nothing was ever diagnosed or treated, but I was definitely the kid who always was glued to my mom's side. And then we have a bunch of mood and anxiety stuff percolating in my family, and some substance abuse on my husband's side, so I feel like my kids are genetically loaded. So when either of my kids are having big feelings and can't seem to get it together, I guess I just worry about what it means down the road, and I kind of freak out."

This makes a lot of sense to me, and I tell her so. She's clearly worried, and mom rage is so often a reaction to our own anxiety.

"Totally. The meltdowns have become such a trigger for me. Like, is he doomed to have crippling emotional issues for the rest of his life? If this is how he is reacting now, what's it going to be like when we add adolescent hormones and social media into the mix? When I see the kids getting upset, I feel this intense pressure to help them out of it perfectly—like this is the moment where I need to be an A+ parent. I worry all the time about what will happen to them if I screw that up."

I agree that it's a ton of pressure for parents when we feel like it's all on us to prevent our kids from developing an anxiety disorder.

Heather nods. "My husband is constantly reminding me that the best way to help the kids to avoid being anxious is for *me* not to be anxious. But seriously—when Liam was born, I remember looking at my husband and saying, 'I don't think I will ever *not* be anxious again.'"

■ ■ ■

Heather's experience is deeply relatable. I find myself having these kinds of conversations more and more, both in my professional life as a clinical psychologist specializing in anxiety disorders and in my personal life as a mother and friend. As the co-director of a clinic treating child anxiety disorders at McLean Hospital, as faculty at Harvard Medical School, and in my private practice where I treat mothers with postpartum anxiety disorders and parenting stress, I consistently connect with parents who are worried about their children's anxiety. I see these concerns mirrored in my friends, colleagues, and acquaintances—individuals and families without formally diagnosed anxiety disorders, or who are not currently seeking treatment, but who still feel paralyzed by the responsibility of helping their child grow up to be emotionally healthy in today's tumultuous world.

It makes sense to be concerned. Let's start with some facts. We know that rates of pediatric anxiety disorders have been steadily rising for the past several decades, and that the COVID-19 pandemic was an absolute gut punch to kids and families that only accelerated this trend. Anxiety disorders are the most common type of mental health concern impacting children, adolescents, and adults. Each disorder is characterized by persistent, excessive fears or worries that significantly interfere in daily life. The source of the fear is what differentiates one disorder from another. We're talking here about separation anxiety disorder, social anxiety disorder, selective mutism, generalized anxiety disorder, specific phobia, panic disorder, agoraphobia, and unspecified anxiety disorders. These conditions are closely related to—but distinct from—obsessive-compulsive disorder (OCD) and post-traumatic stress disorder (PTSD).

While the identification of anxiety disorders has certainly improved, it is highly unlikely that the trends we are seeing are simply due to better diagnosis. A number of arguments have been proposed for *why* anxiety in young people is accelerating—including the dominance of smartphones, the decrease in childhood independence, pressures to achieve, and mental health experts themselves. It's tempting to pin it all on a single culprit. But the global increases in anxiety disorders are most likely due to a number of factors combining to create chaos. To this effect, in 2021, the U.S. Surgeon General declared youth mental health concerns a national public health emergency.

What makes this crisis even worse is the lack of providers available to treat the growing number of kids in need. It's even harder to find clinicians who are trained in evidence-based approaches—treatments that are backed by science. And even though we are getting better at identifying mental health concerns when we see them, the number of kids with unmet healthcare needs is increasing. Less than two-thirds of kids with anxiety disorders receive treatment, and it's even harder for kids from racial or ethnic minority populations, or for kids from low-income families, to access care. Kids are so often languishing on waitlists as symptoms worsen, if they can find a provider at all.

The cost of anxiety can be high. Kids with anxiety disorders can lose pace academically, and they often become isolated from their peers. Lots of these kids avoid important activities, like parties, family gatherings, extracurricular activities, and—most problematically—school. Child anxiety disorders create ripple effects throughout the family. Parents of kids with anxiety report higher levels of stress, depression, and—understandably—anxiety as well. Siblings can be affected, too, as parents shift the focus of their attention and resources to the struggling child. And speaking of costs, families with an anxious child can spend up to *twenty-one times* as much on illness-related expenses compared to families without these concerns.

We know that untreated anxiety disorders put kids at risk for developing depression, substance abuse, self-injury, and suicidal thoughts and behaviors. Alarmingly, longitudinal data from adolescents and young adults highlights that having an anxiety disorder increases the odds of suicidal thinking by nearly eight times, and suicide attempts by close to six times. In short, these conditions are increasingly common, but they are by no means easy to manage.

The Primal Scream

So, many kids are really struggling. And many of today's parents aren't doing that great either. Between 2016 and 2020, there was a significant decrease in the number of parents reporting that they were coping "very well" with the demands of childrearing. In fact, over two-thirds of parents believe that modern parenting is much harder than it was twenty years ago. Things have gotten so bleak that, in 2024, the U.S. Surgeon General released an unprecedented advisory on the decline in the well-being of parents. And new research reinforces this advisory, revealing a decline in maternal mental health that cuts across sociodemographic lines—an alarming indicator of a widespread and deepening crisis.

This is a huge deal. Today's parents are coping with the additive stressors of economic instability, unmanageable time demands, heightened health and safety concerns, the complexity of managing technology, growing loneliness and isolation, and cultural pressures to do everything the "right" way. This all takes a toll on a parent's physical and emotional health, and declining parent mental health is actually another risk factor for youth anxiety. Parents and kids are trapped on an anxiety-fueled roundabout, and it often seems like there's no exit.

If you're a parent who struggles with your own anxiety, or have kids who struggle with anxiety, you want to support your children in any way that you can. As in Heather's situation, you may be worried that the proverbial apple doesn't fall far from the tree, and you don't want your children to suffer as you have. You actively seek knowledge, skills, and support. Enter social media, which is inundated with "experts" with a range of credibility creating content in response to this demand. Delivered in short video or text snippets, these platforms serve up suggestions for managing specific child behaviors or promote a certain parenting style. But these hot takes cloaked in therapist-speak are often inflammatory rather than reassuring. They reduce complex ideas into a one-size-fits-all approach.

Ironically, the hyperavailability of this bite-sized content—which is often conflicting or inaccurate—can lead to even more confusion and anxiety. As one parent shared with me recently, "The advice out there makes me feel like not only do I *not* have the right answer, but I don't even have the right problem. My kid seems way more complicated. It makes me feel like my child must be a total disaster and that my instincts are completely wrong." Today's parents are truly stuck between a rock and a hard place: The problem of anxiety is overwhelming, and many of the available "solutions" are confusing at best and harmful at worst.

Within today's culture of Intensive Parenting, parents are under relentless pressure to always do *more* to promote their child's future well-being and success. Parents feel driven to deliver a wealth of positive emotional experiences and offset any negative ones to ensure their kids' "optimal" development. Parents are inundated with the message that "good" parenting means protecting kids from every possible danger, internal and external, meaning that it's no longer enough to keep your kids physically safe; you are warned of the perils that may arise when your kids experience painful emotions like anxiety, sadness, or shame—emotions that you are told must be processed and problem-solved by the attentive and well-informed parent. You are bombarded with the message that experiencing anxiety will cause kids toxic stress, cortisol spikes, attachment injuries, and any number of other alarming outcomes served up to you as parenting clickbait.

When each negative emotion is seen as a threat, it's easy for you to conclude that whatever *feels uncomfortable* must also *be unsafe*—that feeling bad means something is really wrong. This means that even the normal emotional experiences that you might expect your kid to encounter during childhood can now be seen as hazardous: the pain of social rejection, the disappointment of being cut from a team, anxiety about giving a presentation. These days, you may be convinced that if you don't do something in the moment to "fix" your child's anxiety, you are insensitive at best, neglectful at worst. This manifests in parents who email teachers to get their child out of a difficult assignment, who are in constant contact with their teen when apart from one another, or who walk on eggshells at home to avoid stressing out their kid. For many modern parents, knowing that your child is experiencing anxiety and not *doing anything about it* simply feels like bad parenting.

But something isn't adding up. If being uncomfortable is indeed unsafe, shouldn't child mental health be improving as parents, educators, clinicians, and policy makers work to decrease discomfort in kids? Instead, we are seeing the *opposite* effect as rates of pediatric anxiety and co-occurring conditions continue to soar.

Where did things go wrong?

In this book, I argue that many people misunderstand what anxiety really is, and modern parenting culture often adds to this confusion. Because of this, well-meaning parents may use parenting approaches that, sadly, often end up making child anxiety worse. Ironically, as you try *so hard* to protect your kids and to minimize their distress, you're creating the perfect environment for anxiety to thrive.

This happens for a very simple reason: When you avoid something that makes you uncomfortable, it becomes harder to face again in the future. Avoidance means that you lose out on the chance to learn that, even though it's uncomfortable, you can cope with feeling anxious. And, importantly, more often than not, your worst-case scenario doesn't come true. The basic truth here is that *avoidance fuels anxiety*. And it's just as true for kids as it is for adults.

I specialize in treating anxiety disorders using exposure therapy, the evidence-based psychological practice that encourages you to approach—rather than avoid—anxiety and discomfort. Clinicians who do this work know that being uncomfortable is *not* the same as being unsafe. We know that resilience comes from learning that you can cope with discomfort, and that the most effective way to overcome a fear is to face it. After gradual, intentional exposure therapy, kids who were afraid to sleep without their parents go away to camp. Teens who were afraid to drive go on road trips with friends. New parents who were afraid to leave their baby with a sitter can go on dates again. Discomfort is where the learning happens.

But we are in an era where each negative emotion is treated as a crisis, and where fears of screwing up the parent-child relationship mean that you may be working overtime to minimize any discomfort in your kid—and in yourself. And this is backfiring spectacularly.

The avoidance of discomfort itself is what can ultimately be unsafe. When kids haven't had the chance to practice coping with discomfort in normally stressful situations, they lose out on learning how to deal with their negative emotions and to practice tolerating distress. So they can end up flailing in truly *unsafe* ways when larger challenges come up. On the extreme end of this, we are seeing an increase in young people turning up in emergency departments for suicidality and self-injury, a trend that represents their most troubling attempts to cope with emotions that feel utterly unmanageable. The bottom line is that attempts to shield kids from discomfort can actually worsen anxiety, deepen dependence, and stifle resilience.

What You Can Do Differently

Getting to know anxiety better can help you dispel the myths about this normal, natural, and ultimately helpful emotion. It also can help you to shift your responses to anxiety-provoking situations so that you and your kids can become less avoidant and more resilient. And you are actually doing a ton to protect your kids—and yourself—through this process, as you cultivate the flexibility and fortitude that paves the way to flourishing.

And when you step back, you can begin to see the ways in which contemporary parenting expectations have likely shaped your view of anxiety. Once you recognize the waters in which you are swimming, you can choose to go against the tide. You can make decisions that are right for you, and for your family, rather than giving in to modern parenting orthodoxy when your gut tells you otherwise.

And finally, where anxiety is a clinical disorder, knowledge about how and why the best psychological treatments for anxiety disorders work is empowering. Going into treatment with this understanding gives you a leg up, allowing you to more rapidly and effectively fight against anxiety.

Even in the absence of clinical anxiety disorders—if you or your child has not been formally diagnosed—awareness of these approaches gives you an anti-anxiety framework to apply to your life, helping you to break cycles of anxiety and promote resilience. Simply put, knowledge is power, and theory can be your friend. I learned this lesson early on in my clinical training.

My first patient was Nora, a six-year-old girl with separation anxiety disorder, whom I co-treated during my first year of my clinical psychology PhD program alongside a senior doctoral student named Christina. In this model of psychotherapy training, the senior student takes the lead on the case, with the junior student observing and taking an increasingly active role over time. I had worked with kids before, but this was my first rodeo as a budding psychologist specializing in child anxiety. Nora and her family were suffering, and I really wanted to help.

I prepared meticulously for each session, wanting to ensure a foolproof, step-by-step approach to Nora's treatment, accounting for every "what if" scenario.

"You know that pit in your stomach that you get before a session?" I asked Christina. "Does that ever go away?"

"It gets better," she reassured me.

Then one session, the wheels came off the bus. The plan had been to help Nora practice separating from her mother, staying in one room with Christina and me for five minutes while her mother went into another. But anxiety is unpredictable, and it got loud that day; Nora was *not* having it, and her mother was paralyzed. So was I.

Christina swooped in. She got down on Nora's level, intervening confidently and flexibly, and made a new plan. She validated Nora's anxiety with warmth and also expressed confidence in her strength. She didn't tie herself in knots trying to make Nora feel better. She didn't say too much, honestly. She waited.

After a few agonizing minutes, Nora's sobs lessened a bit. Christina encouraged her and then gave her the choice of trying the original plan, or separating for four minutes instead. Four sounded better to Nora than five, and she practiced separating. The session ended on a high note.

Back in our shared office after the session, I asked Christina in awe, "How did you know what to do?"

She thought for a moment. "I go back to the theory," she said simply, and turned back to her laptop.

"What the hell does that mean?" I thought.

In parenting, as in psychotherapy, there is no way to prepare for all possible scenarios. The scripts we memorize, the strategies we research, the skills we practice—they can work beautifully under perfect conditions. But life is full of curveballs. How can we ever know how best to respond to the infinite possibilities? How do we know how to act in any given moment so that we make the issue at hand better, instead of worse?

I didn't understand it at the time, but Christina was spot-on. You need to know the theory from which you are operating, meaning that you need to understand *why* and *how* suggested approaches and strategies work. Understanding that avoidance fuels anxiety and that emotions are painful but not harmful gave Christina the clarity to support Nora with calm and confidence.

Basic knowledge of how your immune system works helps you make choices to minimize your risk of getting sick. In the same way, foundational knowledge about the emotion of anxiety—how and why it occurs, what is normal and what is cause for concern, factors that make it better or worse, and parent-child dynamics that either promote resilience or prolong disability—provides a framework through which you can respond to curveballs with confidence. This book will help you do just that.

A Road Map and a Tool Kit

In these pages, I offer a practical guide for parents who are seeking to understand and address anxiety in themselves and in their kids. My aim here is twofold: (1) to address how you can most effectively manage your own anxiety, particularly in the context of the parent-child relationship, and (2) to address how you can best support your anxious kids, whatever their age. This is a resource for you if your family is experiencing normal, minimally impairing anxiety. It is also a guide for you if you, or your child, are struggling with a diagnosed anxiety disorder.

The book is divided into three parts. In Part I, I demystify anxiety. We discuss what drives normal fear and anxiety in the body, consider what it looks like on the outside, and highlight the relationship between parent and child anxiety. We debunk the myth that experiencing anxiety is harmful. Instead, we learn how anxiety is either emboldened or defused, based on what you *do* in response to it. We learn the difference between normal anxiety and clinical anxiety disorders, explore how less acute anxiety can become an anxiety disorder over time, and create a framework for intervening before it does.

In Part II, I highlight the powerful impact of cultural beliefs and expectations around parenting in our responses to anxiety. Specifically, we consider the impact of Intensive Parenting—the dominant cultural framework that drives beliefs and expectations around "ideal" parenting practices in much of the world today. Some aspects of Intensive Parenting may be useful for coping with child anxiety. At the same time, parents need to be aware of how Intensive Parenting culture pushes them to respond in ways that actually worsen child anxiety by encouraging overinvolvement, overcontrol, and overpermissiveness. These behaviors and the beliefs that inform them have been culturally consecrated as "good parenting." Anxiety is hijacking this vulnerability, and kids and parents are suffering for it.

A central theme of this book is that the best approach to parenting anxiety within our childrearing culture is to find a middle-path approach, where warmth and empathy coexist with firm limits. How can you achieve this? By developing psychological flexibility, which is the ability to take mindful, values-guided action. It means becoming aware of your outer situation and internal experience, and then choosing to act in a way that is consistent with your values. Psychological flexibility is at work when you resist saying the thing that will really hurt your partner in the heat of an argument, pausing to take some deep breaths instead. It's operating when you allow your daughter to stay up and watch TV with you tonight, even though it's past her bedtime and she's got a test tomorrow, when your gut tells you that you both need this moment of connection. It's present whenever you choose to do the hard, scary thing that you have been avoiding, because you know that doing so will ultimately bring you closer to your goals. Psychologically flexible responses to normal and clinical anxiety are associated with a ton of benefits for kids and parents. Because of this, developing psychological flexibility is a key aim of many of today's leading psychological treatments. We introduce this concept as it relates to parenting in Part II of this book, and it is woven throughout the chapters that follow.

Part III of this book is a deep dive into the evidence-based treatments for clinical anxiety disorders, providing an accessible road map for addressing these disorders in kids and parents alike. We outline the most effective strategies delivered during cognitive behavioral treatment of anxiety disorders and discuss how psychological flexibility helps you apply these approaches to address what you and your family need most.

It's extraordinarily difficult to be a parent. I'm trying my best, and I know you are, too. My hope is that this book gives you practical insights and strategies to manage anxiety in a balanced, confident manner. I know that you are coming to this book with all the tools you need to succeed. Seriously, if you have ever successfully put sunscreen on a screaming toddler, you have what it takes to be successful here. So stay open, get curious, and keep going—you've got this.

PART I

CHAPTER 1

In My Feelings

"I don't want to feel this way anymore."

"I don't understand why I can't just control my irritability around the kids."

"I have no right to be depressed; on paper my life is great."

"My anxiety is completely out of control."

When I ask my adult patients what their goals are for therapy, the majority give me some variation of these answers. In other words, "I want more control over my painful feelings and thoughts." It's not far off from what my child patients want, and they lead with something similar, like "I just want my anxiety to go away."

Totally fair. Emotions can be super painful, and we kick ourselves when we can't seamlessly "snap out of it." We think that our inability to instantly pivot to positivity means that we are weak, broken, or deficient. We assume that something is wrong with us if we don't feel happy—or at least content—most of the time.

We come up with all sorts of strategies to "get better" at negative emotions. Our go-to strategies primarily involve trying to avoid, suppress, or replace painful feelings. We might start a gratitude journal. Or pour a glass of wine to take the edge off. We distract ourselves with social media. We shop online. We recommit to exercise. We focus on self-care. These are all normal and socially acceptable coping strategies, and even if we feel less proud of ourselves for using some than others, they are all recognizable parts of the modern coping tool kit.

The emotional well-being of your kids is arguably even more of a priority for you than your own contentment. It can be gut-wrenching to see your kids struggle with negative emotions like anxiety, sadness, frustration, or shame. And you'd probably attest to the truth of the phrase "A parent is only ever as happy as their unhappiest child."

But it no longer seems good enough for modern parents to merely empathize with kids who are going through a hard time. In a culture that sees parents as the architects of children's happiness and success, child distress seems like an indictment of your parenting. If my kid has a public meltdown, I'm less worried about her being judged for being a chaos goblin—she's just a kid, after all—and way more worried that I am being judged as a bad mom. I am my own worst critic when I fall into the trap of berating myself for my inability to control my kid's emotional experience. I wonder if you ever feel the same.

This burden of being your kid's emotional security guard creates tremendous pressure, breeding loneliness, anxiety, and self-doubt. So you may find yourself working equally hard—if not harder—to avoid, control, or "fix" your kids' negative emotions. Isn't that what good parents are supposed to do?

Wanting control over your emotions, and wanting to teach your children to control their own, makes so much sense; who wouldn't want to feel good all the time, or at the very least never feel bad? Human beings are innately motivated by the deceptively simple drive to avoid the bad, maximize the good. This impulse not only drives your emotional experiences but ensured the very survival of the human species.

And yet deep misunderstandings about emotions—and your ability to control them—can amplify your suffering. The beliefs that you have about which emotional experiences are okay and which are not are translated to your children. They deserve a true story.

You can start to change your relationship to your emotions when you understand where they come from, what they are trying to tell you, and the ways in which you actually have tremendous agency. Understanding the human emotional experience and what drives it is so empowering. It demystifies what we all, *by design,* experience, and provides a foundation for better, more resilient coping with anxiety.

Get the Good, Avoid the Bad

Modern humans are the product of millions of years of evolution. In a nutshell, any biologically based feature that helped our early ancestors survive long enough to make babies was selected for in the next generation—meaning that the qualities that allowed parents to survive would likely be passed along to their children, who in turn would be more likely to survive until childbearing age and pass along their genes.

Our early ancestors who had particularly nimble hands and fingers would have been better able to feed, shelter, defend, and clothe themselves because they were better at making and using tools. Modern humans now have the dexterity to write novels, build intricate watches, play the piano, and embroider tapestries. Emotions evolved in the same way: Any trait that helped our ancestors avoid threats or accumulate benefits was more likely to be passed along to the next generation.

Most scientists agree that there is a set of universal human emotions, experienced and recognized by all humans, regardless of culture, language, and ecology. These "basic" human emotions are communicated through universally recognizable facial cues, vocalizations, posture, and gestures. They remain with us because they helped us survive, or because they enabled social connections that were key to survival. Which indicates that being in psychological distress does not necessarily mean that you have a mental health disorder . . . it means you are human.

At their core, emotions are *signals:* They tell us something about our experience and about the world around us. Perceiving these signals sets off complex changes in our body that affect how we feel, think, and act.

Ultimately, the signal of any emotion triggers an *urge*—we feel strongly driven to *do something* in response to the emotion. Positive emotions like joy, love, or excitement signal to us that there is an opportunity to get something that we want, like, or need. We then have the urge to hold on to, or get more of, that thing.

In contrast, negative emotions like fear, anger, or sadness signal that there is a threat that will bring us something that we don't want, we don't like, or could hurt us—like fear, pain, or loss. We then have the urge to avoid or oppose that threat. In simplest terms, humans are governed by the basic urges to accumulate the good and avoid the bad.

This signal → urge pattern is so deeply ingrained that it can happen without your awareness. If you start to cross a street and a car comes barreling around the corner, you don't stop and think, "This seems dangerous, how can I avoid becoming a road pancake?" Your brain perceives a threat and signals the emotion of fear, which automatically kicks your body into high gear—immediately sending blood to the parts of your body that need the energy to respond, dilating your pupils to help you see better, and tensing your muscles so you can flee. You leap back onto the curb without even thinking about it. This is a profoundly beneficial system.

All of our emotions—even the ones that we think of as the negative or "bad" ones—have a purpose. When you consider three of your basic human emotions—sadness, anger, and fear—you can see why these unpleasant emotions were so crucial for our ancestors' survival. And you can better understand how they continue to impact you today.

Sadness

Normal sadness is not a crisis—it does not mean that you are weak or broken. Sadness signals that you have lost something that was good for your well-being. When you feel sad, you have the urge to isolate, to withdraw from family or friends. Alternatively, you may feel the urge to seek comfort from others. Sometimes it's a bit of both.

The urge to withdraw allows time and space for reflection and problem solving, both of which are often enhanced by being in a sad mood. Humans are not great at interpreting our environment. We are much more likely to take in information that confirms our opinions, versus information that challenges our beliefs, and we are susceptible to a range of biases, stereotypes, and other cognitive shortcuts. These errors are more common when we are in a good mood. But when we are in a mild negative mood, our memory is improved, our judgment is better, and we are less susceptible to biases. Sadness also helps shift our attention, leading to a more faithful interpretation of the world around us.

Another urge triggered by sadness is to seek comfort from others. Feelings that led humans to connect with each other helped foster the relationships and build the societies so necessary for survival. Sadness motivates the connections that humans need to thrive and helps information processing and problem solving so you are less likely to experience loss in the future. Sadness isn't a flaw or a failure—it's just a feeling that has really bad PR.

Anger

Anger signals a threat, urging you to get aggressive and defend yourself. In response to a threat, neurotransmitters called catecholamines prepare your body for a fight by increasing blood flow, heart rate, and muscle tension. Attention, alertness, and focus become sharpened. In times of danger, scarcity, and competition for scant resources, the highly reactive, quick-to-anger early humans were more likely to survive and reproduce. In contrast, early humans who didn't pick up on threats and who didn't have a strong urge to defend what was theirs were less likely to fight and win their resources back, meaning they had fewer resources to ensure survival and reproduction. Chill vibes died out a long time ago.

Fear

Like anger, fear is a response to a perceived threat. We will go into the emotion of fear, and its sister, anxiety, in greater depth in the next chapter. But in short, fear signals danger and prompts you to avoid its source. If you can't do that, you prepare to defend yourself. This is the fight-or-flight response that you learned about in biology class. It makes sense that if you were to perceive something dangerous, you would be motivated to avoid it now, and in the future.

Like sadness, anger, and the range of other negative human emotions, fear is natural and normal . . . and it feels *awful*. However, when you understand how this ancient system operates in your modern emotional life, you can start to create a road map for coping most effectively.

Ancient Circuitry, New Environment

Emotions, with their characteristic signals and urges, persisted across the ages because they enabled human survival in a threatening world. But things have changed. The closest thing to a dangerous animal in my neighborhood is the birdseed-stealing squirrel who drives the dog nuts.

Even in the absence of ever-present danger, ancient human emotions are at work in modern humans. When you perceive a threat, your primal emotional circuitry automatically kicks in. You feel physically anxious, experience anxious thoughts, and have the urge to flee, *regardless of whether the situation is actually dangerous*. Your teen's classmates aren't actually going to abandon him to die alone in the wilderness, but it can *feel to him like they might* when they start teasing him. The modern inputs are different, but the emotional experience is still universally recognizable—and, contrary to many conflicting messages, inescapable.

Controlling the Uncontrollable

The human brain is an incredible evolutionary advantage that propelled the development of civilization. Thanks to the neurological genius machines at the top of our necks, humans harnessed fire, pioneered agriculture, invented the wheel, mastered seafaring, and developed penicillin. Given how adept our species has been at mastering our environment, it's tempting to think we should be able to master our internal worlds as well.

But this is just wrong. You can't control whether you feel your feelings.

Don't believe me? Consider how useless it is to be told "Just relax," "Stop being so angry," or "Don't be sad." Has anyone *ever* responded to this type of chiding with "Thank goodness you said that. I'm all set now!" Or consider how impossible it would be for you to fall in love with someone random—to immediately feel genuine love for them—just because someone tells you that you should. You can't snap your fingers and just feel something, or *not* feel something, just because you believe you should, even if you want to.

Kind of strange, right? We send humans into outer space, but we can't prevent the wrath that arises when we step on Legos in bare feet. We developed lifesaving vaccines, but we can't halt the lurch of disgust that accompanies a glimpse of a cockroach. My kid can command, "Hey, Google, play Beyoncé," and Google *obeys her*, but I can't stop myself when I feel despondent about my aging body even when I know I *shouldn't* care.

In the absence of ever-present threats to our daily survival, many of us find that we work hardest to avoid the bad in our *internal, emotional world:* avoiding disappointment, anger, guilt, worries, envy, regret, hopelessness, anxiety. You barely consider freezing to death, but you work overtime to avoid feeling shame. Your kid is less concerned about being eaten, more concerned about whether she will feel crippled by anxiety during basketball tryouts. Parents aren't generally up at night worrying that their kids will survive past age five, but they *are* worried that their kids aren't happy.

This is not to belittle these concerns; painful emotions are painful. The point is that the conditions that drive modern emotional experiences are often radically different from those under which they evolved. It's great that your fight-or-flight response still kicks in if you think you might be mugged in a creepy parking garage, but it sure feels less adaptive when it goes off the night before final exams.

Modern humans work *so hard* to avoid or control negative emotions, in ourselves and in our kids, having gotten the message that we *should* have the psychological fortitude to do so. You may believe that if you can't control your emotions, it means you are fragile, inadequate, or broken. You may also believe that uncontrollable emotions are *unsafe*—and no wonder, when your social media feed is inundated with terms like "toxic stress," and you are now terrified of your own cortisol. This leads to a painful-feelings pile-on, where you feel anger, and then feel guilt over your anger; where you feel sad, and then feel shame because of your sadness; where you feel fear, and then become afraid of the fear itself. This pattern of feeling painful feelings, and then condemning yourself *because* you feel painful feelings, amplifies suffering enormously.

Long story short, you can't control whether you experience painful thoughts or feelings, any more than you can determine whether you experience pleasant ones. And as much as you'd like to, you can't change whether your kids experience painful thoughts or feelings. However, you are not powerless. Let's explore a tool that can help you find your footing.

Emotional Mapping

Meet Sophia, a fifteen-year-old girl who is about to start in a new school. Changing schools is hard, and it makes sense that Sophia would experience anxiety. But what does "experiencing anxiety" actually entail? Let's break it down a bit.

The signal of anxiety kicks off Sophia's innate, biologically based anxiety system, priming her to fight or to flee. And she experiences physical symptoms: the feeling of nausea and "butterflies" in her stomach, a headache, muscle tension and tightness all over her body.

If we could identify Sophia's thoughts, we would hear her fears playing out verbally: "The other kids won't like me. They will think I am ugly."

Sophia also behaves in certain ways to cope. She sets her alarm super early and spends extra time getting ready, obsessing over her appearance. She doesn't eat breakfast, both because she feels too nauseated to eat and also because she's running late after she changes her outfit six times.

Sophia's experience of *anxiety* is actually a combination of three components: her feelings, her thoughts, and her behaviors. Sophia's experience isn't unique: Any emotional experience, positive or negative, can be broken down into what you feel, what you think, and what you do. You can map out these factors using what cognitive behavioral therapists call the Three-Component Model of Emotions, or the TCM.

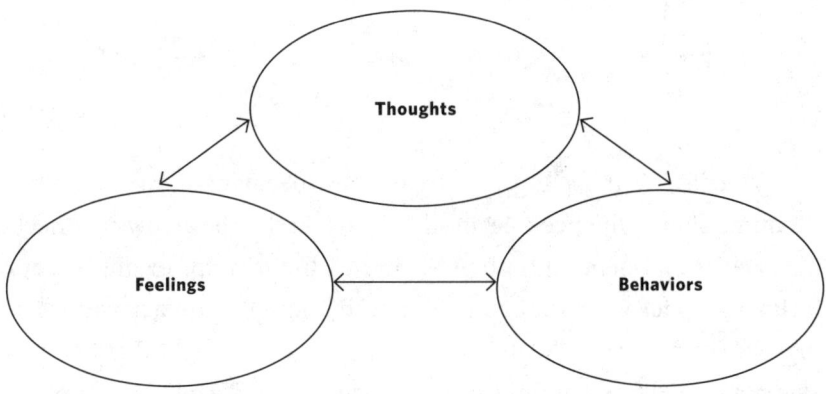

The Three-Component Model of Emotions (TCM)

The *Feelings* component involves the emotions that we feel, as well as the physical experiences that come with the emotion. For Sophia, we would name her anxiety and include the manifestations of the feeling: stomach distress, headache, and muscle tension. The *Thoughts* part of the TCM is made up of the words and pictures in our minds: what someone would hear if they could record our thoughts, and what someone would see if they could capture the pictures in our mind's eye—images, memories, or imagined events. Sophia's thoughts center on the belief that the other kids won't like her because they will think she is ugly and weird. Finally, the *Behaviors* component involves what we *do* as part of our emotional experience, any action that would be visible to the careful observer. Anyone watching Sophia this morning could see that she doesn't eat anything and spends extra time getting ready.

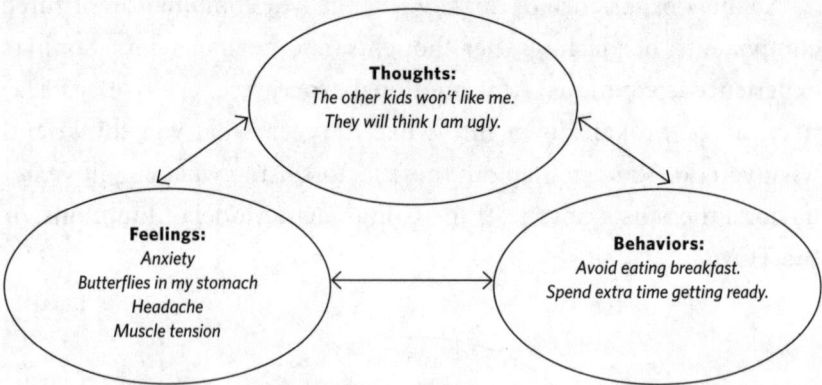

TCM: Sophia's First Day of School, Part 1

Critically, your feelings, thoughts, and behaviors don't exist in a vacuum: They influence one another. This is why the arrows connecting each component go both ways, indicating that, for example, your feelings impact your thoughts, and your thoughts impact your feelings. In Sophia's case, the more she fixates on the thought that her new classmates will find her ugly and reject her, the more intense her physical feelings of anxiety become—she feels more muscle tension and more stomach distress, and she generally feels her anxiety getting worse. As these thoughts and feelings snowball, they impact her behaviors. The more nauseated she feels, the less likely she is to eat breakfast. The more her fears of judgment grow, the more time she spends trying to perfect her look. And these behaviors have consequences that, ultimately, make her anxiety worse.

Having spent so much time getting ready, Sophia gets to school late. Walking into the building solo, she thinks, "People will think I am a weird loner." So she pretends to be engrossed in her phone, figuring that looking preoccupied is better than looking lonely. The impact of skipping breakfast is starting to kick in, and she feels shaky and weak, which increases her headache and stomachache. The worse she feels physically, the more her behaviors are impacted: She withdraws even more, choosing a desk in the back of each class and sinking into her screen.

Of course, being glued to her phone and hiding in the back of the classroom make her appear totally unapproachable to her peers, so no one approaches. As the day goes by and no one engages with her, she thinks, "I can't make any friends. I am a loser." These thoughts confirm her fears that she will be rejected by her new classmates, and now here comes sadness—signaling the loss of opportunities for new and needed friendships. When the solitary first day ends, she thinks, "I can't go back tomorrow." The stage is set for a major conflict with her parents when she refuses to go to school the next day. We can map out these additional feelings, thoughts, and behaviors in the model.

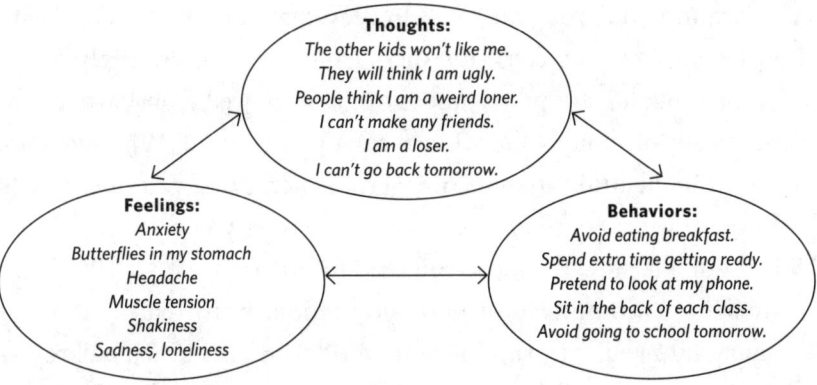

TCM: Sophia's First Day of School, Part 2

Painful emotions, like the anxiety that comes from starting a new school or the sadness of being ignored, can be overwhelming, and it's hard to even know where to begin to cope. The Three-Component Model guides you in mapping out and better understanding your emotional experiences. Having clarified the patterns between your feelings, thoughts, and behaviors, you have taken the first step toward coping more effectively.

The TCM is a useful tool and a great starting place. See the Resources section at the back of this book for blank Three-Component Models, which you can copy and start using when you—or your kid—have an emotional experience, whether positive or negative. Collecting this data to learn more about your experience can guide you to intervene most effectively, shifting your experience from being hopelessly overwhelmed toward coping resiliently.

Swimming with the Beach Ball

If all emotional experiences are made up of feelings, thoughts, and behaviors, which one is the most difficult to control? It's your feelings—I teed this one up pretty hard.

You can't control whether you feel your feelings—your emotional circuitry is hardwired in your body, honed over millions of years of evolution, and now consists of *automatic* responses to what you perceive around you. You can work to reevaluate and better cope with these feelings, but you can't stop them from happening entirely.

Your thoughts are pretty uncontrollable as well. You have a constant stream of thoughts flowing through your mind. When you are bothered by painful thoughts, images, or memories, you often try to suppress or get rid of them. Ironically, the harder you try to suppress a thought or a feeling, the more you tend to experience it.

Imagine swimming in a pool alongside a beach ball that keeps bumping into you, interrupting your good time. The beach ball represents all of your painful thoughts and feelings. To get rid of the beach ball, you try pushing it under the surface. Not only does this take a lot of effort, but the second you let go, it immediately pops back up. The same thing happens when you try to avoid your painful thoughts and feelings—they require a ton of energy to suppress, and you get whacked in the face by them whenever you let down your guard.

This may all seem disheartening, but there is good news. Your feelings and your thoughts can't actually hurt you. Anxiety, sadness, anger, shame, boredom, rage, guilt, hopelessness, irritability, fear—none of these emotional experiences *in and of themselves* are dangerous or destructive. Your emotions are painful—but not harmful.

This may be hard to believe, because we are constantly fed the message that happiness, success, and positivity are the norm. People aren't generally broadcasting their worst moments—Instagram is decidedly *not* reflecting the belligerent circus of our home lives. This has led us, as a culture, to pathologize negative emotions: to see normal negative thoughts and feelings as a defect that must be corrected, a sickness that must be cured, or a personal failure that you'd better get a handle on. So you work really hard to push the beach ball under the water and then berate yourself when you can't keep it submerged.

The answer isn't to lie down and let your negative thoughts and feelings consume you because they aren't controllable. You can learn evidence-based treatment strategies to help you cope with anxious feelings and thoughts, which we will cover in Chapter 8.

But critically, there *is* an element of our emotional experience over which you have agency: your behavior. You can choose what you do and how much power you let your painful thoughts and feelings have over you and your life in a given moment. This is just the lifeline you need to improve your emotional experience and to teach your kids to improve theirs.

Then Why Don't You Act Like It?

Many kids and parents absolutely balk when I share that feelings and thoughts are harmless. They look at me like I am Voldemort and usually say something along these lines:

"How can you say that anxiety isn't harmful? My ten-year-old is so terrified of vomiting that he stopped eating. He had to be hospitalized!" "I am so deeply depressed that I can barely get out of bed—how is that not harmful?" "My worries are so paralyzing that I can't focus on my schoolwork and my grades are suffering—and you're saying that's not harmful?"

For the record: *not Voldemort.*

It is not the feelings and thoughts themselves that lead to distress and disability; rather, it's how you behave *in response to those feelings and thoughts*. You stop eating because you are afraid to vomit. You no longer get out of bed because you are so depressed. You procrastinate on schoolwork and instead scroll on TikTok to cope with your intrusive thoughts.

You drink to dampen your grief. You pick a fight with your spouse because you are angry about work. You stop taking public transportation because you are afraid to catch an illness. You refuse school because you believe you can't handle the discomfort you feel when you are in the building.

How you *behave* in response to your feelings and thoughts is what makes or breaks your experience. You can act in ways that worsen your painful feelings and thoughts—driving you deeper into a painful emotional cycle—or you can act in ways that improve your painful feelings and thoughts, resetting the cycle. Acknowledging this truth—and modeling this truth for your kids—is incredibly powerful.

Behaviors are the key. You'll hear that a lot in this book.

Let's go back to Sophia, starting a new school. After she has mapped out her emotional experience, how can she use her behaviors to shift her painful feelings and thoughts, to take back control over her experience, and to interrupt the cycle of anxiety?

Let's start by acknowledging that Sophia comes by her anxiety naturally. It's an ancient, helpful emotion playing out in the context of radically different modern stressors. As Sophia perceives a threat to her well-being—being rejected by her peers—it makes sense that she can't *just stop* the feelings that accompany anxiety: nausea, muscle tension, headache. Nor can she *just turn off* the thought that "the other kids won't like me." And while it makes sense that she behaves as she does to cope—avoiding breakfast because she feels nauseated, taking extra time to get ready, hiding in the back of the class, pretending to be busy on her phone—these behaviors have consequences. They end up making her overall experience of anxiety worse.

Knowing all this, how could she change things?

By changing her behaviors.

If Sophia eats half a granola bar despite her nausea, she will feel less shaky, and her headache may improve. If she changes her outfit once instead of six times, she won't be late for school and have to walk in alone. If she puts down her phone, she might make eye contact with someone else, who smiles at her, and they then start up a conversation that gives her just enough of a boost to try again tomorrow.

Behaviors are what impact the feelings and thoughts: They alone can calm the emotional storm.

What Can You Take Home with You?

- The feelings and thoughts that you have in response to a painful emotion may be uncomfortable, but they are evidence that your body and mind are reacting the way they are supposed to. Normalizing this fact for yourself—and modeling it for your kids—is an important first step to reshaping your experience with anxiety.
- Start noticing when you experience negative emotions: fear, sadness, anger, shame. What feelings and thoughts come up for you when these signals are triggered? What behaviors do you notice yourself doing in response to your feelings and thoughts?
- Use the blank Three-Component Model pages in the Resources section at the back of this book to start mapping out your emotional experiences. What patterns emerge? Are there certain

physical sensations that you regularly feel, or specific thoughts that tend to come up? Importantly, are the behaviors that you notice helpful to you, or are they making things harder for you? How can you envision acting differently, in ways that might shift your anxious feelings and thoughts?

CHAPTER 2

We're *All* Freaking Out
(and That's Okay!)

"Is anxiety good or bad?"

I posed this question to a classroom full of kindergartners. I was speaking with them as part of their social-emotional learning curriculum. Best talk ever. "Bad!" they shouted.

"Good!" countered one kiddo.

"Why is it good?" I asked, pleased to get this one dissenting view.

"Because it keeps us safe."

"That's right!" I exclaimed. "Anxiety helps to keep us safe and helps tell us what's important. If we didn't have anxiety, would we look both ways before we crossed a street? Would we study for a test? Would grown-ups brush their teeth before they went on a date?"

Resounding responses of "No!" became louder and louder as they got the message.

"Right! We all need a little anxiety to stay safe and healthy. But anxiety can *feel* bad, right? What do you feel in your body when you are scared?"

"Your heart goes fast." "You get butterflies in your belly." "You feel all wobbly." "You cry." "My dog throws up when he is scared. He's on medicine."

I hope that this generation of kids learns this lesson early, and often: Experiencing anxiety does not mean that you "have anxiety." Well, it does; we all do. But feeling anxious and having an anxiety disorder are very different things. I'm all for destigmatizing mental health issues, but we pathologize normal emotions when we treat them as a crisis. When we give emotions too much attention, kids learn that their feelings are the most important thing to focus on in tough moments. But feelings are not facts. And critically, when we catastrophize normal anxiety, we risk accidentally setting the stage for it to become an anxiety disorder.

But anxiety *feels* like a crisis, so how do you not treat it that way? Particularly when it's your kid who is suffering and you feel driven to intervene?

First and foremost, by learning about it. When you understand *why* anxiety feels like it does, and what's going on in your body and in your mind when your anxiety alarm goes off, it makes the experience of anxiety so much less scary. So, in this chapter, we are going to focus on fear and its sister emotion, anxiety. It's why we're all here, right?

Once you acknowledge that your emotions are normal, valid, and ultimately harmless, you stop trying to eliminate them and learn more helpful ways of coping.

Wired for Survival

Imagine you are an early human out foraging and you encounter an ancient predator, like a saber-toothed tiger. If you are an early human without much of a fear response, maybe you think, "Oooo, kitty!" and move in for a closer look. What happens? You get smoked—you do not reproduce and pass on your curious genes.

In contrast, our more cautious early human ancestor who saw the saber-toothed tiger and whose fear response kicked in, causing them to bolt, lived to make babies with the same response. Those anxious babies had anxious babies who had anxious babies, resulting in the modern human species who come equipped with an inborn alarm system. While some alarm systems are more sensitive than others— which may make some folks more vulnerable to anxiety disorders— thanks to evolution, it's an alarm system that we all have.

I once lived in a tiny apartment in Boston with a smoke detector that went off every time the steam from the shower escaped. If I didn't make sure to seal the bathroom door, the alarm would go off in the middle of my shower, prompting a wet, flustered, and objectively absurd attempt by me to fan the steam away from the sensor.

I think about this alarm all the time when I talk about anxiety. As obnoxious as it is for a smoke detector to go off when there is no fire, on the whole, wouldn't you rather have a false alarm that is triggered when there is no threat, as opposed to one that only goes off in the middle of an inferno?

This applies to our fear response as well: It was far more adaptive for our species to have "false alarms" when there wasn't any real danger than to experience the fight-or-flight response only when we were nose-to-nose with a saber-toothed tiger. Evolutionary psychiatrist Randolph Nesse described this principle wonderfully when he explained, "If a successful panic flight costs 200 calories but being clawed by a tiger costs the equivalent of, say, 20,000 calories, then it will be worthwhile to flee in panic whenever the probability of a tiger being present is greater than 1%. This means that the normal system will experience 99 false alarms for every time a tiger is actually present."

Human survival was ensured by the fact that freaking out in response to false alarms was the norm rather than the exception. What this means for you and your kids now, in the modern world, is that you have a very sensitive alarm system operating in circumstances where you generally aren't facing daily life-threatening challenges. Instead, this alarm is going to go off when you fear you might be ostracized by your friends, when you are afraid that you will bomb a job interview, and when you worry that you aren't parenting the "right" way. We are all freaking out, all the time, naturally and by design, because it made sense for our early ancestors to be anxious *just in case* there was an actual threat.

The Anatomy of the "Nope" Reflex

We tend to use the words "fear" and "anxiety" interchangeably, but they refer to two distinct, though related, experiences. Fear shows up in response to an *immediate* threat. Anxiety arises in *anticipation* of a threat. Fear is the emotion you feel when you encounter a bear in the woods. Anxiety is the emotion you feel when you are worried that you *might* encounter a bear in the woods. If fear and anxiety were signals on a traffic light, fear would be the red light and anxiety would be the yellow light. Fear immediately launches your body into fight-or-flight mode.

What goes on in your body when you feel fear? Your heart pounds like crazy; you feel like you can't breathe. You get hot and sweaty; you may feel shaky and dizzy. Your hands and feet may feel clammy and cold. Your muscles clench. Your stomach is a mess. You can't focus on anything else.

This feels awful, by design. If you can nerd out on the science with me, I promise it will be worth it. So many kids and parents find that simply understanding why their body does what it does helps them feel less scared when it happens. It's not a cure-all, but it's a really good start.

Think back to our early ancestor, nose-to-nose with a saber-toothed tiger. What needs to happen, physically, to keep her alive? She needs most of her energy to go to the muscles in her arms and legs so that she can either run or fight. Massively simplifying complex processes here, your body's energy comes from oxygen, which goes from your lungs to your bloodstream and is then shuttled around your body to fuel your cells. When you need this all to happen pronto, you need to breathe faster to increase your oxygen supply, and your blood flow needs to accelerate to get oxygen to the areas that need it most. All of the symptoms that you experience when you feel fear or anxiety are the result of this process. It's uncomfortable but not harmful.

When you perceive a threat, your heart rate automatically goes up, increasing the flow of oxygenated blood to your large muscles. The highways of your blood flow—arteries, veins, and capillaries—expand, and as blood pulses through these expanded throughways, you feel hot. You start sweating. You get flushed as expanding capillaries draw blood closer to the surface of your skin. As blood moves toward the muscle groups that need energy, it also moves away from the areas that need it less, and this shift can cause trembling, shakiness, or the sensation of "cold feet" and clammy hands.

Your breathing patterns also change automatically when you perceive a threat. Sometimes these shifts are really subtle. Other times you clearly pick up on them: You hyperventilate, you can't catch your breath, or you have the sensation of choking. These changes alter the ratio of oxygen to carbon dioxide in your body—not in a dangerous way, but in a way that can make you feel dizzy or lightheaded, see spots, or have a headache.

As your heart rate and breathing change, your muscles become tense, priming you for action. This muscle tension can stick around for a while, because if you just survived a threat, it's helpful for your muscles to be ready in case the threat comes back around. This is why people can feel ongoing muscle tension for several hours after a panic attack, or why you may feel that you are "tense all the time" if you are in a season of high stress. You may also have trouble falling or staying asleep because your body is keeping you in a sustained, low level of alertness, tension, and readiness for action. Super adaptive. Not fun at all.

As part of this process, energy is diverted away from systems that are less essential to survival in the moment. So your digestive system slows down as your heart rate and breathing speed up. You feel nauseated, your tummy roils, and you may vomit or have diarrhea. These . . . unpleasant . . . side effects are helpful if you are in life-threatening danger, because you don't want your body wasting precious energy on digesting lunch when you need energy to fight or flee. When you aren't in serious danger but are still anxious, you can still feel stomach distress. So frequent bathroom trips or food aversions are just part of your fight-or-flight response. Again, this is unpleasant, even embarrassing, but not dangerous.

There are also cognitive changes that happen in response to fear and anxiety. Just as a good watchdog alerts you to potential danger, anxiety automatically shifts your attention so that you are laser-focused on potential threats. This "watchdog effect" means that you are more likely to misinterpret things when you are anxious; you are more likely to think a friend is angry with you, to think that someone is lurking outside your door, or to read vague text messages as negative.

All of the unpleasant feelings and thoughts that you experience when you are anxious are the result of a purposeful, helpful process—to get energy to where you need it in your body if you are in danger. It means that your body and your mind are working the way they're supposed to, trying to keep you safe.

When Knowledge Is Power

Recognizing that the shadow in your bedroom is the lamp and not an intruder makes a huge difference in how you feel about the shadow. Similarly, when you understand how anxiety shows up in your body and how it impacts your thoughts, you have power over anxiety, rather than anxiety having power over you.

The physical feelings of fear and anxiety are the same as the feelings you get when you are exercising: Your heart rate increases, you breathe heavily, you are hot and sweaty, and your muscles are tense. If you aren't alarmed by these physical feelings, you can take a sip of water and let them pass in their own time. Why? Because of context. You *expect* to feel this way when you exercise.

What if you had the same expectations when you were anxious?

A colleague of mine shared that she once noticed some uncomfortable physical symptoms while driving: Her heart was pounding, she was having a hard time catching her breath, and she noticed hot flashes. She recognized that she was having a panic attack. Knowing that anxiety—like all of our emotions—tends to increase, peak, and decrease, she pulled into a parking lot and waited. "It sucked," she told me later. "I panicked. Then I had a good cry. And then I went on to work."

Without this knowledge, her experience could have turned out differently. If she had simply thought, "I can't breathe, I can't see straight, why are my hands shaking? Something is really wrong with me," she would have likely catastrophized this experience, believing that there was something truly wrong with her. She would have started scanning her body, looking for more confirmation that she was having an acute medical crisis, and likely would have taken herself to the emergency room.

And I promise you, if you expect to find a sensation, you will find it.

Try this quick exercise with me. Bring your attention to your body right now and find a place that itches . . . did you find one? Several? Did you scratch? I find myself scratching my right shoulder as I write this. My left elbow as I reread. Bringing your attention to something makes it more likely to be noticed. You probably weren't aware of your itch before I asked you to notice it. And there it is.

Similarly, if you don't understand what goes on in your body and mind when you feel fear or anxiety, it makes sense that you will assume that something is really wrong with you. You will likely notice sensations that confirm your fears, amplifying the experience of anxiety simply by *looking for it*.

These feelings feel awful and scary—because they had to in order to motivate the fight-or-flight behaviors that kept our ancestors alive—but these symptoms are not dangerous, and they can't hurt us. When you know the symptoms of anxiety and panic, you can recognize them for what they are, name them when they arise, and have confidence that they are not dangerous. And you can model this for your kids, emboldening them with the same knowledge that can bring confidence in managing anxious feelings.

Kids and parents may understand that normal anxiety isn't harmful but worry that anxiety disorders are a different story. How does this change if you, or your kid, have a clinical anxiety disorder?

All of this still applies! Your anxiety alarm may be more sensitive, and it may be going off more frequently and intensely, but your body is still doing what it's supposed to be doing . . . just at the wrong time, and more often. And if you or your kid struggles with higher anxiety than the average bear, such that anxiety gets in the way of daily life, there are things that you can do to cope more effectively. Moreover, the choices that you make about what you *do* in response to anxiety can alter the course of anxiety in a positive way.

Let's start with validation. *Validation* is a way of communicating to another person that their emotional experience makes sense to you in a given situation. This crucial coping skill is rooted in compassion and is the first step in turning the volume down on a strong emotional response. And the compassion needed to validate well comes more easily when you can genuinely acknowledge that the emotion makes sense: that anxiety is a primal alarm system going off in response to modern stressors. Validation, along with the recognition that anxiety is normal, natural, and harmless, takes the power away from your kids' anxiety (and your own).

It Makes Sense That . . .

There is a general understanding that validation involves naming what you think someone else's emotion is in the moment: "Aw, sweetie, I can tell that you are feeling frustrated." This is, broadly, true. Many parents feel that validation is just expected within a solid parent-child relationship and is part of teaching kids about emotions. It has become a marker of informed parenting, the cherry on top of secure attachment. As one of my friends said, "Isn't validation just what parents are supposed to do now? When I was upset, my parents just told me to get over it, so this is just how we are parenting better. Now my kid knows I care, right?"

Yes, effective validation can show your kid that you care about how they feel, which is certainly good for the relationship. However, as validation has become a part of modern parenting expectations, its purpose has become misunderstood and its benefits diluted. Understanding why and how it's effective is key to optimizing its usefulness.

Emotions are like the weather. Sometimes it's seventy-two degrees and sunny. Other times it's a raw, rainy day with a biting wind. A storm can appear suddenly and unexpectedly, and you can't do a damn thing about it. Same thing with emotions. Emotions arise, sometimes unexpectedly, and sometimes inconveniently. They stick around for a while, and they fade. During an emotional storm, the challenge is to ride it out without making your situation worse: to avoid *behaviors* that have lasting and negative consequences.

Validation communicates "It makes sense to me that you feel this way. I see you, I hear you, I believe you." Validation builds, strengthens, and reaffirms relationships. You communicate validation through your words and through your actions, your tone, and your body language. It is an anchor during an emotional storm, decreasing the likelihood that the person you are validating will make choices that ultimately worsen their situation.

In contrast, *invalidation* communicates that another person's emotional experience does not make sense or is not worthwhile. You feel it when you are told to "calm down," "don't be so angry," and "just focus on all the good things that you have in your life," or that "there is nothing to worry about." Often you might find yourself invalidating others accidentally when you are trying to help them solve a problem or reframe their thinking in ways you hope will be beneficial. Or you might invalidate unintentionally through your actions and body language, perhaps by checking your email while your kid is telling you something hard about the school day. Invalidating statements and behaviors typically worsen the emotional experience, prolonging the storm.

Validation helps the brain reregulate during times of high emotion. There are two areas of interest in the brain here. First, there is the "emotional center" of the brain, located deep in its core, which involves structures like the amygdala and the hippocampus. Then there is the prefrontal cortex, the "rational center" of the brain behind your forehead. When you are calm, the pathways between the emotional center and the rational center of the brain are like open highways informing one another, helping you make good decisions.

However, when you experience an emotional storm, the communication between the emotional center and the prefrontal cortex temporarily goes offline. This process has been called *amygdala hijack*. During amygdala hijack, you are, for a time, largely governed by your emotions. This is the reason why we often say we "can't think straight" or that we behave unexpectedly during a moment of intense anxiety, bitter sadness, explosive rage, or all-consuming joy. But validation helps to get the prefrontal cortex back online more quickly.

Validation often involves naming the emotional experience, which is helpful on a brain-based level because naming the emotion is one way to reengage the prefrontal cortex. It helps to reestablish communication between the rational and emotional centers of the brain. Acknowledging "here is anxiety" begins to lower the anxiety. Naming the emotion isn't going to halt the emotional storm in its tracks, but it's a solid start.

There is no perfect prescription for validation; in fact, latching onto a script that you use every time is going to end up being invalidating because it's not going to be nuanced enough for each person and each situation. Validation should be genuine, and other people—especially teenagers—can sniff out insincerity like a hound dog. Instead of trying to memorize a script, think about the goal of validation: to communicate to the other person that their emotional experience is acceptable and understandable. And go from there.

Here are some more concrete guidelines for validation. An abbreviated "cheat sheet" is available in the Resources section at the back of this book.

How to Validate

- **Pause, pay attention, and actively listen.** Face the other person, make eye contact, and nod while they are speaking.
- **Get curious.** Observe what the other person may be feeling. Look for a word or phrase that describes that experience and reflect it back to them without judgment; for example, "You

seem so stressed," "This must feel really scary," or "That sounds so upsetting."

- **Reflect.** Sometimes it helps to reflect back to the person why it makes sense for them, in this moment, that they feel the way that they do. For example, "It makes so much sense that you are anxious about your test; you care about doing well at school." Or "It makes sense that you are angry with me when you don't have a smartphone and many of your friends' parents have given them one."
- **Look for the grain of truth.** Remember that emotions are signals that tell us something about our environment or present experience. Even if the emotion doesn't fit the facts in the moment, there must be a grain of truth that is driving the experience. Why does it make sense, for this person, in this moment, to be feeling this way?

Phrases to Get You Started

- "You seem [emotion]."
- "I wonder if you are feeling [emotion]."
- "It makes sense that you would feel [emotion]."
- "I believe you that you are [emotion]."

What to Avoid During Validation

- Less is often more. Sometimes just actively listening, without speaking, is enough. If it feels right, you can use gentle touch, like a hand on their shoulder or a hug. Resist the urge to fill the space with lots of talking, which can easily deteriorate into invalidating or unhelpful behaviors—like attempting to solve the problem, sharing examples from your own life, or reframing the situation. These responses can be helpful *outside* the emotional storm but can fuel it in the moment.
- Be mindful of your reactions. Resist invalidating behaviors like multitasking, sighing, eye-rolling, or making light of something.

- Avoid the phrase "I understand how you feel." It seems great but can easily be read as invalidating, particularly for teenagers who believe that *no one* could possibly understand how they feel.

Pro Tips

- If you aren't sure what the other person is feeling, you can take a guess or get curious. Describe what you see without judgment. When all else fails, remarking that the other person feels upset and asking, "Am I getting that right?" can help to nonjudgmentally gather more information.
- Use "and" instead of "but." Using the word "but" ends up negating all the great validation that came before it. Using the word "and" allows us to hold two seemingly contradictory ideas at once. For example, consider how differently the sentence "You feel nervous about starting school, but I know that you can do hard things" lands when compared to "You feel nervous about starting school, and I know that you can do hard things."
- Don't assume that you know what the other person wants or needs in the moment. It's a great idea to ask, "What do you need from me right now? Would it be helpful to problem-solve together, or do you just need me to listen?"

Validating someone's experience does *not* mean that you agree that the emotion fits the facts of the situation, or that you need to capitulate to the emotion. When you won't let your preteen go to a concert with her friends on a school night, you can validate her feeling of anger—it makes sense—but that does not mean that you agree that she should be allowed to go. If your child with separation anxiety is anxious about you leaving him at a birthday party while you dash to the pharmacy and back, you can validate the feeling of fear—which is genuinely awful—even when you know you'd never abandon your kid. When you validate, look for the grain of truth within the other person's experience: Why does this experience make sense for this person, at this given moment? You can validate the emotion—"You feel scared because you are worried that I won't come back"—while also showing that feelings are not facts when you add, compassionately but firmly, "I will be gone for ten minutes, I will be back, *and* I know that you can handle this." Then, as the birthday boy's dad gives you a nod in solidarity, you go to the pharmacy. And you come back when you say you will.

While there are lots of things that you can validate—emotions, of course, but also desires, thoughts or beliefs, efforts, and effective behaviors—you do not want to validate dysfunctional or ineffective behavior. You would not validate your teen's risky behavior by saying, "It make so much sense that you got absolutely plastered at that party because you are nervous about fitting in." You can instead affirm what is valid while still setting expectations: "It makes sense that you are nervous about fitting in, and we need to talk about how you can make safer choices when you are uncomfortable." Validation doesn't excuse misbehavior.

Many folks find validation to be difficult. If it's unfamiliar, it can be an uncomfortable way of communicating. This is particularly true if you didn't get a lot of validation growing up, or if validation isn't typical in your culture. If this rings true, I'm here to validate you. And I would ask you to consider how you communicate with the important people in your life, particularly those closest to you—your kids, your partner, your own parents. Does communication around tough issues improve the situation for everyone, or do things unravel further when hard subjects come up? If communication is not a slam dunk all around, are you willing to try something different?

Though it may be uncomfortable at first, your efforts to validate will pay off over time. I have sat through heartwarming sessions where a parent is attempting validation, making earnest efforts to counter a lifetime of invalidation. As they work to communicate in a new way, it's incredible to see the look of astonished amusement cross their child's face as they see their parent working to do something new for their benefit. Validation shows your child that you care about the relationship—enough to work on communicating in a way that can be new, and even uncomfortable.

Let's put this all together by revisiting Sophia from the last chapter, our fifteen-year-old who was anxious about starting a new school. Behavior change is key to altering her experience, but validation has a role to play as well. First, let's acknowledge that it's super common for kids to express discomfort about going to school—whether at the start of a new school year, when beginning a new school, or even if just going back after a weekend. In these circumstances, well-meaning parents can invalidate like crazy: "You love school!" "You're going to have the best day!" "Your new teachers will adore you!" But ultimately these responses land as dismissive, and now not only do kids feel anxious about school, but they feel shame when they get the message that they "shouldn't" be anxious.

So how could Sophia's parents validate her anxiety before the first day of school? By acknowledging the ways in which her anxiety is normal and valid, and by communicating "It makes sense that you are feeling nervous; you care about making friends. Starting a new school is hard." Taking the time to attentively listen and validate is relationship-affirming. Naming the emotion for her, with compassion, helps Sophia acknowledge and accept the emotion for herself, which is part of restoring the pathways between the emotional and rational centers of the brain. Compassionately validating, without jumping in to try to "fix" the emotion, models for Sophia that her anxiety is not a crisis—it's a normal, natural, and harmless feeling that she is capable of handling.

But how do you know whether a given anxiety-related experience is normal? How do you know whether, and when, to intervene? In the next chapter, we will take a closer look at how to distinguish between normal anxiety and clinical anxiety disorders.

What Can You Take Home with You?

- Having learned about the biological basis of fear and anxiety, get curious about what physical feelings of anxiety come up for you when you are anxious. Are there certain sensations that you tend to notice more often? How does knowing why your body is reacting this way change your interpretation of those sensations? This knowledge often makes these sensations less scary, which helps de-escalate the anxiety cycle.

- Talk with your kids about the fight-or-flight response. Explore with them the ways in which our bodies and minds automatically react when we think we are in danger. Personalize it by asking about the feelings that they feel most often when anxious. Share your experience and link it all back to the fight-or-flight response. Emphasize that while anxiety feels awful, it can't hurt you.

- Validation is a skill that gets better with practice. So start practicing. Consider why an emotional reaction makes sense for a given person in a given moment, and communicate that to them, with warmth and compassion. Reference the validation "cheat sheet" in the Resources section at the back of this book if you need help. As you practice validating, keep an eye out for invalidation and try to minimize it.

- It is tempting to jump into problem-solving mode while validating, but remember—unless you are specifically asked for advice, now's not the time. If your teenager is crying because she was excluded by her best friends, naming other people with whom she could hang out instead will land like a lead balloon. Stick with validation and be with her in her sadness without trying to change it. It can be hard to resist the urge to try to "fix" a loved one's emotion. But getting better at tolerating your own discomfort in the moment models good emotional coping for your kids.

CHAPTER 3

Is This Normal?

Parents constantly ask me to weigh in on whether a given anxiety pattern is "normal." And I get it. I started asking myself a lot more questions about what "normal" looks like once I became a parent. Really, what we are asking is, *Should I be concerned? Should I be intervening in some way? And what happens if I don't?*

In this chapter, we discuss how to distinguish between normal anxiety and *clinical anxiety*—meaning anxiety that meets diagnostic criteria for an anxiety disorder. There is no nasal swab or spit test to determine whether anxiety for a given person, at a given time in their life, under given circumstances, is normal or clinical. But there are some conditions under which it's normal to see a temporary increase in anxiety. This knowledge can help you respond with calm and confidence when you notice increased anxiety in yourself or a loved one. And how you respond to anxiety is important, particularly within the parent-child relationship.

When you treat normal anxiety like it's a catastrophe, your kid views it as a catastrophe: something over which they have no control, that they can't handle, and that needs to be fixed immediately. This mindset inflames the situation even more, because now everyone has (unnecessary) anxiety about their anxiety. And, sadly, that increases the risk of reacting in ways that will make anxiety worse in the long term.

I was reminded of this shortly before my daughter lost her first tooth. One morning while she was brushing her teeth, she started screaming. I rushed in, and she showed me her mouth, where an adult tooth had broken through behind her baby teeth. "Holy sh*t, she's a shark," I thought. I've worked with a ton of kids with all sorts of needs, but this one was new to me. So my mind went to the worst-case scenario—the one in which she is a medical mystery with rows upon rows of teeth, all chance of a normal life obliterated. But my sweet little daughter, tears streaming down her face as she gawked, mouth agape, in the mirror, was looking to me to make sense of this. Regardless of the outcome of our dental drama, I knew that how I framed it was going to impact how she thought about her ability to cope. "Oh my gosh!" I exclaimed. "I bet you are about to lose a tooth!" Bolstered by my apparent confidence, she left for school, excited to show off her shark tooth to the rest of her class, and a quick call to the dentist confirmed that shark teeth aren't just for sharks.

Your response to curveballs gives those around you information and informs their reactions. So, when you know that increased anxiety, while never fun, can be normal, you can react proportionally, in a way that helps everyone respond more resiliently. It sets a framework for your kids to understand that feeling anxious doesn't necessarily mean they have an anxiety disorder and lowers the temperature on the response.

Let's explore three broad circumstances where anxiety is the shark tooth—a challenge for sure, but still within the realm of normal, and something that tends to resolve on its own.

Fear's Greatest Hits, by Age

There are certain stages of development where anxiety and fears are normal and expected. For example, it is normal and beneficial for babies to start showing separation and stranger anxiety at eight or nine months of age, once they realize "Mom still exists even when I do not see her, and I want her all the time." Anxiety about being away from primary caregivers is typically a marker of secure attachment;

clinicians are actually concerned when young children *do not care* whether their caregivers are around. Separation concerns stay common throughout early childhood and can wax and wane. So, during that period where your little one only wants you, and all you want to do is lock yourself in the bathroom and eat an unholy number of Oreos, know that it is a normal, adaptive, and typically brief stage in their development. Also, leaving for short periods of time and returning teaches your child that you *will* come back, a fact that they will not learn if you never leave in the first place.

Many kids find that structure and routines lend some predictability to an otherwise uncontrollable world. As a result, rigidity and inflexibility can be common, particularly during the elementary school years. At this stage it's normal for kids to show anxiety in the face of the unexpected, or when trying new things, given the uncertainty involved.

As children develop, "what if" fears become increasingly common: "What if there is a war?" "What if you die?" "What will happen because of climate change?" Such questions may increase when kids are coping with other mild stressors, such as at the beginning of the school year. And this makes sense: When any of us feel upheaval in our lives, we search for certainty where we can. As much as we all wish we could assuage our kids' fears by reassuring them "Don't worry, you will never live through a war," or "Grandpa is actually a force of nature who will never die," we can't make these promises, and it erodes trust to do so. Instead, you can respond in ways that acknowledge the reality of a world where sad or scary things happen sometimes, while also highlighting the ways in which the adults in your child's life are prioritizing their safety and well-being.

As kids become preteens and teenagers, their primary influences shift from parents to peers. Unsurprisingly, anxiety around social situations becomes common. This is also when we see the "spotlight effect," a cognitive bias where teens overestimate how much others are paying attention to and judging them. I still remember, as a teen, when my father burst a balloon at a school function, and everyone's head whipped around. I thought I was going to die of embarrassment, right there in the auditorium. It's easy for adults to dismiss teens' social fears, but this can feel deeply invalidating and fuel more parent-child conflict. So instead, acknowledge that your teen's anxiety is influenced by brain-based changes over which they have no control.

Life's Vibe-Killers

It's common to experience high anxiety when you have a life transition, even a positive one. You may feel more anxiety after a recent move, when changing schools, or when starting a new job. Anxiety often increases around marriage, divorce, or shifts in living situations, like when a new baby joins the family, a grandparent moves in, or the oldest sibling leaves for college. Increases in anxiety are common during pregnancy and the postpartum period, given the many role transitions, biological changes, and new responsibilities that come with pregnancy and parenting infants.

Anxiety levels can also shift at different times of the year. For example, some kids feel more anxious during the school year, given the stress of academic and social pressures, and summer brings relief. For some kids, it's the opposite; they feel more anxious during the summer or on holiday breaks because of the lack of structure and routine, and getting back to school is helpful in relieving anxiety. Anniversaries of a loss can also be tough times where low mood and anxiety can worsen.

If you expect that you may feel anxious or stressed about any of these environmental changes, you are less likely to catastrophize anxious thoughts and feelings. You can also set these expectations with your kids and use them to validate. For example, you can communicate to your kid, "You're feeling really stressed right now. It's normal for anxiety to increase when things change, and you've been dealing with a lot of changes recently."

The Art of Not Falling Apart

Whenever your body is run-down, you are more vulnerable to feeling anxiety. You simply have less bandwidth to cope, and so you may feel more easily overwhelmed by anxious thoughts and feelings. Anxiety often increases in response to getting sick, and you are certainly likely to feel more anxious if you are coping with a chronic illness or healing from an injury. Hormonal changes—the ones that occur naturally during puberty, menstrual cycles, pregnancy and the postpartum period, menopause, or in response to certain medications—can be accompanied by increases in anxiety. General health factors can impact anxiety a ton. If you aren't getting good sleep, if you are eating lots of processed foods, if you aren't moving enough, or if you are putting too many substances like caffeine, alcohol, or drugs into your body, you are unlikely to feel your best to begin with, and this also makes you more vulnerable to high anxiety.

Do not dismiss this advice. I know you have heard it a hundred times—get better sleep, exercise more, eat healthy foods—and it's easy to ignore. When anxiety gets loud, people look to solutions like therapy or medication, and these interventions may be needed. But overlooking these basic health factors means that you may be handicapping yourself when you do begin therapy or medication.

Insufficient sleep is just bad news, all around, for child and adolescent health and wellness. Pretty much everything gets worse for kids with poor sleep—injuries, emotional regulation, obesity, depression, learning problems, suicidality, and anxiety. The flip side of this is that pretty much everything gets better with better sleep. So when your kid's anxiety increases, making some improvements to their sleep is likely to pay off. The American Academy of Sleep Medicine recommends that kids ages six to twelve should get nine to twelve hours of sleep, and teenagers ages thirteen to eighteen should get eight to ten hours of sleep.

Recognizing When Anxiety Is Normal

Taken together, if you notice increases in anxiety that broadly fall within these circumstances, it is reasonable to assume that this is a normal, common, and time-limited shark-tooth challenge. Note that "normal" does *not* mean easy, painless, or unworthy of empathy. But anxiety within these circumstances often resolves on its own, in a relatively short period of time, because humans—even small humans—are incredibly resilient.

Understanding that it is normal to experience fluctuations in anxiety can help you approach painful thoughts and feelings with more self-validation and less fear and concern. It also helps you to be better prepared. Let's say you recognize that it is normal for your ten-year-old to have more anxious thoughts and feelings at this stage in his development. And you get that he is even more vulnerable to anxiety because his best friend recently moved away and the start of fifth grade has felt rocky. Expecting that your son is likely to be having a harder time impacts how you will respond to his anxiety, helping you to normalize and validate his experience. When he says, "I am worrying too much to fall asleep. Why can't I just turn off my brain, Dad?" you might say, "You are really worried, buddy, I see that. You are right at an age where kids start worrying about lots of things, because of all the amazing changes that are happening in your brain and all that you are learning about the world, and sometimes that feels scary. Also, you're missing your best friend, and change can be tough. It can be hard at night when you are noticing a lot of worried thoughts, and I know you will fall asleep eventually."

This is a message full of empathy and validation, but it's more than that. It also educates him and normalizes his experience in a way that helps your son to see that, while he is struggling, he is not broken.

What if you can say this all to your son, but you aren't sure you believe it? What if you're concerned that his lack of sleep is going to impact his brain development, you fear that he won't find a new best friend, and you worry that he will devolve into isolation and despair?

Here is where self-compassion and self-validation comes in. You ac-knowledge your own anxiety about the changes you see and validate your feelings of being concerned: "It makes sense that I would be wor-rying more about my son. I adore him, he's having a rough time, and I don't want him to suffer." You monitor, projecting a casual confidence that you may not totally feel but is important to model.

Time often gives us the answers. You wait and see how things develop.

What If Anxiety Goes Beyond Normal?

One of the challenges in figuring out what is normal anxiety and what is a clinical anxiety disorder is the word "anxiety" itself. Unlike the clear distinction between "sadness" and "depression," the term "anxi-ety" is used interchangeably to describe both a normal emotional re-sponse and a diagnosable disorder. It's confusing.

Anxiety exists along a continuum. Imagine your level of anxiety at any given time like water in a drinking glass, where an empty glass represents no stress or anxiety. The more water in the glass, the greater your anxiety levels. An overflowing glass represents an anxi-ety disorder.

None of us has an empty glass. We all come into the world with some water in the glass given our genetic inheritance. And life stress-ors build on that. There are times in your life when the glass is less full, and times when you feel like you are about to overflow. Stressors add up, and the more stressors with which you are coping at any given time, the more water in the glass. Sometimes the glass does overflow, anxiety becomes a clinical disorder, and intervention is needed.

So how do you know if the glass is overflowing or just pretty full? Again, there is no simple test. Instead, we are tasked with drawing a line—however blurry—between normal and clinical anxiety along a spectrum where everything blends together. And that's tricky. Good diagnostic assessment achieves this, but how do you know whether assessment is needed?

To answer this question, consider three factors to better understand the scale and impact of your anxiety: To what degree are the symptoms interfering with your life, how much distress are they causing, and how long have they been present at this level?

Interference

Anxiety disorders really take a toll on your life. There are places you won't go, people you won't see, activities that you won't engage in, responsibilities that you neglect, and goals that you give up. Or you develop new behaviors and routines purely because of anxiety, so that managing anxiety becomes your focus. If life has changed significantly for you, and often for those around you, because of your anxiety, you are likely no longer dealing with normal anxiety. This is clinically significant interference.

Now, when I talk about "clinically significant interference," I mean that anxiety is messing up your life in ways that are out of proportion to the stressors you are facing. If you are enduring a tremendous stressor—a serious illness in the family, for example—of course your life is going to go off the rails. But this interference makes sense, given the stress that you are facing; this is unlikely to be disordered anxiety.

And it is normal for anxiety to get in the way of your life to some degree. For example, if you are a college student plowing your way through a challenging semester, it makes sense that your anxiety would be high. Your routine might change to prioritize studying, and anxiety might be interfering with your sleep schedule and your social life. However, this interference is not unexpected, and pulling a few all-nighters in college is not uncommon.

In contrast, if you are working so hard that you are regularly pulling all-nighters and your sleep is completely disrupted, if you are the only one of your friends staying in on weekends to prioritize schoolwork, if you are neglecting meals or showers to study, and if you are restructuring your life to avoid being anxious in a way that messes things up for you, anxiety may have shifted from normal to clinical, interfering more than most people would reasonably expect, given your current life stress.

Common clinically interfering behaviors in young people with anxiety disorders include dropping out of extracurricular activities, avoiding social situations, texting parents nonstop for reassurance, making unhealthy changes to eating or bathing routines, refusing to sleep alone, or avoiding school. Similar patterns of impairment show up for adults struggling with anxiety disorders. Adults turn down job opportunities, bow out of the dating scene, or limit communication with friends because of clinically interfering anxiety. Or they remain dependent in unhealthy relationships, use substances to cope, or rigidly stick to rules and routines.

For adults who are struggling with anxiety with regard to parenting specifically, clinically interfering anxiety often looks like massive overinvolvement in your kid's life in ways that limit parent and child independence and well-being. This could mean going with your kid to activities when a parent isn't needed, avoiding socializing or traveling without your kid, or refusing to let other adults care for your child. It could look like overengaging in your kid's schoolwork, spending excessive time on internet deep dives about parenting, or deprioritizing important relationships—spouses, friends, other family members—in favor of your child. These behaviors may not be a sign of a disorder if they happen every once in a while. However, if they occur repeatedly and really get in the way of life, it may be time to think about options for treatment.

Distress

Anxiety by nature comes with discomfort or emotional pain, but how upset—or how distressed—you feel, relative to the stressors you are facing and the symptoms with which you are coping, is a key differentiator between normal and clinical anxiety. Unlike normal stress, clinical anxiety doesn't just feel tough—it feels like it's too much to handle, like it's totally running the show, rather than being hard but still manageable.

Distress is hard to measure because it's so personal and subjective. It can't be measured by the number of times you cry, the number of days you are extra irritable, or how often you say "I feel horrible because of my anxiety." So it can be useful to compare current distress to a baseline; in other words, how different is your level of distress now, compared to your "normal" emotional experience? If you are generally an emotive person who has a cry pretty regularly, distress that signals a clinical anxiety disorder is likely to show up as *lots* more crying. In comparison, a single episode of tearfulness for a person who rarely shows any negative emotion may be just as much of a red flag.

There are also developmental considerations. A young child's distress tends to come through in more tantruming, clinging, and crying. Other children or adults who are in distress may seem more irritable or angry. They may be more standoffish or completely shut down. They may just not "seem like themselves."

Emotional, irritable, and standoffish? Sounds like your average teenager. This overlap is one of the reasons why it can drive parents batty to try to figure out whether their teen's experience is "normal." It's also why relying solely on the degree of distress caused by anxiety isn't typically enough to identify a clinical disorder: Being really upset isn't usually sufficient to warrant a diagnosis. This is why anxiety disorders are assigned only when symptoms cause significant distress *and* interference over a certain time period.

Duration

Clinically significant anxiety *lasts*. In order to result in an anxiety disorder diagnosis, symptoms need to have been present for at least a few consecutive weeks to months without much improvement. And the symptoms stick around even when things are generally going well, meaning that they persist without periods of meaningful symptom relief.

But how long, specifically, do the symptoms have to be interfering and distressing in order for them to no longer be "normal" anxiety? It depends on the symptoms and the disorder. See the Appendix at the back of this book, where I dive into the different anxiety disorder diagnoses in more detail, for specifics. But as an example, symptoms of social anxiety need to be present for at least six months to warrant a diagnosis, whereas symptoms of panic disorder need to be present for one month. And there are sometimes different time requirements for children versus adults; symptoms of separation anxiety need to be present in adults for six months to warrant a diagnosis, but only for four weeks in children.

Don't worry about getting too precise in determining exactly how long you—or your child—have been struggling with anxiety symptoms as you consider whether it meets the clinical threshold. It can be useful to recognize that most anxiety symptoms need to be present and interfering for one to six months before warranting a diagnosis. Here are some questions that you can ask yourself—or reflect upon for your kid—to help determine whether to seek treatment.

DIY Anxiety Assessment

Interference:
- In what ways is anxiety messing things up for you in your daily life?
- Are there things that you are doing, that you wouldn't ordinarily do, because of anxiety?
- Are there things that you are *not* doing, that you ordinarily would do, because of anxiety?
- How much has your daily routine changed because of anxiety?
- If you weren't struggling with anxiety, how would your life look different?

Distress:
- How upset are you, on average, because of anxiety? How bothered are you, on average, because of anxiety?

- Do you believe that you are way more distressed than most people your age, and in your circumstances, would be? Or do you think most people would be reacting in the same way if they were in your shoes?
- How hard is it for you to control your anxiety-related distress?

Duration:
- For how long have you been feeling anxiety/fear/panic at this level of distress?
- For how long has anxiety been causing interference or impairment in your daily life?
- How many days per week, on average, are you feeling this level of anxiety?
- Within that time period, have there been times when you didn't feel anxiety-related distress or interference at a high level? Have there been any periods where you felt like yourself?
- If your anxiety arose in response to a stressful life event, is that stressful event ongoing? If it's no longer occurring, for how long are you continuing to feel anxiety after the stressor has stopped?

If anxiety is messing things up for you in your daily life—if it is leading you to change your behaviors and your routine in ways that you otherwise wouldn't—if it's causing you uncontrollable distress, and it's been interfering without relief for several weeks to months, anxiety may have shifted from normal to clinical. And it's worth speaking with a medical or behavioral health provider.

Suspecting that you or your child may have a clinical anxiety disorder can feel scary. But there are many reasons to be hopeful. Truly, a diagnosis of an anxiety disorder does not have to be a life sentence, and there are very good options for treatment. Assessment and diagnosis is the crucial first step to clarify what's going on and to direct a treatment plan. I encourage you to start by speaking with a trusted health provider to consider your options. You can also find more information on the assessment and diagnosis of anxiety disorders in the Appendix at the back of this book, which provides you with a road map for what to expect if you do seek professional guidance for yourself or your children.

The silver lining of the fact that anxiety disorders are so common is that there has been a ton of research into treatment for these conditions. And with treatment, these conditions can vastly improve, as can your confidence in managing them.

The most effective treatments are based on the knowledge that what you *do* in response to anxiety—your behavior—impacts whether anxiety gets better or worse over time. In the next chapter, we unpack this principle so that you can begin to apply it to support yourself and your family in breaking the cycle of anxiety.

What Can You Take Home with You?

- The way you respond to anxiety shapes how your child perceives it. If you react to normal anxiety as if it is a crisis, your child is likely to see it as something overwhelming and unmanageable, rather than something challenging that they can learn to navigate.
- When you or your kid are showing higher anxiety, pause. Consider whether it might be a result of health issues, life stressors, or normal developmental periods when anxiety naturally increases. If so, start by normalizing the experience—not to dismiss it as easy or unimportant, but to frame it as something painful, manageable, and likely temporary.
- During periods where higher child anxiety is likely normal, parents should always start by empathically validating—why does it make sense that your kid feels more anxiety right now? Keep track of the symptoms to see if they are worsening or improv-

ing. Log symptoms daily in a journal or on your phone to keep an accurate record of interference and distress over time.

- Don't dismiss the impact of your kid's sleep hygiene. Taking some steps to improve their sleep can be a simple but surprisingly meaningful way to intervene.
- Reach out to your child's pediatrician to let them know what you are seeing; they know your child and your family and can help you figure out whether your child's symptoms are normal and time-limited or need direct intervention.
- When anxiety gets high, resist the urge to shut down life completely. Tapping out from life in these moments may feel good but is likely to make things worse in the long run, because avoidance fuels anxiety.

CHAPTER 4

How Avoidance Fuels Anxiety

Much of the experience of anxiety feels uncontrollable. You can't erase millennia of evolution, genetic vulnerabilities, or stressful life events. Sometimes your glass overflows and you develop an anxiety disorder, largely due to these ungovernable factors. But often there are things that you may do—behaviors in which you may engage—that make anxiety worse in the long run.

This doesn't mean that your story is written for you—you have power to shape your experience with anxiety, because you can control your behaviors. And this means that you actually have tremendous agency, and the ability to build and strengthen an anxiety-fighting skill set. Your kids do, as well.

In this chapter, we will explore the ways in which our actions set us on a course that can either protect against greater anxiety or worsen anxiety. While avoidance was vital for our ancestors who faced ever-present danger, avoidance in the absence of lethality is often the thing that leads to most problems in modern daily life. I will show you how to apply this knowledge to better understand your own anxiety and to support your kids. Understanding the relationship between avoidance and anxiety opens the door to a completely new approach to your emotional life.

Pushing Pain Away

Humans are great at finding ways to avoid discomfort in our environment. We leave a room to avoid unpleasant smells, layer up to avoid unpleasant temperatures, spit out unpleasant tastes, unfollow unpleasant people. This makes sense and is adaptive, as it's consistent with our basic human drives to accrue the good and avoid the bad.

The drive to avoid unpleasant things translates to our internal, private world as well. Psychologists call the tendency to avoid unpleasant thoughts and feelings *experiential avoidance*. We all do it, all the time, but some folks rely on it more than others. Noticing your own experiential avoidance—and teaching your kids how to notice theirs—is hugely helpful on the journey to improving resilience and combating anxiety.

If you consider an image or memory that brings up negative emotions—fear, sadness, guilt, shame, anger, or regret—you will likely notice the urge to shove that memory away, or to distract yourself from it. I still find it painful to recall when my beloved childhood dog collapsed in front of me and died in my lap, and I still cringe when I remember falling out of my chair on a first date and seeing the appalled face of a man who I was sure would never call again. When uncomfortable thoughts, images, or feelings come up, we try to replace them with other thoughts, or we try to distract ourselves to block out the pain. And like the beach ball in the swimming pool, despite our efforts to submerge our painful thoughts and feelings, they inevitably pop back up.

In addition to searching for mental tools to suppress our negative thoughts and feelings, we look for behaviors—things to *do*—to avoid our negative emotional experiences. Some of these behaviors are pretty harmless in moderation—like binge-watching, stress-eating, or losing ourselves in the social media vortex. Sometimes they become deeply problematic. People often abuse alcohol and drugs because those substances can turn down the volume on unpleasant thoughts and feelings in the moment. Eating-disordered behavior, like bingeing

and purging or excessive exercising and restricting food, is often behaviors that people do to avoid or replace unpleasant thoughts and
feelings. People who engage in self-injury by, for example, cutting or
burning themselves typically report that they turn to these behaviors
to try to minimize emotional pain. And we know from research that
people who work hardest to avoid negative emotions are more likely to
experience mental health conditions, including anxiety disorders.

What Happens When We Push Anxiety Away

Humans come up with all sorts of avoidance strategies to turn the volume down on fear and anxiety. Afraid of dogs? Avoid dog parks.
Afraid of heights? No glass elevators for you. Nervous about sending
an email to your manager? Ask your partner to review it before you
send the message. Afraid of feeling anxious? Your life gets smaller and
smaller as you avoid more and more things that *may* cause anxiety.

Notice that some of these avoidance strategies are obvious, like
when you avoid being around dogs or heights because you are afraid
of dogs or heights. Others are a little sneakier, such as seeking reassurance that your email is okay before sending; on the surface, it doesn't
look like avoidance, but getting your partner's blessing on your email
is an anxiety-driven behavior that serves a purpose: to minimize your
fears of saying the wrong thing.

What's the problem with avoiding things I don't like? Nothing, if it
doesn't mess things up for you. If you have a life where you don't ever
need to be around dogs, go for it—avoid dogs (but you're missing out).
If getting reassurance on your email is a onetime thing that helps you
send a tough email, no problem. Avoidance isn't always a recipe for
anxiety problems. However, avoidance is a slippery slope—and I am
not immune.

I moved to Boston for graduate school, and then to New York City
for my clinical internship and postdoctoral fellowship. Living in these
cities, I spent nearly eight years rarely needing to get behind the wheel
of a car. This didn't start off as deliberate avoidance—I didn't drive

because I didn't need to—but as time went on, I felt less and less confident in driving. This prolonged period of de facto avoidance meant that I gradually felt more uncomfortable when I did have to drive. But the more I avoided driving opportunities, the less confident I became. When I finally was in a position where I had to drive again, I was pregnant. Now I was afraid that I was going to crash my car and kill myself and my unborn baby in the process.

I didn't. And for the record, I have never been in an accident, though I have scraped up some nice rims. The point is that avoidance fuels anxiety. Even if avoidance is not deliberate, it can sneakily cause impairment over time. The link between avoidance and anxiety doesn't come with age restrictions either; these principles are just as relevant for kids as they are for grown-ups. The good news is that if you understand the relationship between anxiety and avoidance, you can take steps to help prevent avoidance from snowballing into an anxiety disorder.

Avoidance Fuels Anxiety

Imagine that your kid has been placed in an honors math class for the new school year. You and he were proud when you heard the news over the summer, but he had some doubts that he could handle the work. His anxiety kicks in when he shows up to the first class. As he sits at his desk, trying to make sense of the material flying at him, he thinks, "I don't understand any of this." His stomach flutters with anxiety, his muscles tense, and he notices a bit of dizziness. As he feels increasingly lost and uncomfortable, he has the urge to flee from the classroom.

Our Three-Component Model that follows illustrates the feelings, thoughts, and behaviors driving his experience.

At the peak of his distress, he raises his hand and says he feels sick, and asks to go to the school nurse. He gathers up his things shakily and heads down to the nurse's office, still noticing feelings of dizziness and worrying because it's hard to catch his breath as he walks down the

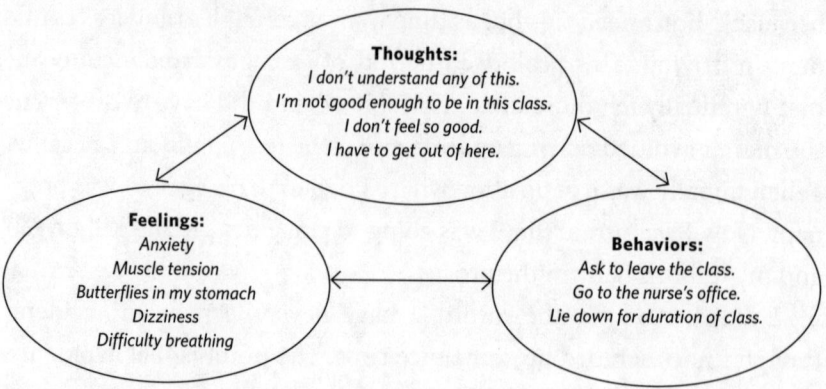

Breaking Down the Emotional Experience of Honors Math

hall. He tells his symptoms to the nurse, who takes his temperature—normal—and suggests that he lie down for a bit. As time ticks on, he begins to feel better, and he feels able to join his friends for lunch and finish out the rest of the school day.

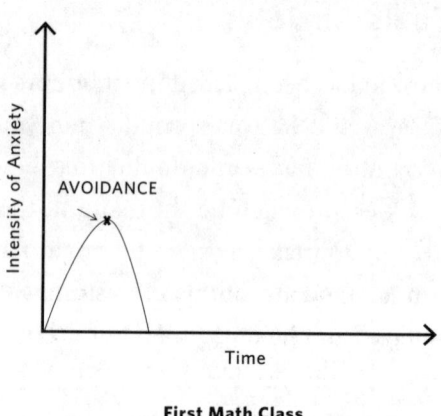

First Math Class

Anxiety Levels and Avoidance During the First Math Class

Avoidance is a quick and powerful way to decrease anxiety, and the relief that it brings is super reinforcing. In the preceding figure, you can see how decamping to the nurse's office rapidly dialed down the intensity of your son's anxiety. By the time math class was over, he was back to baseline.

But his avoidance has consequences. New learning has taken place: He has evidence suggesting to him that he can't handle honors math class. This sets the stage for him to arrive at Math Class #2 even more anxious than he was for the first. He is on high alert for any feelings in his body or thoughts in his mind that confirm that he is too anxious to stay in the class. And because of his distraction, it's even harder for him to follow the lesson. It doesn't take long for him to notice worried thoughts and butterflies in his stomach.

As you can see in the following figure, his anxiety increases more quickly and dramatically than the first time. So what has he learned that he needs to do to cope? He raises his hand within the first few minutes of being in the classroom and heads to the nurse. Once again, the relief that he feels only reinforces this cycle. As he lies down in the nurse's office, his relief is mingled with shame and self-doubt. "I'm too dumb to be in this class. Why is this so hard for me?"

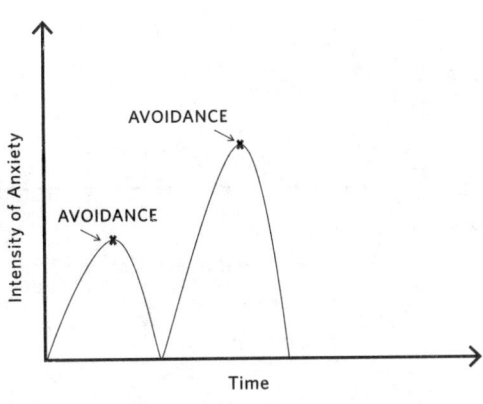

Anxiety Levels and Avoidance During the Second Math Class

Beliefs about his inability to cope become more entrenched as the pattern plays out again: greater anxiety before Math Class #3. But this time, he has so much anticipatory anxiety that he feels overwhelmed even before he enters the classroom. In fact, he notices butterflies in his stomach as soon as he wakes up that morning, and you and he have a tense and tearful argument about going to school that day. He makes it into school, carrying a pit of dread in his stomach all morning. On the way to class, he feels his heart pounding in his chest, he has trouble catching his breath, and he feels hot and clammy and tense and miserable. So he goes straight to the nurse's office, without even attempting to enter the classroom, only noticing his anxiety start to improve when the school nurse calls home to have you come pick him up for the day. And here is the bottom line: Short-term avoidance fuels long-term interference.

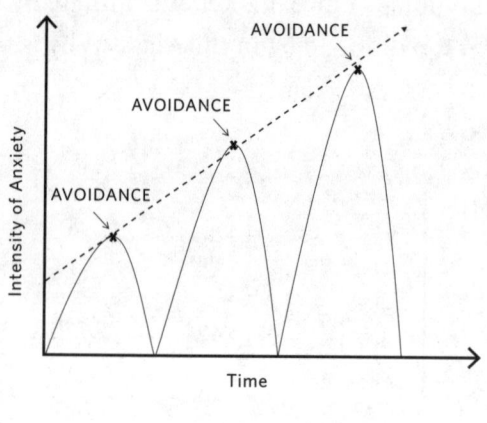

Third Math Class

Anxiety Levels and Avoidance During the Third Math Class

The relief that we feel when we avoid something anxiety-provoking is a powerful motivator of future behavior. This means that relief reinforces the avoidance behavior, and we call this the cycle of anxiety.

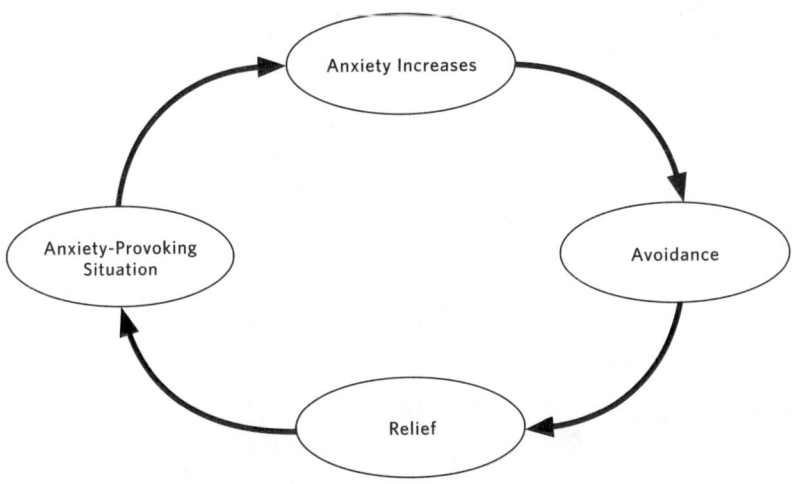

The Cycle of Anxiety

Starting on the left, you encounter an anxiety-provoking situation. Your fight-or-flight response kicks in, urging you to avoid the situation, and when you do so, you feel relief. The positive feelings of relief reinforce this cycle, making it more likely that the pattern will repeat whenever the same anxiety-provoking situation comes up again in the future. Not only does this cycle repeat over time, but it gets bigger and badder: This is how your son gets from leaving math class to feeling unable to go to school at all. The key process at play here is *negative reinforcement;* when you experience relief from distress after a certain behavior, that behavior is more likely to occur in the future.

It's a vicious cycle—but it's a cycle that you can break.

The Alternative Ending

I sometimes ask kids to draw for me what they think will happen to their anxiety if they don't avoid or escape from an anxiety-provoking situation. Most of them have never really thought about it, but when asked, they often draw something like this:

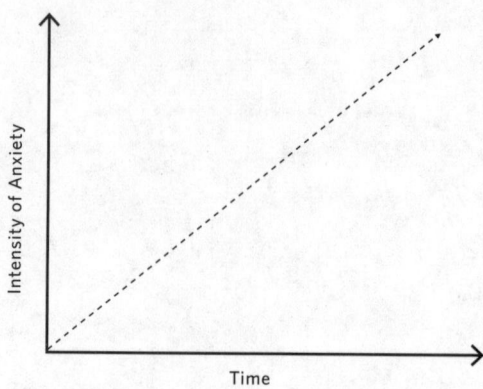

Predictions About Anxiety

We'll take a look, and I'll say something like, "So you think your anxiety would keep going up and up and up, getting worse and worse over time, unless you did something to stop it?"

"I guess."

I acknowledge that this would be pretty awful. But then I ask them to think about what that would actually mean—what would happen to their body or their mind if their anxiety went through the roof and never stopped.

"I don't know, really . . . I guess I would have a heart attack and die? Or I wouldn't be able to control my body at all, and maybe I would freak out and try to jump out a window or something. Or I would go crazy. Like my brain would break. I would completely lose my mind and be in a coma or need to be in a hospital or something for the rest of my life."

This is when I validate those assumptions while also pointing out that there is almost no chance that their feelings of anxiety will hurt them in the moment—and if anything scary or unusual did happen, it would be due to an underlying medical vulnerability.

Your emotions rise, peak, and fall like waves. They don't—they *can't*—stay elevated for too long. This is because your body strives for balance, for homeostasis. Feedback loops in your body elevate you into the fight-or-flight response, then trigger changes to bring you back to baseline. Instead of distress going inexorably up until you die or lose your mind, the most likely scenario by far is this one—even if you do nothing but wait:

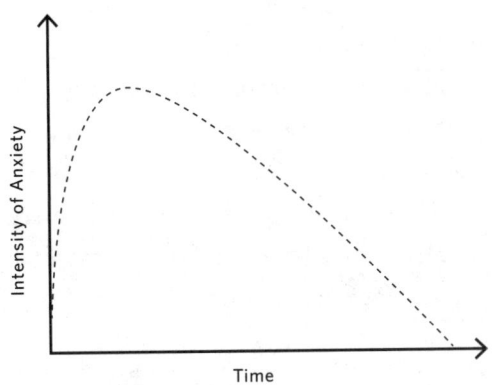

Anxiety in Reality

What would have happened if your son hadn't left math class? The most likely outcome for him if he hadn't left class that first time is this: His anxiety would have risen, possibly quite high, and eventually peaked and plateaued before starting to decrease, slowly. He might have become tearful, and maybe some of his classmates or his teacher might have noticed, which might have felt embarrassing. But it's likely that his teacher actually cares about how he is coping and may have approached him after class. Maybe the two of them would have set up some time to meet one-on-one to review the basics, and your son would see that he does, in fact, understand the material— or at least he has the capacity to understand it, with some extra time and help.

The point is that it is way more likely that your son will be able to cope with his anxiety if he resists the urge to avoid than it is for him to kick the bucket from a heart attack at age thirteen. But when he avoids, he loses the opportunity to learn that his "worst-case scenario" predictions typically do not come to pass. And he also loses the chance to learn that he can, indeed, cope with the tough situation. It certainly is much quicker and easier for him to feel better by leaving the class. But the short-term relief from distress sets the stage for longer-term problems.

Learning that avoidance fuels anxiety gives you a path toward a different ending: one where discomfort brings opportunity, where challenge builds strength, and where anxiety loses and you win. Granted, doing hard things is hard, but leaning into rather than away from anxiety is actually the key to reducing its power. There are ways to approach this challenge so that you are more likely to succeed, and we will get there. But first, let's talk a bit about how you as a parent can model resilient coping in the face of anxiety for your kids.

Modeling Matters

You are your child's first and most enduring barometer for understanding the world; they look to you for information about how they should interpret and respond to their environment. What happens when your toddler takes a tumble—they look to you, right? Kids get a ton of information about what to be afraid of from their caregivers, starting at an early age. Observing their parents also gives them important information that helps them form beliefs about how capable they are of handling tough things.

This means that what you actually *do* matters: Modeling brave beliefs and resilient responses to anxiety sets your kids up to have brave beliefs and resilient responses of their own. The opposite is true as well; your kids are likely to adopt your negative beliefs and avoidant coping strategies.

So, once you understand (1) that avoidance fuels anxiety and (2) that doing the hard thing feels awful but won't hurt you, you then have a tool. You can model brave beliefs and behaviors to positively influence your kid's relationship to their own anxiety.

Modeling healthy beliefs about anxiety

Your response matters when your child is feeling overwhelmed with anxiety. Imagine they are crying, having trouble catching their breath, and telling you that their heart is beating quickly. What does it communicate to them if you respond with panic: "Oh my gosh, what's wrong, are you okay? Let me check your pulse. Jeez, you are really hot. Calm down! I seriously need you to calm down. If you don't calm down, you will make yourself sick!" This response is adding major fuel to the anxiety fire, amplifying the painful-feelings pile-on and creating more anxiety about anxiety.

What if, instead, you take your kid's hands, look them in the eye, and validate with confidence. "You feel really scared; I see that. Anxiety feels awful. At the same time, it can't hurt you. This will pass. I am right here with you, if you want me to be."

Consider how impactful it is for your kid to see that you are so confident in their coping abilities that you would actually encourage them to sit with—rather than run from—their distress. When you model calm during an emotional storm, you are helping your child to write their own story of resilience.

Modeling bravery when you are anxious

Confession: I am an anxiety disorder specialist who is also scared of bugs. (There are many of us, actually.) Once I became a parent, I didn't want my kid to learn from my reaction that bugs were scary or dangerous. I know they aren't. And I understand that it was helpful for my early ancestors to have a strong fear reaction to prehistoric insects that were likely to be dangerous, and that I've inherited this response. So I push myself really hard to assume a convincing poker face when she points out a spine-chilling beast with a thousand legs on the living room wall. As my insides are tying themselves in knots, I try to sound convincing when I say, "Wow! Look at all those legs! I bet he is fast! Let me put him outside where he belongs. . . ." We make friends with ladybugs. We observe bees and talk about how much they help the planet. I am getting better at it, but I'm still a work in progress.

It is helpful to model brave behavior, like modeling calm curiosity around bugs. And it is also important to model for your kids that you, too, can be afraid. In fact, modeling healthy responses to the range of negative emotions helps our kids feel less vulnerable and unmoored when they experience those same feelings.

Anxiety can make us feel terribly alone. When we believe that we are the only one struggling, we can feel like we are damaged and defective, weird and incapable, and we can worry that our anxiety will define us and our future. It is such a gift to be able to share with your kids about times in your life when you felt frightened, worried, uncertain, or terrified, but—crucially—when you rose to the challenge, resisted the urge to avoid your anxiety, and instead fought back. I did this recently and it went something like this:

"A kind of scary thing happened to me today. My manager called me and asked if I could give some updates on a project during a big meeting this afternoon. I felt nervous, because I didn't have much time to prepare, and I knew I would be speaking in front of people who are important for my job. In the moment, I wanted to make an excuse to get out of presenting somehow. But I didn't want my anxiety to stop me from doing something important, and so even though I felt nervous, I presented. I was sweating the whole time, and I definitely tripped over some of my words. But it actually went fine, and it showed me that I can do hard things, even when I don't feel confident. And that feels good."

Modeling a balance of bravery *and* vulnerability is the key. When something anxiety-provoking or unexpected happens, you should be mindful of what your response communicates to your children, knowing that your reactions are likely to influence their developing view of their world. However, you shouldn't come across as a placid, unflappable robot either.

If your kids never see that you feel fear, anger, shame, or sadness, they are more likely to feel alone and broken when they experience these emotions themselves. Modeling balanced responses to negative emotions—rather than having your kids believe that you never experience them—can be the foundation of flexible and healthy emotional narratives for your children.

It's important to consider a child's developmental stage and emotional maturity in the process. It's one thing to say to your nine-year-old, "I'm feeling a bit stressed about some of the stuff in the news these days, and I know I can handle it," and another to share, "I am pretty sure this is Armageddon and I'm totally freaking out." While it's impossible—and not actually all that helpful—to shield kids entirely from the bad stuff, you want to be mindful about what you share, and model how you are coping with your hard feelings.

Modeling confidence in your child

You know your kid so well that you can often anticipate their reactions. For example, if your child tends to feel anxious in large social situations, you might watch them at a holiday party with wide-eyed trepidation, waiting for the other shoe to drop. You might check in with them repeatedly to see if they are all right. You might give them an "out" ahead of time: "If it feels too hard, we can go whenever you want. I'll just tell Aunt Vicki that I'm not feeling well."

If your kid notices that you are on high alert for their reaction, they are more likely to notice uncomfortable thoughts and feelings themselves (remember, when you look for an itch, you will find one). If you check in with them repeatedly to see if they are all right, it communicates that you think that there is something about this situation that is *not* all right. If you give them an "out," they know that you don't think they will be able to cope. In effect, you are modeling your belief that they won't be able to handle a given situation that everyone else in the room can handle. That means either that the situation must be dangerous or that they are too fragile to cope, or both.

But I know my child is going to struggle in this situation.

First, you don't *know*. Your child could surprise you!

But more importantly, even if your child does struggle, each anxiety-provoking situation is an opportunity to shape a healthy anxiety narrative. What do you hope your child learns from this tough situation? How can this experience take them closer to the goals that you and they share, for them to grow up to be a confident and capable young person?

Both validating your kids' anxiety *and* expressing confidence in their ability to cope with tough feelings are key to modeling a healthy response to anxiety. This is a situation where we can use a skill called a *supportive statement.*

Supportive statements are a tool used in evidence-based treatments for child anxiety that help parents model and encourage effective coping in the moment. A supportive statement is based on the following equation:

$$\text{Support} = \text{Acceptance} + \text{Confidence}$$

To create an effective supportive statement, you want to do the following:

1. First, communicate acceptance and understanding by *validating* (accepting) your child's experience.
2. Next, express your *confidence* that they can rise to the challenge.
3. Connect the phrases using the word "and," to model how seemingly conflicting truths can coexist: fear and bravery, discomfort and persistence, anxiety and strength.

In the holiday party situation discussed earlier, a supportive statement could sound like any of the following: "I see that you are uncomfortable. It can be hard to be around a bunch of people, and I know you can do hard things even when you feel uncomfortable." "It makes sense that you are anxious, and I have seen you fight back against your anxiety many times. You've got this." "You are struggling now, and I know you can get through this."

The goal of the supportive statements is *not* to magically eviscerate your child's anxiety in the moment—it's not verbal Valium. Rather, the goal is to communicate how *you* view your child. It is a shorthand that you can reach for when your kid is anxious and you don't know what to say or do, but you want to do something that helps.

Supportive statements plant seeds. In the moment, it does not matter if your child believes that they can handle this situation—what is important is that they know *you* believe in them. You are modeling acceptance of their experience, and modeling confidence in their abilities. This then becomes their story over time.

■ ■ ■

Avoidance is on-brand for humans, but so is rising to the challenge. My sincere hope is that, having read this first part of the book, you are seeing negative emotions like anxiety or sadness in a different way—not as personal shortcomings or dangerous experiences that must be avoided, but as formative challenges within our collective human experience. I hope that you have begun to identify your feelings, thoughts, and behaviors in response to an emotion and to recognize the power of actions in shaping your experience. Armed with the knowledge that avoidance fuels anxiety, you can begin to push back on the notion that what is uncomfortable must also be unsafe and model this approach for your kids.

However, none of us are operating in a vacuum. Anxiety in parents and in kids must be understood within the broader landscape of modern parenting. Many of the dominant messages of modern parenting culture impede resilience and worsen anxiety. This makes trusting your parenting instincts while combating anxiety that much harder.

But you can do hard things. In the next part of the book, we will explore the modern practice of Intensive Parenting and the challenges that it presents for anxious kids and parents. We will see why building a coping skill set grounded in psychological flexibility helps you move forward with confidence.

What Can You Take Home with You?

- Begin to notice the ways in which you may work to avoid painful internal experiences. How is avoidance impacting your life? Are there ways in which it's getting in the way of your goals and your values?
- Challenge yourself to resist the urge to avoid in some low-stakes situations—tackle some things you have been putting off, lean into that hard conversation you need to have, practice sitting with some discomfort.
- Start pointing out to your kids the relationship between avoidance and anxiety. Help them understand that while avoidance helps decrease distress in the short term, over time it can make anxiety and distress worse. Create an ongoing dialogue in which your kids know that you view anxiety as uncomfortable but tolerable—an opportunity for growth, rather than a signal to avoid. Share stories about times when you felt anxious and faced your fears. This is a topic worth repeating.
- Practice supportive statements with your loved ones. Remember that the two ingredients of a supportive statement are acceptance and confidence, so first validate their experience to show acceptance, and then communicate confidence in their ability to do hard things.

PART II

CHAPTER 5

The Intensive Parenting Paradox

Imagine you are hosting a party for your mother's seventy-fifth birthday at your home. You have been planning this for over six months. Family and friends are traveling from out of town to celebrate. You are looking forward to the event, but you are also stressed. You want your mother to be happy, and you want to represent your home and family well.

As the party approaches, you realize that the biggest X factor is your teenage son. He has been "off" recently, struggling for the past few months in a way that seems beyond what you have come to expect from teenagers. He is stressed about his schoolwork, despite solid grades. He has been taking forever before school each morning, obsessing about his appearance. He is complaining of headaches and has missed several school days as a consequence. He spends most of his time holed up in his room, glued to his phone.

In rare forthcoming moments, he shares with you that he feels stressed around people these days. He isn't sure why, but he says he feels overwhelmed and kind of sick when he is "put on the spot." And here you are, bringing a big group into your home with whom you expect him to interact graciously.

You empathize with him for feeling anxious, and you have suggested that he talk to the school guidance counselor, or maybe even his pediatrician. But he shuts you down, and you don't want to push.

He becomes more and more anxious and withdrawn, and you really start to worry about how he will behave on the day of the party.

In the weeks leading up to the event, in addition to helping Aunt Cynthia arrange a rental car and planning a vegan dinner option for your cousin, you are also scouring the internet for advice on how to better understand and help your son. You comb through parenting articles, Instagram posts, Facebook threads. Anxiety and withdrawal can be due to *so many things*. You try to open the door for him to be honest. *Did something happen at school? Are you in trouble? Has anyone hurt you— like,* really *hurt you? You can tell me anything.* He recoils from all your questions and repeats that he is "stressed" and wants to be left alone.

The weekend before the event, things come to a head. You are running around like the house is on fire, barking at your family. Everyone else is helping out. But your son refuses to get his hair cut. That same night, he won't come downstairs for dinner. Tension gets the better of you and you snap. Using some words you regret, you tell him he needs to shape up before next weekend. That's when you learn that he's not planning on coming out of his room for the party. He can't do it, he says. He *won't* do it, point-blank.

What would you do in this situation? What *should* you do?

Before we get to what you would *do*, let's consider what you might feel: Anxious. Angry. Helpless. Worried about your son. Worried about what others might think. Worried about doing the wrong thing in response. You're thinking, "He is obviously going through something right now and needs support. He's a good kid, and something about this situation is clearly hard for him." Which leads to "No, this is ridiculous—it's a family party, not a firing squad! You show up for family, end of story."

You imagine the reactions of your guests. "What if I insist that he come out and we get into a screaming match in front of everyone? Will I be seen as a domineering, insensitive parent? Or if I don't insist that he be a part of the event, will they say I am coddling him? If we admit he is going through a hard time, what will everyone think of him? And of me?"

What *Is* My Job?

At the intersection of child anxiety and parenting anxiety is a question: What is your primary job, as a parent, when your child is anxious or distressed? When do you push your kid to face their fears, and when do you back off?

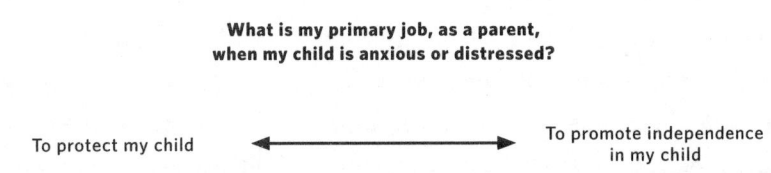

Parenting Dialectic Part 1

It's helpful to consider the answer to this question along a continuum. On the one hand, your primary job as a parent is to protect your children. You started doing that before your kids were even born—remember all those delicious cheeses you passed up while pregnant?—and you are biologically predisposed to do so until the end of your days. On the other hand, your job is to promote independence in your children, to prepare your baby birds to leave the nest, to ensure that they grow up to be functioning, well-adjusted adults.

This represents a critical parenting *dialectic*. A dialectic occurs when two things that seem contradictory are actually true at the same time. For example, "I am a capable person, *and* I need support." "I love my child, *and* I am upset with their behavior." "I love being a parent, *and* I don't like many of the activities of parenting." Dialectics are really helpful ways of approaching mental health, and many of today's most effective psychological treatments integrate dialectics into the work of therapy. The supportive statement skill discussed in Chapter 4 is an example of a dialectic approach (e.g., "I see that you are worried, and I know you can handle this").

In the case of our parenting dialectic, both of these answers are true. Sure, you may prioritize independence more for your fifteen-year-old than for your five-year-old, but your job as a parent is to protect your child *and* to promote their independence. The problem is that anxiety can pit these two truths against each other as if they can't coexist.

As we know, anxiety shows up when we believe that we need protection from danger. When kids' anxiety alarms go off, they seek safety, often through closeness with their parents. Anxiety therefore pulls very, very hard at the left side of this parenting dialectic, urging you to prioritize protection. It can elevate the false belief that whatever *feels uncomfortable* must also *be unsafe,* hijacking your deep-seated biological drive to protect your children, even from their own feelings. Parenting anxiety can urge you to move heaven and earth to help your child feel better in the moment. Translation: You let your kid skip the birthday party.

At other times, anxiety seems so irrational that it feels absurd to let it control the situation. You know that it is important to help your kid build resilience, and you worry about the long-term consequences of their inability to cope with difficult situations. Parenting anxiety can therefore urge you to put your foot down, leaving little room for emotions. Translation: You make your kid come to the party by any means necessary.

Parents often have the experience of ping-ponging between these two poles in response to their child's distress. You may find yourself oscillating between protection and independence, particularly if you are anxious or stressed yourself. You start by trying to do the warm, understanding thing. You take a deep breath and validate. *I want him to know that I believe him when he says he is struggling. If I give him love and support, he will get through this.* And then at some point you hit a limit, where the irrationality of your child's anxiety, the interference of your kid's emotions in daily life, and your fear for their future—governed by anxiety—pushes you to the opposite pole. *I have been bending over backward to try to make things easier for him and nothing is getting better. I am babying him, and he is too old for this.*

Sound familiar? If so, you are not alone. When anxiety is high, thinking tends to get more polarized and less flexible. This makes it even harder to decide when to push back versus when to give in to your child's distress. It often seems like there are no good options.

What's even worse is that the risk for child anxiety increases at either end of this parenting dialectic. On the left-hand side, parenting characterized by lots of warmth but few clear limits or expectations for the child's behavior is associated with child anxiety. We can call this pole the *overparenting* side. It typifies the behavior of parents who tend to swoop in to manage their kids' distress, often because they fear the child can't handle it itself. While loving efforts to protect kids from their own anxiety improves their distress in the short term, it decreases their chances to build resilience. Over time, this decreases self-efficacy and self-confidence, and kids can become increasingly anxious and dependent on others.

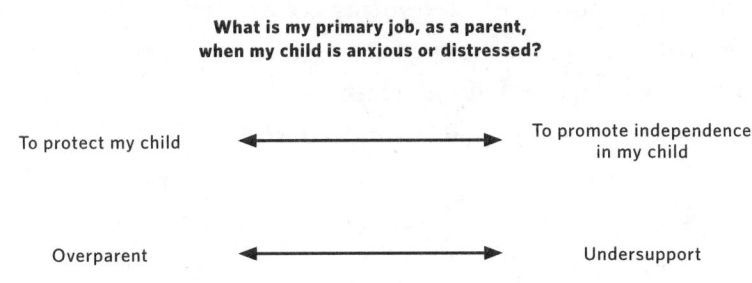

What is my primary job, as a parent, when my child is anxious or distressed?

To protect my child ⟵————————⟶ To promote independence in my child

Overparent ⟵————————⟶ Undersupport

Parenting Dialectic Part 2

On the right-hand side, parenting characterized by lots of demands and low warmth is also a risk factor for child anxiety. We can call this pole the *undersupport* side. While, often, parents' well-meaning goal on this side is to encourage their kids to become self-reliant and independent, if kids don't yet have skills to cope independently, they are likely to be unsuccessful. These kids are pushed into the deep end of the pool before they can swim. Demoralization, depression, and greater anxiety can follow.

The Lure of the Insta-Fix

So, what is the best way to parent when you or your child are anxious? Today's parents are bombarded with advice, often propagated by internet content creators with varying degrees of credibility and a boatload of apparent confidence. Sometimes the information that you find is helpful, and online support can be a lifeline. Other times, however, information-seeking that is intended to alleviate your anxiety can have the opposite effect.

Years ago, searching for how best to address my infant daughter's sleep regression, I stumbled upon a parent seeking advice for how to stop her toilet-training child from hiding "number twos" under the dresser. It hadn't ever occurred to me to worry that my home could become a giant litter box once I had a child. "It doesn't matter if I ever get her to sleep," I remember thinking, numbly. "As soon as I do, I'll wake up to some other fresh parenting hell." I was totally despondent. Granted, I was also totally sleep-deprived. And my fears from that day never materialized, thankfully. But the point is that sometimes what you find online can amplify your anxiety.

Researchers are starting to study this effect. A 2021 UK study found that higher levels of anxiety were associated with more engagement with "InstaMum" accounts—the social media accounts of mothers made famous via Instagram—particularly for women with lower self-esteem or who were more prone to comparing themselves to others. This suggests that increasingly anxious parents are seeking information online that makes them more anxious, prompting more online engagement. A vicious cycle indeed.

Today's parents are understandably perplexed by inconsistent guidance about how best to parent in the context of anxiety. The available parenting advice is well-meaning but often contradictory. Critically, it often aligns with either end of our parenting dialectic, urging parents to either overparent or undersupport their anxious kid. Because there is truth on both sides of the dialectic, you can find compelling arguments to support any opinion. But whether this advice is served up to you through an article, a meme, a reel, or a podcast, it's a one-sided conversation. Advice is framed in a one-size-fits-all approach via "parenting hacks" that feel reductive and sometimes even accusatory. This leads to more anxiety for parents seeking clarity.

In seeking advice for the birthday party dilemma, you could easily find support for viewpoints that align with either end of our parenting dialectic. On the one hand, some might say that if you "force" your teen to show up to the party, you are showing him that you don't care about his feelings, and he won't feel like his home is a safe space. You will be causing a fundamental attachment injury, he will withdraw even further, and the trust between you will be irrevocably broken.

In contrast, others might say that he needs to learn how to do things even when he doesn't feel like doing them. You are reminded that the adult world is full of examples of when he'll have to do things even when he doesn't want to, or even when he feels like he is unable to. He can't just not show up for work whenever he is "stressed." If you don't help him learn this now, you are putting his whole future at risk.

You feel damned if you do, damned if you don't—either way, you notice the "I'm a bad parent" story coming up for you in your thoughts. Because, for reasons that you can't quite put your finger on, you believe that "good" parents have "good" children who are well-adjusted, emotionally mature, gracious hosts, and team players. What does it say about you if your son isn't able to fulfill that role? You wish you didn't care what other people think about your parenting . . . but you do.

Contemporary parenting advice is strongly influenced by the dominant parenting culture of the moment. To make choices along our parenting dialectic that are right for us and for our family, and to better navigate parent and child anxiety, we need to zoom out and consider the broader landscape of modern parenting culture in which we all exist.

Culture Is Context

In the 1990s, U.S. sociologist Sharon Hays was studying beliefs and expectations about what makes an "ideal" mother in Western countries. She found that modern society equated good mothers with "intensive" mothers—those who place their children at the center of their life and devote tremendous time, energy, and emotional and financial investment into childrearing as a moral enterprise. She coined the term "intensive mothering," which we now broadly understand as "intensive parenting."

In her book *The Cultural Contradictions of Motherhood*, Hays notes that "the ideas [of Intensive Parenting] are certainly not followed in practice by every mother, but they are, implicitly or explicitly, understood as the proper approach to the raising of a child by the majority of mothers." In other words, whether or not you agree that "good" parenting means Intensive Parenting, these are the norms and expectations that are percolating in your culture; they are bound to influence you. Many other familiar parenting approaches that have emerged within the last few decades—helicopter parenting, snowplow parenting, or gentle parenting, to name a few—broadly fall under the umbrella of Intensive Parenting.

A quick disclaimer: The study of Intensive Parenting is an entire discipline, and I can't do it justice here. I want to lay out a snapshot of Intensive Parenting, particularly as it relates to parent and child anxiety in our culture today. Recognizing the themes of the Intensive Parenting ideal can help you better understand the current context of increasing parent and child anxiety and their interaction. I now find it impossible to look at contemporary parenting anxiety—and child anxiety by association—without considering how it has been impacted by idealized parenting norms. Once you identify the Intensive Parenting waters in which you are swimming, you can begin to push back against its currents when it doesn't serve you, your kids, or your community. This is an empowering—and ultimately an anxiety-busting—approach.

What Is Intensive Parenting?

Intensive Parenting is structured on a few principles. First, children are seen as sacred, precious, and in need of protection from the corrupting influences of a dangerous world. Parenting is both an active responsibility and a selfless, natural instinct that requires the all-encompassing efforts of parents—primarily mothers. "Good" parents intensively parent in ways that are child-centered, emotionally absorbing, labor-intensive, expensive, and expert-driven. Let's explore each of these in turn.

First, Intensive Parenting is "child-centered," meaning that the needs of the child should always come first in the family. There is some good stuff here: We know that forming *secure attachment*—a strong parent-child emotional bond that is marked by parental warmth, availability, and responsiveness—is the keystone for healthy child development. Secure attachment becomes the foundation for how well children can trust and thrive in their environment, and a template for how they relate to other people as they grow. Parents who want securely attached kids prioritize building an affectionate, responsive parent-child relationship. And this is fantastic for kids. At the same time, this fuels expectations that "good" parents drop everything to respond immediately to their child's needs (and wants), over and above all else. It opens the door for anxiety and guilt if you prioritize your partner's needs—or, heaven forbid, your own—above your child's demands in any given moment.

Second, Intensive Parenting is an "emotionally absorbing" endeavor, requiring a boatload of involvement and investment. This centers on the expectation that you should devote tons of mental and physical energy to becoming deeply emotionally involved in your child's life as a marker of "good" parenting. This means being attentive to your child's emotional experience, which can help them feel valued and supported. But it leaves little room for separation between your kid's emotions and your own, and that's not always a plus. It's harder to steady the ship when you are feeling just as overwhelmed as your kid.

This principle also has implications for your sense of self, with expectations that parenthood should become the most important part of your identity, the place in which you should naturally find complete personal fulfillment. The flip side of this is that parents who don't feel blissed out by parenting can feel that they are "bad" parents.

Parenting is expected to be "labor-intensive," in terms of time and emotional energy. And more is always assumed to be better. We see this trend in cross-national data indicating that modern parents dedicate way more time to childrearing activities than the parents of previous generations, particularly parents with higher levels of education. How much more labor-intensive is it to make your own baby food from scratch, to take time off from work to do carpool shifts, or to plan a Pinterest-worthy sleepover for your tween . . . all of which society equates with "good" parenting when you see it glorified in a highlight reel? Relatedly, Intensive Parenting is also "financially expensive." Modern parents feel compelled to spend money to enrich their children as a marker of devotion, and many parents worry that they aren't doing enough. Critically, it's not clear that labor-intensive and expensive parenting always leads to better outcomes for kids, or whether it's worth the very real costs to parents. But the anxiety of *not* doing enough keeps many parents on the hamster wheel of expending more time, effort, and money on parenting.

Finally, the Intensive Parenting ideal is also "expert-driven." Devotion isn't enough; the Intensive Parent should be knowledgeable and highly skilled. This is parenting as brain surgery. Seeking out expert advice is now another marker of a "good" parent, and the internet has made it increasingly easy to do so—more often than not, this advice is served up to you on your social media feed even before you choose to search for it. And expert advice is often protective. It helped me to immediately dismiss the advice of my very dear father, who suggested that we put my newborn on her belly to sleep because "Elkinses sleep on their stomachs." (Not before they can roll over, Dad.) The fact that you are reading this book means it's likely that you identify with the instinct to seek out expert advice as part of parenting. But it's increasingly tough to discern whether the guidance is fact or opinion, and whether it should apply to you and your family.

Intensive Parenting is so deeply baked into our culture that its principles may seem unassailable: *Of course* children are precious. *Of course* good parents are responsive to their kids' needs. *Of course* experts know more than your great-aunt about child development. But cultural norms, by definition, feel self-evident—which is all the more reason to give them a careful look.

Even if you disagree with these assumptions and pointedly reject the tenets of Intensive Parenting, the very act of choosing to reject them shows how profoundly they influence your choices. Because, like it or not, Intensive Parenting ideals are the yardstick against which modern parents are judged by others—and by themselves. In other words, it's virtually impossible to be immune to this concept.

What's most relevant to our discussion here is that Intensive Parenting is interlaced with anxiety. And if you are a parent who runs anxious to begin with, this approach is doing nothing to alleviate your anxiety. In fact, it may be influencing your behavior in ways that actually make anxiety worse for you and for your kids.

Modern Intensive Parenting

Though identified in the 1990s, Intensive Parenting is by no means a cultural relic. As recently as 2019, the headline of an article in *The Atlantic* proclaimed "'Intensive' Parenting Is Now the Norm in America." In fact, we are seeing the *intensification* of Intensive Parenting in the twenty-first century, particularly in the United States and the United Kingdom but in other countries as well. This intensification is driven by the sense that today's children are even more vulnerable than in previous generations, and that they need parents to provide them with constant intellectual stimulation and opportunities for success. This practice is known as *concerted cultivation*.

In addition, today's parents are even more likely to believe that their parenting choices are make-or-break for their children's long-term success and happiness. Seventy-one percent of parents of young adults in the United States say that their children's success and failure reflect directly on their parenting prowess.

It's impossible to dismiss the seething undercurrent of anxiety here. It seems that, at any point, parents might do the "wrong" thing, setting their child on a path toward an adulthood that is emotionally bereft and unsuccessful and condemning them to some worst-case scenario that they will be dissecting in thirty years with their therapist (or their corrections officer). This is perhaps an exaggeration, but my point is that within this culture, parents feel overwhelming pressure to ensure their child's future happiness and success, all on top of managing the general goat rodeo that is modern parenting.

The Range and Impact of Intensive Parenting

There is a range in how Intensive Parenting pressures and beliefs play out across different identities, family systems, and communities. In general, parents from across social classes show similar, positive attitudes toward Intensive Parenting practices—so while families may have unequal resources, we all want to parent in ways that we hope will help our kids be happy, healthy, and successful. The problem is that Intensive Parenting assumes a position of privilege—to "do it well," parents need to be able to devote a lot of time and resources to enhance their child's outcomes. This naturally disadvantages low- and middle-income households, or communities that have more limited access to education, extracurricular activities, and expert support, all of which exacerbates inequity.

The physical and emotional labor required to parent intensively is way more difficult to come by in circumstances marked by deprivation or discrimination. And sadly, the Intensive Parenting lens can become a vehicle for judging the parenting of folks from historically disadvantaged or marginalized groups. Because these approaches are upheld as the universal example of "best parenting" practices, if you don't parent intensively—because you deliberately choose not to, or because you , simply can't—our culture derides you for not "doing enough" for your kids.

Moreover, in the United States at least, the emphasis on individualism places the responsibility for manifesting this idealized form of childrearing firmly on parents' shoulders, with very little social and material support. Modern Intensive Parenting practices are now seen as a form of "status safeguarding." Intensive Parenting today is not seen merely as a marker of devotion, but as an anxiety-fueled rat race to secure resources and opportunities for your kids in an increasingly competitive, economically uncertain era. In effect, the work of modern Intensive Parenting is often about creating an individualized safety net in societies without social safety nets. This further privileges the privileged.

So why aren't we, as a society, calling it quits with Intensive Parenting? In a 2022 *Atlantic* article, Nate G. Higler argues that the Intensive Parenting approach isn't going anywhere because access to opportunities valued within the Intensive Parenting construct—small class sizes, extracurricular opportunities, test prep, and access to quality basics like food, sleep, and clean air—does benefit children's physical health and achievement, and parents aren't going to just stop caring. "The problem," he argues, "is that we impose these costs on the wrong people: individuals. This ensures that only the richest, most highly educated parents can manage everything without breaking their lives in half."

You might be happy to sacrifice yourself on the altar of Intensive Parenting if it meant that your kid would come out well-adjusted and set for life. However, studies to date don't show a clear link between Intensive Parenting styles and immutably good child psychological outcomes over time. A 2021 study investigated the extent to which Intensive Parenting approaches impacted children's physical and psychological health outcomes. Drawing data from the Millennium Cohort Study, which followed more than eighteen thousand children in the United Kingdom born between 2000 and 2001 from birth to adulthood, the authors could *not* conclude that an Intensive Parenting approach led to better psychological health outcomes for kids compared to the children of parents who adopted an "intermediate parenting" approach—those who were more moderately involved with their kids. The authors conclude, "The focus on probable risks for children's health may urge parents to become 'intensive' parents, but effects on children's health seem negligible." More isn't always better for psychological health.

In contrast, we do know that Intensive Parenting can negatively impact parents' mental health and well-being. Specifically, mothers who identify more strongly with Intensive Parenting report greater levels of parenting stress, burnout, and lower life satisfaction. There is such a clear link here that our culture of Intensive Parenting was cited by the U.S. Surgeon General as a major contributor to parenting stress.

You may not be willing to shelve Intensive Parenting, but having an awareness of its role in your life and in your parenting choices—particularly in the context of anxiety—is a whole new way of seeing your circumstances and making decisions for yourself.

Circling back to Grandma's birthday party, it becomes clear that what's going on is more than just your son's anxiety and your own parenting anxiety. This situation is also impacted by the dominant messages of modern parenting culture. Depending on how closely you identify with Intensive Parenting ideals as part of your own sense of who you are as a parent—or who you believe you *should* be—your response is probably impacted by these cultural norms.

If you reject these norms (and many cultures do), then the answer to the birthday party dilemma is pretty clear: His attendance at the party is nonnegotiable. But if you are firmly in the Intensive Parenting camp, I would wager that you are likely to lean toward the left-hand side of the parenting dialectic—toward overparenting. That means you will probably do some combination of the following: You will see your son's needs and wants as primary in this situation, and will get pretty emotionally absorbed with your son's experience—if he is happy, you are going to be happy; if he is miserable, you are going to be miserable. I'd guess that you will spend a ton of time, energy, and emotional bandwidth that you don't have attempting to understand and solve this dilemma. You are likely to fear that his emotional distress is somehow unsafe—or at least suboptimal—for him, and that you are responsible for protecting him from these feelings. Informed by these Intensive Parenting notions, I'd bet that you will defer to his distress and to agree that he can stay in his room for the party.

Because that's what a "good" parent would do, right? Hang tight, as we will come back to this a little later once you have more of the tools you need to resolve this dilemma.

■ ■ ■

Intensive Parenting has significant implications for parent and child anxiety. When something this influential is left unspoken, it can quietly shape your experience—bringing it to light helps you deal with anxiety more skillfully, whether it's everyday worries or something more serious.

In the chapters that follow, I argue that the dominant beliefs and practices of contemporary Intensive Parenting encourage parents to lean toward the left-hand side of the parenting dialectic—toward overparenting—which feeds into the avoidance that fuels anxiety. Having understood this pattern, you are better prepared to address this parenting dilemma and manage parenting anxiety.

What Can You Take Home with You?

- Identify where you tend to fall along the parenting dialectic: Are you more likely to trend toward overparenting or to under-supporting in the face of child anxiety? Are there times when you are more likely to lean toward one pole versus the other? What tends to be the outcome—for you and for your kids—of responding in either way?
- If you have a partner or co-parent, where do they fall along this parenting dialectic? It's not unusual for co-parents to have

different go-to responses. These differences can be a major source of conflict when addressing child anxiety disorders, so get it out there. Have a conversation with your co-parent to gauge where you both tend to fall, and—using your validation skills—try to understand the beliefs, fears, or motivations that drive your respective behaviors.

- Consider how Intensive Parenting impacts you broadly—your sense of yourself; your parenting values, beliefs, and practices; the norms and expectations of your peers and your community. For some folks, Intensive Parenting resonates deeply, while others see it as less of a factor in their daily life. As we move into discussing Intensive Parenting and anxiety more specifically in the next chapter, it will help to have collected your thoughts.

CHAPTER 6

Overparenting

Whether we like it or not, Intensive Parenting is embedded into conversations around "how best to parent" in many modern societies. It is the patina that coats our parental thoughts, beliefs, conversations, and actions. So it makes sense that it would influence both parent and child anxiety. But how, exactly?

We unfortunately don't yet have data measuring the degree to which parents live by Intensive Parenting ideals and how that impacts child anxiety over time. But the absence of published studies does not mean that there isn't an association—it just hasn't yet been investigated. That said, what I'm seeing as a clinician is troubling to me. There is a profound mismatch between what parents and kids need to be resilient in the face of anxiety and the dominant beliefs and practices of contemporary parenting culture. The long-term impact of these pressures is likely to play out differently for you, depending on whether higher anxiety is part of your family's equation. This means that if your child doesn't regularly struggle with anxiety, giving in to their distress when they unexpectedly do is unlikely to matter much in the long term. But for a kid who trends anxious, the link between avoidance and anxiety is a bigger deal. And if cultural pressures are making it more likely that you will help your kids avoid things that make them anxious, you may be kneecapping their future resilience. All the more so if you run anxious as well, as we will see shortly. So, what are you to do?

Start by looking critically at Intensive Parenting. Consider the parts of this parenting ideal that protect against anxiety and those that are likely to exacerbate it. Once you lay out the pieces, you can develop a set of strategies to help you flexibly choose a path forward that is right for *you* and *your family,* knowing there is never a one-size-fits-all solution.

First, the Good Stuff

The Pew Research Center's 2023 survey of U.S. parents found that 44 percent reported that they are trying to raise their children differently from how they were raised. Most of these parents said that they were trying to give their children more encouragement, support, and outward praise than they received as a child. This can be viewed as a rejection of parenting marked by harsh discipline and hierarchy, in which children's negative emotions were dismissed or criticized (factors more closely tied to the undersupport side of the parenting dialectic introduced in the previous chapter).

Broadly speaking, this move away from the undersupport pole via Intensive Parenting is a good thing for child anxiety. For decades, studies of child development have acknowledged that harsh criticism, low warmth, and insufficient support are risk factors for child anxiety. So the "warm and fuzzy" vibe of modern Intensive Parenting is welcome in this regard.

And there is more good stuff here. Intensive Parenting is theoretically linked with many factors that can protect against child anxiety, such as strong familial bonds, emotional awareness, warmth and affection, encouragement and positive reinforcement, and high-quality parent-child communication. I will focus here on three factors that fall under the umbrella of the Intensive Parenting ideal and are broadly protective against child anxiety disorders: a positive parent-child relationship, emotion socialization, and parental involvement. These are the parts of Intensive Parenting that may help your kid in the face of anxiety.

Positive parent-child relationship

Any way you slice it, a strong parent-child relationship is good for kids. Securely attached kids—those who are part of a parent-child relationship marked by parental warmth and responsiveness—are less likely to struggle with anxiety disorders. Additionally, parental warmth, which is a cornerstone of secure attachment, is a protective factor for child anxiety. The Intensive Parenting ideal elevates a strong parent-child attachment and a warm and loving relationship, and that's terrific for kids and parents. The other side of this coin is that parent-child relationships that are marked by insecure attachment, a lack of parental bonding early in life, or little parental warmth can mean a higher risk for developing anxiety disorders.

We also know that strong social support can protect against child anxiety. Children are at a greater risk for developing anxiety disorders following exposure to traumatic, negative, or stressful life events—violence, abuse, and natural disasters, as well as stressors such as divorce, the death of a family member, or repeated family relocations. Fortunately, research shows that the risk for developing anxiety disorders after such a life event is reduced if the child has positive social support from family. Strong parental support can cushion the blow of negative life events for kids. The Intensive Parenting lens primes parents to be aware of and attentive to their kids' emotions, encouraging them to show up in ways that buttress children against life stressors.

Emotion socialization

Emotion socialization, or the way that parents attend to, model, teach, and discuss emotions with their children, has important implications for managing anxiety. As seen through an Intensive Parenting lens, "good" parents are expected to be responsive to their child's emotions. Parents who are high in an "emotion coaching philosophy" view kids' emotional experiences as teaching opportunities, or opportunities for parent-child connection. They also tend to be more aware of their own emotional experiences, as well as those of their child, and tend to be invested in using skills like validation. Approaches that fall under the Intensive Parenting umbrella, such as gentle parenting, emphasize the concept of emotion coaching.

Evidence suggests that parents with better emotion regulation skills—like greater emotional awareness or better emotion-coping skills—are more likely to have warmer, less hostile relationships with their children. (Notice that I said *better* emotion regulation skills—not *perfect* emotion regulation skills. This does not necessarily mean that your child is doomed to a lifetime of anxiety if you lose your cool every so often.) Importantly for our purposes, these parents are also less likely to have children who struggle with anxiety.

Relatedly, we know that there are ways that parents can respond to children's emotions that are truly helpful in the context of anxiety. Responding to children's emotions with validation is nearly always beneficial, and teaching parents how to effectively validate their child's emotional experience is a cornerstone of family-based treatment for anxiety. If the Intensive Parenting approach encourages parents to fortify their emotion coaching and validation skills, that's a plus in my book.

Parental involvement

The Intensive Parenting framework places high value on parental involvement. It encourages parents to be actively involved in their child's life by wearing many hats: protector, nurturer, provider, teacher, playmate, coach, Uber driver, personal assistant, life coach.

The result of all of this involvement is often positive for kids' long-term health, emotional well-being, or economic success. Tutoring can help kids academically. Participation in structured extracurricular activities is often beneficial for kids' well-being. These activities tend to require some organization, involvement, and investment from parents. Money can't buy your kids happiness, but there is a relationship between more financial resources and greater well-being in adulthood. So modern parents are unlikely to stop being involved and invested anytime soon.

There is also some indication that the fruits of this labor can be associated with lower rates of anxiety. We know that kids who participate in extracurricular activities, particularly ones that include physical activity, are less likely to have anxiety disorders than those who do not. And some parental involvement in kids' school life—volunteering at school or attending school events—is associated with a lower likelihood of child mental health concerns. A degree of parental monitoring of kids' activities and whereabouts also appears protective. While this doesn't mean that knowing where your kid is on a Friday afternoon ensures that they won't develop an anxiety disorder, there is certainly a notable correlation.

The point here is that we have evidence that some degree of parental involvement in kids' lives seems helpful in offsetting the risk of anxiety disorders and other child mental health concerns. But is more always better? If some emotion coaching is good, is more emotion coaching better? If some parental involvement is good, is more involvement better?

There are many reasons to think not.

The degree of parental involvement can be imagined as an upside-down, U-shaped curve, where either too little or too much parental involvement is associated with problematic consequences for kids. This is absolutely consistent with what we see in child anxiety research: Too much or too little parental involvement places kids at higher risk for child anxiety. And parental *overinvolvement*—something that Intensive Parenting sanctifies—is closely linked to a number of factors that make child anxiety worse. Let's take a closer look.

When Too Much Is Too Much

The Intensive Parenting approach strongly encourages parents to do *more*. More meals made from scratch, more holiday magic, more Instagram-worthy parties, more family vacations, more activities. This is what Judith Warner refers to as "too-muchness" in her book *Perfect Madness: Motherhood in the Age of Anxiety*. In clinical settings, my colleagues and I are increasingly seeing connections between the "too-muchness" of Intensive Parenting and parenting styles and behaviors that can inadvertently worsen child anxiety disorders.

What's the mechanism here—*how* does this happen?

Overparenting—a term that I will use to characterize both over-involvement and overprotection—sends the message that the world is an unpredictable and dangerous place, and that your kid is incapable of managing challenges on their own. While the short-term outcome of overparenting is that your child has more support from you in the moment, the long-term outcome is that they don't get to fully experience normal stressful situations, don't have the chance to learn that they can handle tough situations without being chauffeured through them by a parent, and, of course, then have limited confidence about their ability to cope. This breeds more dependence on you, as their parent, to solve their problems, to intervene in their stressors, and to help them handle their own negative emotions. Of course, this prompts you to step in and manage life for them, and the cycle of anxiety and dependence continues.

We see this play out in studies showing that mothers of anxious children are more likely to jump in and assist their child in completing complex tasks than mothers of nonanxious children. There are a million examples of this in daily life—for example, not allowing your child to play with friends in the neighborhood without adult supervision; not allowing them to use a knife to cut their own food; taking over your child's household responsibilities when they are stressed out; or writing college essays for your teen. Let's be clear, I'm not advising you to give your three-year-old free rein with a steak knife. But in circumstances where the risk to their health and safety is low, and where the child has the ability to manage independently (even if they don't *want to* manage independently), a pattern of overparenting often backfires.

Let's imagine a father concerned about his daughter's academic success. With the well-meaning goal of making sure that she fully understands the course material, Dad is a regular participant in homework. It makes sense that giving his daughter extra support would help her perform better in school. It's also a lovely way to spend time together, at least in principle. Here we have our child-centered, labor-intensive, emotionally absorbed Intensive Parenting in full effect.

But Dad's involvement has downsides. His daughter doesn't have the chance to solve problems independently. She doesn't have the experience of getting stuck and working through an issue by herself. She doesn't have the opportunity to experience frustration, to tolerate that unpleasant emotion and move forward. Moreover, Dad's presence implies to her that *he doesn't believe that she is capable* of doing the work without help. And it sends the message that the stakes here are super high: An imperfect assignment seems somehow dangerous, otherwise, why would Dad be spending his time on this? The seeds of perfectionism, academic anxiety, and dependence are planted through this benevolent overinvolvement.

When kids lose opportunities to try to manage their own experience, they believe that they can't cope independently. The resulting anxiety makes sense; if you have been getting messages throughout your childhood that the world is an unsafe place that you are incapable of handling, you are going to feel anxious whenever you are outside your comfort zone. Whether this manifests in panic, separation anxiety, or any other anxiety disorder, there is often a core fear of being unable to cope independently, a difficulty tolerating distress independently, a challenge with managing uncertainty independently.

I worked with a sixteen-year-old, Anthony, who was struggling with generalized anxiety disorder and panic attacks. He was worried that he needed his parents to help him calm down when he had a panic attack, and so he started to struggle when he was apart from them. He was terrified of being home alone, and he worried about how he would ever manage an independent adulthood that was fast approaching. Through our work together, we learned that a driving fear contributing to Anthony's anxiety was his belief that he couldn't cope independently in a crisis. He believed he wouldn't be able to function when the stakes were high, that he would freeze up or black out. This belief fueled the sense that he needed other people around him to rescue him.

Part of what maintained this belief was his lack of experience doing things for himself. We recognized that his loving parents had managed his life in such a way that he hadn't had the opportunity to develop the building blocks for more independent functioning. And as his panic disorder worsened, his parents took his few responsibilities off his plate entirely because they didn't want to further stress him out when he was struggling.

This does not mean that his parents caused his anxiety disorder. For a kid with emotional vulnerabilities, well-intentioned overparenting may feel like the kindest thing a parent can do. But this type of involvement can easily become a double-edged sword if it prevents kids from learning life skills.

Therefore, in addition to addressing Anthony's anxiety symptoms in treatment, we worked on independent coping activities. He made phone calls to order pizza. His parents taught him how to do laundry. He learned how to change a tire. Learning to do the tasks of adulting may seem like an odd approach to anxiety treatment—but independence-focused therapy has increasing support.

If you feel like you might be overparenting, you are not alone. A recent survey on parenting found that 45 percent of U.S. parents describe themselves as overprotective, and 35 percent believe that they give in too quickly to their children's demands. These approaches to parenting are common enough that they have been assigned tags such as "helicopter parenting," "snowplow parenting," and, more recently, "gentle parenting."

Researchers have begun looking into links between some of these parenting styles and child anxiety. Studies have emerged linking "helicopter parenting"—defined as parents' overinvolvement in improving their kids' academic and personal success—with parenting behaviors that have significant associations with child anxiety disorders. For example, a 2021 study found that parents who endorsed higher levels of helicopter parenting were also more likely to jump in to alleviate their kids' distress in the moment—behaviors known as *parental accommodation*. We see that college-aged kids who perceive their parents to be helicopter parents are more likely to be medicated for anxiety or depression. Both helicopter parenting and "tiger parenting"—a parenting style marked by demands for a child's excellence in academics and behavior—are repeatedly identified as parenting approaches that increase the likelihood of child anxiety. Tiger parenting is a bit of a double whammy, as it blends both ends of our parenting dialectic: undersupport *and* overparenting. It's parental involvement, but without the warmth and with a dose of (implicit or explicit) criticism.

These trends are tightly tied to the fact that children at high-achieving schools are now officially considered an "at-risk group," given the mental health outcomes of extreme pressures to excel. Think about this for a second: Other recognized "at-risk groups" of young people are those most vulnerable in our society, like children living in poverty, in communities plagued by crime and neighborhood violence, or those with incarcerated parents. It feels absurd to lump kids from high-achieving schools, who typically come from privileged families, in the same risk category as kids in the foster care system. But the data is clear: Kids at high-achieving schools are more likely to struggle with mental health than the general population, highlighting some of the unhappy ways that overparenting can play out among different populations.

What's the Deal with Gentle Parenting?

There is very little published research to date on gentle parenting. Wild, I know, given how significant this construct is in modern parenting discourse. The gentle parenting movement is not the product of scholarship. Unlike attachment theory or positive parenting approaches, which have their roots in academic study, gentle parenting is largely a product of the internet age. The popular British childcare author Sarah Ockwell-Smith is often credited as the founder of the movement, which has largely emerged from the internet within the past decade and is fueled by parenting influencers on social media.

To date, there is one enlightening, exploratory study where researchers attempt to define the gentle parenting construct by surveying a sample of one hundred U.S. parents about their perceptions of their own parenting. Researchers Anne Pezalla and Alice Davidson found that nearly half of their sample identified as "gentle" in their parenting approach. Clearly this idea is percolating for today's parents. By examining the behaviors of the parents who defined themselves as "gentle," Pezalla and Davidson conclude that gentle parenting is marked by the following: an emphasis on parents regulating their own emotions and helping kids to regulate theirs, prioritizing affectionate responses to children, and avoiding "harsh" discipline strategies in favor of "boundary setting." What these boundaries are, and how they are enforced, remains unclear. Relatedly, "gentle" parents were more likely to align with an indulgent parenting style, which is related to overpermissiveness, as it captures a tendency to "give in" to children's demands. The authors found preliminary evidence suggesting that parents who identify as "gentle" report slightly more parenting satisfaction. But there was a catch: Parenting satisfaction and self-efficacy were lower for gentle parents who were more self-critical.

There is no data yet on how gentle parenting impacts kids over time. But we can make educated guesses, based on what we know about Intensive Parenting. Gentle parenting's emphasis on affection and emotion coaching are likely good things for reducing the risk for child anxiety disorders. On the other hand, readily giving in to kids' demands and having unclear expectations for their behavior suggests that gentle parenting is also likely tied to overpermissiveness, which we know increases the likelihood of child anxiety disorders.

Overparenting behaviors are often driven by a parent's own feelings, beliefs, and motivations. Importantly, these interactions are amplified for parents who are coping with their own anxiety and who are swimming in the waters of Intensive Parenting beliefs and practices. And it's bad news for anxious kids in the long run.

The Perfect Storm of Parent and Child Anxiety

It has long been established that having a parent with an anxiety disorder is a fundamental risk factor for child anxiety—this is due to both nature and nurture. Yes, there is a genetic component, but nature doesn't begin to explain all of it. The estimated heredity of anxiety disorders is only about 30 percent, leaving plenty of room for other factors to help explain the link.

While you can't control the "nature" part of the equation, the good news is that many of these "nurture" factors are parenting behaviors—over which you do have control. The first step is to learn about factors operating within you that are tied to anxiety. We can call these "parent factors," and they can help explain the transmission of anxiety between parents and kids. Some of the most impactful parent factors are threat sensitivity, beliefs around anxiety, and two key emotion regulation factors: distress intolerance and experiential avoidance.

If you are a parent who struggles with your own anxiety, know that these factors may be hot-button areas for you. Awareness brings clarity and purpose and is a great first step in making some changes that can really help your kids. Even more so when you recognize the links between these tendencies and our Intensive Parenting culture.

The monster that isn't there

Folks with anxiety disorders are more aware of potential threats in the environment. If you are a parent with anxiety, you are more likely to see situations as dangerous for your child than a nonanxious parent— the playground is a death trap rather than a fun outing. Of course, you are going to be motivated to limit your child's exposure to those situations you view as threatening.

We've already touched on modeling: Parents who see monsters everywhere communicate more frequently and urgently about the potential dangers in a child's environment. Their kids then internalize these messages into their own set of anxious beliefs about their world. So if you are a kid whose parents have spent your entire childhood talking about how cities are dangerous places, and they glue themselves to you on family trips to a city, you are likely to feel afraid of cities yourself. It is very likely that parental anxiety and heightened threat awareness, plus the cultural consensus that children are increasingly vulnerable, is leading to the decrease in the freedom we are giving kids to spend time on their own without an adult—a cross-cultural trend that is on the rise.

Knowing that you may be extra threat-sensitive, can you check yourself before you communicate your fears to your kid? How likely is it that there is a monster here? And consider modern parenting culture—would this have been an activity that you would have been allowed to do, but that no longer *feels* safe for kids? What would it be like to start letting your kid take a few developmentally appropriate risks in situations that are actually pretty safe?

Worrying about worry

How parents think about anxiety—how they believe that the emotion of anxiety "works"—impacts how they parent. Anxious parents are more likely to hold negative beliefs about anxiety: They are more likely to believe that experiencing the emotion of anxiety is somehow harmful or dangerous, or will lead to negative consequences for their child. This is where that false belief that whatever feels uncomfortable must actually be unsafe comes into play. Anxious parents are more likely to become scared if they observe their child becoming scared, and anxious parents are more likely to feel that they are "bad" parents when their child is stressed out. It makes sense that parents who hold negative beliefs about anxiety are also more likely to help their child avoid anxiety, which fuels the cycle.

We also have evidence that anxious mothers are more likely to expect that their children will be anxious in any given situation. If you are an anxious parent who expects your child to have a hard time, you will probably clock each time your child appears reserved, assume that this means they are struggling, and check in with them repeatedly: "Are you okay? Do you need to go home?" The message communicated here is that the child is *not* okay and *does* need to go home. Any kid with even a slight bit of discomfort—or boredom—is likely to take you up on that offer to bail.

Anxious parents tend to feel an outsized responsibility for their child's actions and well-being. A UK study found that mothers with anxiety disorders felt a greater sense of responsibility for making sure their kids had positive experiences and for protecting their child from harm than nonanxious mothers did, and intervened more intrusively, and with less warmth, in interactions with their child. Here we find ourselves swimming in the Intensive Parenting waters again: an outsized sense of a parent's responsibility for child outcomes, and a direct link with parenting anxiety. If you believe it's your responsibility to "fix" your child's distress, of course you are more likely to intervene.

Seriously examine your beliefs about anxiety. Do you believe that it is harmful for your child to feel nervous or scared, or when they are nauseated or panicky? If so, why? What are you afraid will happen if your kids feel anxiety? And how do your worries about your kid's worries impact your feelings about yourself as a parent? Does the "bad parent" story come up for you if your kid is anxious? And how do any of these beliefs and perceptions impact your parenting behaviors? What would you be doing differently if you were confident that anxiety wasn't harmful?

I can't even

Parents with anxiety also show higher levels of *distress intolerance*, which is the perceived inability to tolerate negative feelings. Folks with high distress intolerance feel like they can't handle painful experiences. And because parents are wired to be attentive to their children's emotions, if you have high distress intolerance, you likely feel extra overwhelmed when your kid is upset because you don't believe you can handle how your kid's distress makes you feel.

Relatedly, many parents who have a child with anxiety disorders report high levels of *experiential avoidance*. Recall that people who engage in a lot of experiential avoidance try very hard to avoid feeling any negative feelings, or they work really hard to suppress or change negative feelings when they arise. Naturally, parents with this tendency also try hard to avoid their child's negative emotions. It makes sense that if you are more experientially avoidant, you will be motivated to make changes to your environment so that your kids won't experience anything that will bring up negative thoughts and feelings . . . and which would consequently provoke negative thoughts and feelings for you.

Unsurprisingly, higher levels of both distress intolerance and experiential avoidance are common in people with anxiety disorders. And there is a clear relationship between anxious parents seeing their child upset and getting involved to try to "fix it": overparenting in a nutshell.

If you read about these emotion regulation factors and think, "Yep, that's me," know that you are not alone. Acknowledging what is going on for you internally and then choosing how you are going to act in the face of it all is the core of psychological flexibility—the game-changing emotion regulation strategy that we will introduce in the next chapter. Start by getting curious—what does distress intolerance or experiential avoidance feel like to you? What unique feelings, thoughts, or behaviors signal that you are in the "I can't even" headspace? You can use the Three-Component Model worksheets in the Resources section at the back of the book to map this out for yourself.

■ ■ ■

Let's put the puzzle pieces together here. All parents struggle to cope with negative feelings when our kids are distressed—it's not a fun experience. But if you are an anxious parent who is extra sensitive to potential threats to your child, who believes that experiencing anxiety is fundamentally bad, or who feels deeply responsible for your child's emotional experience, *of course* you are going to be on high alert for situations that you believe will provoke anxiety for your child.

This response makes so much sense—because your own anxiety means that you likely struggle to tolerate distress and use avoidance strategies to cope with negative thoughts and feelings. And so it's even harder to resist the urge to jump in and rescue your child from distress—because when you do, you are also reducing your own distress. Win-win.

The perceptions, feelings, beliefs, expectations, and emotion regulation factors that come along with parent anxiety disorders motivate overparenting behaviors. Critically, the urge to do so is culturally reinforced, because responsiveness to children's emotions and curating all things positive for your kids is seen as "good" parenting in our Intensive Parenting culture.

This is *such* a hard landscape for parents to navigate. Everything inside and outside of you is screaming for you to give in to avoidance, to accommodate your kids' anxiety. This leads you down a rabbit hole into deference to every distressing childhood emotion. And yet you now know that avoidance fuels anxiety, and that your kids need you to help them face their fears. How can you possibly combat all of these pressures? How can you fight your own internal distress, your children's pleas, and your culture's demands all at once?

Treatments that work for anxiety recognize the dialectic between overparenting and undersupport—and advocate for a middle-path approach. At their core, they teach *psychological flexibility*—the ability to be fully aware of and open to your experience in the moment, and to choose to act in values-consistent ways. Psychological flexibility is a skill that can be developed, and one that you can start applying to your life now. The next chapter outlines how to begin making informed, values-based choices that best serve you, your child, and your family, particularly in response to anxiety's challenges.

What Can You Take Home with You?

- Lean into the good stuff that comes with Intensive Parenting: the positive parent-child relationship, emotion socialization, and (moderate) parental involvement. If one of these areas could use a touch-up, how can you strengthen it? This does not have to be a massive change to have an impact. It could look like setting an intention to put down your phone and check in mindfully with your kid each day after school. Or it could be getting involved in an activity your kid does—but only if it might actually benefit your relationship with your kid. Involvement for involvement's sake helps no one.
- Keep the upside-down U in mind when it comes to your parenting around anxiety: Too little is too little, and too much is too much. Start striving for balance—*some* protection, *some* independence.
- A practical way to start countering the dominance of overparenting is to start encouraging more independence in your kids. Give them a grocery list of items to find in the store while you wait in line at the deli counter. Send them into the post office by themselves to buy stamps. Have them call and order takeout for the family. Teach them how to fix a blown fuse. This shouldn't be framed as a punishment, because it's not. In fact, you should get kids' input here—what are some grown-up things that they would like to learn how to do . . . *without you*?

CHAPTER 7

The Flexibility Factor

Imagine that you have a six-year-old kid who is signed up for soccer and is *not* having it. They freak out before practice and then spend the entire time crying on the sidelines and begging you to take them home. What would you do?

Your answer lives somewhere within our parenting dialectic, which centers on that key question: What is my primary job, as a parent, when my child is anxious or distressed?

If you lean to the overparenting side and decide to drop soccer, which protects your kid from hard feelings in the moment, you are not alone. Many of us would feel compelled to call it quits. And pulling out of soccer in deference to your kid's distress is largely consistent with an Intensive Parenting approach, prioritizing emotional warmth and following the child's lead. Because isn't your kid feeling seen and heard by their parent more important than playing soccer? And frankly, won't the other parents think you are an absolute monster if you stand on the sidelines, seemingly unmoved while your kid wails?

Maybe so. Maybe what your kid really needs from you in this moment is to prioritize protection over independence. So you eat the registration fee and quit the season.

On the other hand, your instinct may be to lean more toward the undersupport side. You may feel strongly that you don't want your kid to learn that they can quit something before they give it a solid try, no matter how hard it is. Okay, great, but how can you get them over the hump? You can't force them to stop crying and get their butt on the field. You scan your mental filing cabinet for that script you saw on TikTok that you think would give you *just the right* language in this situation, but it escapes you.

What else is in your arsenal? Should you threaten to remove screen time? Dessert? Hiss at them that they are making a scene? Your parents would have never tolerated this nonsense. But Boomer parents were allowed to be mean.

This might be your dilemma for a nonanxious kid who is resisting soccer. For these kids, maybe they just really don't want to play soccer but would happily get involved with tennis, and so your decision to hang up the cleats may not reinforce anxiety in an impactful way. But how might your dilemma change if you have a child who trends anxious? Particularly once you understand that avoidance fuels anxiety?

In this case, your anxious kid probably needs more encouragement to build their independent coping skills. They tend to have a harder time in new situations, and their urge to avoid will be stronger. Anxiety is rarely self-correcting, meaning that if your kid is anxious about this soccer situation, they will likely be anxious about something similar in the future. As a consequence, helping your child to avoid a totally safe but anxiety-provoking activity like soccer means that it's harder for them to get involved with another anxiety-provoking activity in the future. The equation is always a little different for a kid who has higher anxiety.

Knowing this, your values may point you toward finding a way to fight back against anxiety and to compassionately but firmly persist in taking your kid to soccer. While you don't want to embody the "quit whining and get out there, or else" parenting stance of the past, you understand the need to resist the overparenting urge that is so normalized in the present.

Here is where the rubber meets the road: How can you possibly do this—firmly encourage while compassionately validating—when everything and everyone around you is pushing you in the opposite direction? Your kid is pleading with you with tears in their eyes to take them home. The other parents observing from the sidelines—and the Intensive Parenting culture that informs their views—are horrified that you might permit your precious child to endure such distress. And frankly, your stress is sky-high; all you want to do is give in to the anxiety and say, "Okay, you don't have to do this anymore." How can you be effective in doing what is *right* for you and your kid in this context?

The hard truth is that there is no easy solution. There is no parenting hack or magic phrase that is guaranteed to make your kid no longer anxious about soccer, or make you no longer care that your kid is anxious about soccer. But there is a principle that can help you to navigate these waters. It's called *psychological flexibility*.

What is psychological flexibility? It's not exclusively a trait—something that you are either born with or without. It is a skill that can be cultivated, a muscle to be strengthened. Folks with greater psychological flexibility have a range of strategies that they can call upon to help them manage tough emotions and make good choices. It is a way to approach the most challenging circumstances in your life, and in your role as a parent. It can also be modeled for your kids so that they can develop it themselves. Greater psychological flexibility helps you live a more meaningful and fulfilling life. Because of this, it's a central focus of many of today's leading evidence-based psychological treatments.

In this chapter, we will explore psychological flexibility—and its inverse, psychological inflexibility—as it relates to parenting and anxiety. Then we'll talk about how to start building it in yourself so that you can model it for your kids.

On a personal note, psychological flexibility is a construct that I try to keep top of mind as I parent. One of my most fervent hopes is that I can help model and cultivate it in my daughter, because I think it will help her respond more effectively to the curveballs life throws at her. Habits form character, and I hope psychologically flexible habits will help shape and strengthen her as she grows. The jury is still out on how good a job I am doing. She might be doomed anyway because she has a psychologist for a mother. But I'm trying.

What Is Psychological Flexibility?

A quotation attributed to Austrian neurologist, psychiatrist, philosopher, and Holocaust survivor Viktor Frankl reads, "Between stimulus and response there is a space. In that space is our power to choose our response. In our response lies our growth and our freedom." This is the essence of psychological flexibility, which is the ability to nonjudgmentally notice your present-moment experience and to mindfully choose to act in values-consistent ways. It is the ability to be aware of and open to your experience—no matter how painful—and to choose to act in ways that are consistent with who you are and what you care about.

This is heady, so let's break it down. Psychological flexibility starts with *noticing* your experience in the present moment and gently paying attention to what's happening for you. Your internal experience is made up of your physical sensations, thoughts, feelings, emotions, memories, and urges. It is whatever is going on inside you right now that no one else can see.

Try it with me now . . . seriously, just humor me. Bring your attention to your internal experience, to everything that is happening now, in this moment, that is not directly observable to other people. Notice any physical sensations that you feel in your body: any tightness, tingling, tension. Notice also any emotions that you are experiencing. Gently name each feeling to yourself—maybe stress, alertness, boredom, relaxation, fatigue, or worry.

Try to bring your attention to what you are feeling *without judgment*. This is the difference between labeling your experience as good or bad, something to be pursued or avoided, versus simply noticing it for what it is without qualifying or assigning a label. Noticing *with* judgment might play out along the lines of "I am so tired. I hate being tired. Why am I so tired all the time? Being tired is the worst!"

In contrast, noticing your experience *without* judgment might sound like "I notice that I am tired. I feel heaviness in my belly and tightness in my shoulders. I notice the feeling of being frustrated because I am tired, and I notice the thought that I shouldn't feel tired because I got decent sleep last night." It can help to assume a stance of curiosity so you can notice without judgment. Observe your experience in this moment as if you've never checked in with yourself in this way before. For example, if you noticed feeling tired, get curious about how you *know* that you are tired. What does *being tired* feel like to you? The first part of psychological flexibility is awareness and acceptance of your thoughts, feelings, and urges—even the painful ones.

The second part of psychological flexibility is to mindfully choose to act in values-driven ways. Let's say you notice that you feel tired and have the urge to go to sleep. But there is a pile of dishes in the sink that need scrubbing, which you promised your partner that you would handle. And you value being an honest and responsible partner. Being psychologically flexible in this example would be to drag yourself to the kitchen and get scrubbing. You are mindfully noticing your internal thoughts and choosing to act in a way that aligns with your values—even if it means not doing what your thoughts and feelings are urging you toward right now.

If you value determination, you are showing psychological flexibility when you choose to keep up your job search despite the disappointment you feel after a rejection. If you value meeting the goals you set for yourself, you are showing psychological flexibility when you choose to push to the finish line of the half marathon despite every muscle screaming at you to quit. And if you value modeling resilient coping for your kids, you are showing psychological flexibility when you choose to resist the urge to email your kid's teacher to protest a disappointing grade.

Psychological flexibility isn't about doing the "right thing." And it's not necessarily about doing that hard thing when you don't want to—although it often plays out that way. Psychological flexibility is about making a choice to do the right thing *for you* based on *your values* in *this context*. In fact, psychological flexibility can help you push back more confidently on what others think you *should* be doing and to prioritize what is right for you and for your family. In a world that's oversaturated with parenting advice, psychological flexibility encourages you, as a parent, to reconnect with your instincts and to listen to yourself.

Psychological flexibility is context-dependent, meaning that your psychological flexibility will vary based on the values that you hold for a given set of circumstances: The values that guide your behavior in the workplace or in your friendships may be different than the values that guide your parenting behaviors. You can think of psychological flexibility within parenting as the ability to accept feelings like anxiety or frustration, thoughts steeped in guilt or self-doubt, or the impulse to yell or retreat, while still choosing to act in ways that promote a warm parent-child relationship and also provide appropriate limits for your kid's behavior.

Psychological flexibility is essentially an emotion regulation strategy. From a parenting perspective, it is a resource to help parents manage negative thoughts and feelings that naturally arise on the life-affirming and soul-sucking journey that is parenting.

There are compelling reasons to focus on strengthening your own psychological flexibility while parenting. Parents with more psychological flexibility are more likely to use parenting practices that are good for kids. They show more warmth and affection, high-quality parent-child communication, and more encouragement of their children, and—importantly—they set reasonable limits and provide clearer directions. This "love and limits" parenting style, otherwise known as *authoritative parenting,* is consistently linked with positive outcomes for kids. And parents with more parenting psychological flexibility have more positive attitudes toward parenting. Taken together, a parent's ability to be mindfully aware of what's going on for them on the inside and to parent in values-consistent ways leads them to make more positive parenting choices. Unsurprisingly, greater parenting psychological flexibility often translates to kids who are less likely to struggle with anxiety disorders and depression.

Psychological Flexibility and Intensive Parenting

Intensive Parenting and its offshoots—helicopter parenting, snowplow parenting, and gentle parenting—aren't *necessarily* inconsistent with psychological flexibility. But there are some real tensions. Because Intensive Parenting is a set of norms around what makes the ideal parent in our culture, it carries a lot of baggage in the form of "shoulds." Good parents *should* put their kids' needs and wants above all else. Good parents *should* work to minimize their kids' negative feelings. Good parents *should* always do more—of everything—and be happy about it.

This can bump up against psychological flexibility because it naturally means guilt, anxiety, and self-judgment for parents who feel that they should be doing more, better, and with a smile. They are also encouraged to parent intensively, regardless of the cost to self. This translates into everything from staying up to create Elf-on-the-Shelf magic when you are beyond tapped out, to bailing on your best friend's birthday celebration because your kid doesn't want you to go out, to going without medication you need so you have the money to pay the registration fee for league baseball this year.

This self-sacrifice can mean tremendous costs to parents' well-being. And critically, it's harder to be psychologically flexible and parent in ways that are good for kids when you are stressed, burned out, anxious, and guilt-ridden. When parents are under stress, they are more likely to use parenting strategies marked by either avoidance or control—avoiding distress by being overly lenient, or exerting control through harsh and inconsistent discipline. Intensive Parenting pressures can make it harder to parent effectively and then lead you to feel awful when you don't live up to your own standards. No wonder Intensive Parenting made it to the U.S. Surgeon General's report of factors that are negatively impacting parents' well-being. The pressure from these cultural norms makes psychological flexibility in parenting more difficult to achieve—and more necessary to cultivate.

Before we discuss how to build parenting psychological flexibility, it's important to take a closer look at psychological *inflexibility*, along with its relationship to anxiety and parenting practices.

Getting Hooked: Psychological Inflexibility

Let's say that you are having one of those days when nothing seems to go right. Your mind might tell you how you've screwed everything up, and there's nothing you can do about it. If you get sucked into these negative thoughts and feelings, how might you behave? What might you *do*?

I would probably find myself ruminating on how badly I messed up, tell myself over and over what a trash person I am, and really beat myself up internally. I'd probably end up barking at those I love most and maybe eat too much chocolate, which would only make me feel worse. It is *not* values-consistent for me to snap at my loved ones or to binge on junk food, but when my negative thoughts and feelings get really loud, I find it's much easier for me to choose to act in ways I later wish I hadn't. It often feels like I don't actually have a choice in how I behave when I am in these moments.

But we can always choose how to behave—it's just not always easy.

Part of the reason why it can be so hard to act in values-consistent ways when negative emotions are high is that human beings are wired to become *less* flexible during times of stress. Experiencing negative emotions has the side effect of limiting your attention, restricting your focus, and narrowing your options for thinking and responding. In the dangerous environment of our early ancestors, this inflexibility helped them to take quick action that could be lifesaving. Psychological inflexibility helped to augment the usefulness of painful emotions like fear, guilt, or anger that helped our early ancestors to survive.

In the modern world, your driving emotions may feel the same as they did for your ancestors, but the circumstances and the stakes are vastly different. It's not adaptive to bolt from the hospital if you have a panic attack during a routine blood draw. It's not useful for the "fight" part of the fight-or-flight response to lead you to doggedly refuse to accept help on a task when you could benefit from support. And if your kid trends anxious, it is often not helpful to fuel avoidance by bailing on soccer. Psychological inflexibility leads to impulsive, emotion-driven action, stubborn resistance to change, unwillingness to consider alternative actions, and getting stuck in our own negative spiral.

One way to think of this is "getting hooked." Getting hooked by your negative thoughts and feelings means that you fuse with them, you really believe them, and you let them jerk you around like a fish on a line. They then dictate how you think and feel and—most importantly—what you do. Often you end up acting in ways that take you in the opposite direction of your values. In the context of parenting anxiety, getting hooked makes it more likely that you will behave in polarized ways that ultimately aren't helpful, by either overparenting or undersupporting your kid.

A few moments ago, we explored what it would be like to notice feeling tired and wanting to tap out, even when you promised your partner you would handle the dishes. Psychological inflexibility in this instance could be letting your negative thoughts and feelings around being tired—maybe compounded by feelings of frustration with the task, or with your partner—"hook" you so that your actions are completely driven by them. Your mind might tell you all the reasons why you shouldn't have to do the dishes, what a terrible day you have had, how your partner doesn't do what they say they will do anyway so why should you, that your bed is just too cozy to leave. All of these thoughts and feelings may be true, but letting them dictate your actions takes you further away from your values. Maybe it's no big deal to leave the dishes tonight . . . but maybe it leads to an argument with your partner tomorrow.

Psychological inflexibility can show up in everyday situations like these. It also tends to be more pronounced in folks struggling with a range of mental health conditions like substance abuse, eating disorders, depression, and yes—anxiety disorders. This is understandable— when you're trying to avoid or control distress, it's easy to get hooked and respond inflexibly. And most mental health challenges, by nature, involve getting stuck in behaviors aimed at escaping or suppressing discomfort.

When uncomfortable thoughts and feelings come up, the fastest way to relieve them is to avoid whatever is causing the discomfort. The urge to avoid negative thoughts and feelings leads people with anxiety disorders to develop a pattern of responding with avoidance. Then avoidance becomes the go-to coping strategy, and this restricted pattern of feeling, thinking, and behaving becomes entrenched and automatic. In short, folks struggling with anxiety can get stuck in a perpetual loop where they get *hooked* by anxiety-driven thoughts and feelings and increasingly respond inflexibly.

How Can You Recognize Psychological Inflexibility?

The language you use—in your thoughts and spoken words—can alert you to when psychological inflexibility is at play. If you can learn to recognize it, it can be like a little red flag popping up, reminding you that you are going off-track and encouraging you to pivot. In particular, labels, all-or-nothing thinking, *should* statements, and extreme pronouncements are red flags that inflexibility may be percolating.

"I can't handle this right now."
"No one ever considers what I need."
"I should be able to control myself."

"This situation is an absolute nightmare."
"I am the worst parent."

These statements may signal that you are getting hooked by your negative thoughts and feelings, which makes you more likely to act in ways that ultimately may not help you or your kid. They are a sign to pause, to take a moment and notice what is happening—to notice that you are getting hooked—and to reset your actions to align with your values.

Get curious about your own patterns of thoughts and speech. Do you have go-to phrases or thoughts that pop up for you in times when you are less flexible and more reactive? Rather than suppressing them, can you start using them as markers that encourage you to pivot and make a values-consistent choice?

Connecting the Dots—Even When It's Hard

If you tell me that you never have any negative thoughts or feelings about parenting, I am going to call your bluff. This stuff is *hard*. And how you feel about your painful thoughts and feelings around parenting matters. Parents with poorer psychological flexibility tend to judge their parenting—and their parenting stress—more negatively and often use unhelpful strategies that involve control, avoidance, or suppression to cope. This suggests that parents with poorer psychological flexibility are avoiding negative emotions in themselves.

Unsurprisingly, researchers find that parents who report more experiential avoidance and psychological inflexibility are more likely to engage in parenting strategies that aren't great for kids. They are more likely to get hooked by negative thoughts and feelings around parenting, and then they parent less effectively because they are coping less well with those negative thoughts and feelings.

This makes sense, doesn't it? If you are having a tough, highly emotional interaction with your kid, you are going to experience painful thoughts and feelings. If you judge these feelings negatively by, for example, condemning yourself for being frustrated or believing that you *just can't handle* this stress right now, you are going to be more motivated to find a quick solution that minimizes pain. And your general level of stress can amplify this pattern. A Portuguese study showed that parents under high levels of stress also had lower parenting psychological flexibility, which in turn was related to using parenting strategies that aren't great for kids, highlighting how your ability to be psychologically flexible can vary depending on your stress level. Psychological flexibility isn't a fixed quality that you either do or don't have; instead, it is an emotion regulation skill that can be harder to access when emotions are high.

How does psychological inflexibility in parents translate into more child anxiety? By encouraging parents to lean too far toward either overparenting or undersupport, both of which increase the risk for child anxiety.

Let's circle back to our soccer dilemma. A psychologically inflexible response that might play out on the overparenting side of our parenting dialectic would be to give in to distress in the moment. To agree that this is just too hard, we are leaving right now, and why don't we stop for ice cream on the way home? On the undersupport side, a psychologically inflexible response might play out by angrily snapping at your child, demanding that they stop crying and get on the field or else no screens for a week.

Now, maybe these responses are consistent with your values; you'd consider them A+ parenting. But I would guess that most of today's parents would struggle to fully endorse responding in either way. These responses are impulsive, emotion-driven, and likely values-inconsistent. Crucially, both responses increase the risk that your child will continue to struggle with anxiety.

Unfortunately, parents can model psychological inflexibility for their kids. Monkey see, monkey do. A parent's inability to be psychologically flexible can lead to kids who struggle to tolerate their own painful thoughts and feelings and who consequently struggle to respond effectively in line with values. This means more avoidant coping, more distress intolerance, and more vulnerability to developing anxiety disorders. So when you cultivate psychological flexibility in your parenting, you help yourself resist the pull of polarization, which pays off for your kids in so many ways.

A Middle Path

If psychological inflexibility is linked to polarized parenting practices, a middle-path approach to parenting—one that blends sensitivity to kids' needs with consistency in limit-setting—is a hallmark of parenting psychological flexibility.

Let's think through our soccer situation. Psychological flexibility when your anxious kid is anxious about soccer means first *pausing* when your kid is sobbing on the sidelines. It means taking stock and recognizing that you need to adapt to the demands of this situation. It means noticing your thoughts, feelings, and urges in the moment, reconnecting with the value you place on taking a firm but kind approach to a child who trends anxious. By allowing yourself this space between stimulus and response, rather than allowing yourself to get hooked by your negative thoughts and feelings, you can connect with your values in this moment and make a parenting choice that is right for your child.

You might acknowledge that there is truly no threat to your child's life or well-being here—it just *feels* like there is, because their anxiety alarm is going off when there is no danger. Pausing gives you the opportunity to acknowledge that the way you respond in this moment will either confirm for your child that their anxiety was justified if you agree to leave, or give them new information about their ability to tolerate hard things if you stay. You may determine that your anxious child needs your love and limits here; you choose to remain compassionately firm in the expectation that they go to soccer practice.

You know that this means you will have to tolerate a boatload of distress—your child's distress, the judgments of others, your own discomfort and self-doubt—when it would make everybody happier to bail on soccer. You are choosing to go against some Intensive Parenting norms here by holding firm in the face of your child's distress. But in this space when you commit to tolerating your own distress, you can choose to look your child in the eye and sensitively and genuinely validate their feelings. Then you can tell them that you believe they can handle this situation, and that it is not a choice to go home early; you intend to stay on the sidelines until the end of practice.

Now let's circle back to an earlier story, the one about your teenage son's reluctance to attend his grandmother's party. What could a psychologically flexible approach look like here?

With curiosity and self-compassion, you can acknowledge your own anger, helplessness, and stress. You might notice that the urge to demand that your son participate is competing with a softer urge to let him stay in his room. Maybe you notice that many of the messages around you encourage a deference to your son's distress, and the thought that a "good" parent would give up any expectation that he show up if he is so clearly upset by having to do so.

At the same time, you connect with your values. Values differ, of course, but for the sake of the example let's suppose that family loyalty is really important to you, meaning that family members show up for one another. For you, acting in a values-consistent way means encouraging some interaction between your son and his family at this party. It means you are open to tolerating your son being pissed at you, and your sister thinking that you are a coldhearted harpy.

You choose to talk with your son before the party. Well, it's more like talking *at* your son, who is lying face down on his bed and refusing to speak. Psychological flexibility here might be noticing a feeling of annoyance, and as much as you feel the urge to lecture, you commit to expressing your thoughts calmly and with compassion.

You could first acknowledge that you see that he is really struggling, and validate that it makes sense that the party would feel awful if anxiety is telling him he can't handle big gatherings. *And* you and he both know that showing up for family is important, that it will mean so much to his grandmother to see him on her birthday. Taking a love and limits approach, you can compassionately and firmly set the expectation that you two need to find a way for him to be a part of the gathering. Maybe he can come down and visit with Grandma one-on-one at the beginning of the event, take a break, and come back down for cake. Or maybe he can be on dishwashing duty so that he is around, but a bit more removed from the chaos by being in the kitchen. The point here is that it's not an all-or-nothing situation; you set the expectation that he participate in some way *and* also stress that you believe that he is stronger than his anxiety. If it's helpful and values-consistent to identify a reward for following through with the plan—and consequences for *not* following through—that's fair game, too.

Then you leave your son's room. This means fighting the Intensive Parenting–fueled expectation that you become completely absorbed in his emotional experience, sitting with him to process his feelings . . . even if he is nonresponsive. You notice your discomfort with leaving him. But by setting an expectation and giving him space, you are sending the message that you believe he will make the right choice to show up for his grandmother, and also that you believe he can handle this tough feeling independently.

In these types of situations, you have the opportunity to handle a tough feeling, too—to tolerate your own distress when your kid is upset with you, particularly as you notice lingering doubts about whether you are doing the right thing. While it never feels good when your kids don't see the wisdom in your parenting choices, it's not your kids' job to help you feel better about your decisions. Psychological flexibility is not about making your kid do what you want them to do; it's about cultivating the ability to respond more fluidly and effectively to tough circumstances. Modeling this for your kid can pay dividends over time.

Where Do I Start?

To begin developing your own psychological flexibility, you want to pay attention to two things: mindfulness of your internal experience and values-guided actions. You can start integrating small mindfulness practices into your daily routine, and you can clarify your values in your parenting role.

First, *mindfulness* is an attention process. It means shifting your attention in the moment to notice your experience, and doing so with openness, curiosity, compassion, and flexibility. Anyone can practice mindfulness anytime, anywhere, for any length of time. Right now, for instance, by bringing your attention to the way your body is positioned in space, by noticing every point of your body that is touching something else, you are practicing mindfulness. Bonus points if you notice any thoughts or feelings that are happening in this moment and making room for whatever they are, instead of working to suppress them. Right there, that was mindfulness.

You don't need to carve out ten minutes a day to sit on a mat and listen to a guided meditation. Practicing a mindful, attentional shift for several moments a day while you are doing whatever it is that you happen to be doing is a great way to start. Integrating this approach into your daily routine makes it more accessible when you really need it in moments of stress, when your flexibility is in jeopardy.

I began tying mindfulness to holding my daughter's hand. This action became a signal reminding me to notice my experience in the moment, and I would use it as a prompt to nonjudgmentally connect with whatever I was experiencing. One benefit of this practice was that I could become mindfully aware of the sweet, tender feeling of my daughter's little hand in mine, and by being more present with it, I got to enjoy it more. The older she gets, the less often it happens, but I'm conditioned to be mindful when it does. It helps me to enjoy the increasingly rare experience more fully.

Second, you want to clarify your *values*. Values are terms that describe how you want to act both in this moment and on an ongoing basis. Dr. Russ Harris defines values as "your heart's deepest desires for how you want to behave—how you want to treat yourself, others, and the world around you." Values are like an inner compass; no matter how far you have strayed from your intended destination, you can always pivot, turn toward your values, and start walking back in the right direction. They serve as our guide, a source of motivation, and they give us a sense of purpose. Values are often summarized by one or two words, like "friendship," "independence," "hard work," "justice," or "creativity."

Values are different from goals. Think of it this way: Goals are the destination, and values are the way you want to get there. For example, you may have a goal to save money because you value adventure and want to have the means to travel. The same goal might also be driven by a value of family responsibility, and you are saving money because you want to ensure your family's financial security.

Start by clarifying your values around parenting. Take a look at the Common Parenting Values checklist in the Resources section at the back of this book to help you. Emily Oster discusses how to clarify parenting values by creating what she calls a family mission statement in her book *The Family Firm: A Data-Driven Guide to Better Decision Making in the Early School Years*. I *love* this approach. Reconnecting with this mission statement in times of uncertainty is like pulling out your compass when you wander off the trail. It helps to reorient you with what is truly most important for your own life. It helps you filter out the noise and deprioritize the judgment of others, the chatter of your social media feed, and the cacophony of the Intensive Parenting ideals that may not serve you or your children well.

■ ■ ■

Psychological flexibility is not built in a day. Like any muscle, it will alternatively strengthen or weaken given how much you work to fortify it across time and circumstance. And it's a factor worth cultivating for your benefit as well as for your kids.

In the next section of this book, as we explore clinical anxiety disorders and their treatment, all chapters include a Flexibility Factor section, which will help you think about anxiety-related parenting challenges through a lens of psychological flexibility and will support your development of this important skill.

What Can You Take Home with You?

- Think about the times when you have been the least psychologically flexible—when you have gotten hooked by your painful thoughts and feelings and acted in impulsive, emotion-driven ways—and identify your red flags: tip-offs that you are getting hooked. These could be thoughts, images, internal monologues, behaviors, sensations . . . anything that you can earmark as a signal that psychological inflexibility is at hand, and that can be your sign to pause and reset.

- Build mindfulness practices into your daily life. It helps to tie mindfulness into a single action or behavior that you do regularly. For example, you could practice mindfulness every time you are folding laundry—notice your movements as you go through this routine, what the texture of each piece of clothing feels like, the thoughts and feelings that go through your mind as you fold. If your mind wanders, gently bring it back to the present.

- Clarify your values around parenting. Using the List of Common Parenting Values in the Resources section at the back of this book, identify the top five to ten values that you hold for your parenting journey. Watch out for the tendency to mix up values and goals. A goal might be to raise polite kids; the corresponding value might be respect for others. Or a goal might be to raise resilient kids; the value might be perseverance. If you have a co-parent, do this exercise together.

- Recognize that it's harder to be psychologically flexible when you are under stress, making it more likely that you will parent in ways that aren't great for child anxiety. While there are many sources of parenting stress over which you may not have control, buying into Intensive Parenting pressures when they don't serve you isn't one of them. Challenge yourself to get more comfortable with the discomfort that comes from pushing back on Intensive Parenting norms, knowing that doing so can be helpful for you and for your kid.

PART III

CHAPTER 8

The Gold Standard

I first met Maddie when she was fourteen, when her world had imploded. Her parents had taken her to the emergency room four months prior because Maddie was convinced that she was having a heart attack. But nothing was physically wrong with Maddie; after a workup, the physicians told the family that Maddie's symptoms were due to anxiety. By the time we met, three months later, she had lost ten pounds.

Maddie began high school shortly after this trip to the ER, which she told me was a nightmare. A well-liked, solid student who never had to work very hard to get good grades, Maddie suddenly felt like the academic work was beyond her capabilities. Also, she witnessed a student vomiting in the hallway early in the year, and other students posted a video of the event online. The kid who vomited was brutally ridiculed. Maddie became terrified that the same thing would happen to her, so she refused to eat before or during the school day.

The feelings that initially landed her in the ER hadn't gotten any better either. She had ongoing panic attacks, which occurred most mornings before school and increasingly while she tried to do schoolwork. She started staying home from school because of these symptoms, and by the time we met she was missing two to four days of school per week. That also meant that she was frantically trying to keep up with the snowballing academic demands. She quit the volleyball team and was barely seeing her friends outside of school.

As anxiety took over her life, Maddie felt increasingly hopeless and depressed. She was no longer interested in things that she used to enjoy; everything felt sort of flat. Her parents also noted that she was extremely irritable and that there were frequent tiffs at home about little things. They felt like they were losing their daughter, that their vibrant, engaging Maddie had been replaced by a deeply unhappy kid who was either riddled with panic, snapping at family members, or holed up in her bedroom. Maddie tearfully shared that she felt like she was a burden to her family. She told me that she sometimes wished that she could just go to sleep and never wake up. No one should have to feel this way.

Based on her symptoms, Maddie met criteria for social anxiety disorder, panic disorder, agoraphobia, and depression. You can learn more about the assessment and diagnosis of anxiety and related disorders in the Appendix at the back of this book. I recommended that Maddie meet with me weekly for a round of cognitive behavioral therapy (CBT), with an emphasis on exposure therapy.

I suggested this treatment for several reasons. First and foremost, because it is the recommended, frontline approach to treating anxiety disorders in kids and adults—it's considered the "gold standard." Second, because Maddie was engaged—while she was understandably a bit hesitant about therapy, she wanted help—I was optimistic that an active treatment approach where she could learn more about her experience and develop skills to manage her symptoms would be effective.

In this chapter, we unpack CBT so that you understand what it is and what to expect if it's a treatment option that you seek out. We will discuss how CBT is different from other treatments, explore how and why it works, and introduce the core components of CBT that target anxiety.

A Solid Starting Place

As with treatment for any condition—medical or psychiatric—there is no such thing as a one-size-fits-all approach. The best treatment for anxiety disorders for *you* or for *your child* should be determined by carefully considering the many factors that may impact how well any given approach may work. But knowing what's most recommended is always a solid starting place, and for the treatment of anxiety disorders, that's cognitive behavioral therapy.

CBT is an evidence-based treatment, meaning that we have solid evidence from clinical trials to support its use. Results of the Child and Adolescent Multimodal Treatment Study (CAMS), a massive clinical trial of kids ages seven to seventeen in the United States, found that kids who were treated with either CBT, an antidepressant medication in the form of a selective serotonin reuptake inhibitor (SSRI), or both CBT and medication all improved over a twelve-week treatment period. This is good news—it gives families options. But the kids who had a combination of CBT plus medication were doing better twenty-four and thirty-six weeks after treatment ended. And when researchers followed up with kids over time, kids who had received *any* CBT—either alone or in combination with medication—had better outcomes than kids who only took medication.

The take home here is that while both CBT and antidepressant medications by themselves are likely to benefit anxious kids, the combination of the two is often even better. Another key point is that the benefits of CBT are likely to lead to longer, stronger positive impacts over time. The reasons for this become clearer once you understand what's involved in CBT.

For adults, the story is largely the same. CBT is the first-line psychotherapy recommendation for adults with anxiety disorders, and SSRIs are the first-line medication recommendation. In contrast to treatments for kids, there is no current consensus on the "best" approach to treating adult anxiety, simply because adults have more life experience and complicating factors that can impact decisions about which intervention might be best for a given person. We need to consider factors like age, comorbid mental and physical health conditions, pregnancy, current and past treatment, and access to and cost of different forms of care, to name a few, before selecting the best treatment approach for a given adult.

What qualifies treatment as CBT? Let's return to our Three-Component Model (TCM), which highlights how any emotional experience can be broken down into three components: what we feel, what we think, and what we do.

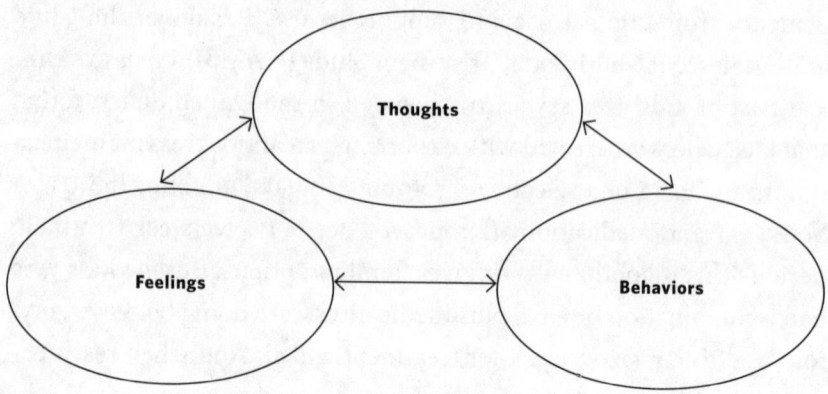

The Three-Component Model of Emotions (TCM)

Generally speaking, you seek treatment for anxiety because you don't like how you are *feeling*. In order to shift how you feel, you need to shift *what you think* and *what you do* in response to your anxiety. Here are the *C* and *B* of cognitive behavioral therapy: the cognitions (thoughts) and behaviors that impact your anxious feelings. CBT for anxiety focuses on changes that you can make to your behaviors in response to anxiety. It also addresses how you can change your relationship to your thoughts: how much you let your thoughts influence you, hook you, and drive your experience. By making targeted changes to your cognitions and behaviors, you shift how you feel—hopefully for the better.

Get Off the Couch

What comes to mind when you imagine a therapy session? Many people imagine a version of what we have all seen in movies. Maybe this is a patient lying on a couch saying whatever comes to mind while a bespectacled therapist takes notes. Or a session of play therapy, where a kid enacts their experience with toys or through drawing. Many of the examples of psychotherapy in the media aren't fully reflective of what to expect in CBT.

CBT has several key features that differentiate it from alternative therapies. First, it is present-focused, meaning that CBT therapists are most concerned about tackling how your symptoms are messing things up for you *currently*. That's not to say that CBT ignores or devalues your history—in fact, many of your anxiety-driven thoughts and behaviors are rooted in your past, and so understanding these patterns can be important—but exclusively rehashing the history of your anxious thoughts and feelings is less helpful than *doing something now* with your anxious thoughts and behaviors to lessen their impact on your life.

So, in CBT, you learn skills and techniques to address symptoms, which you practice during your session and also at home. That means that treatment sessions tend to have a teaching component where knowledge, skills, and strategies are discussed. "Homework" is often assigned, meaning that you and your therapist come up with a plan to practice therapy components between sessions. This may seem like a lot of work, but it leads to increased self-confidence in managing your symptoms; you feel good because you recognize that *you*—rather than a medicine or the superior skill set of your clinician—are the author of your improvement. Indeed, CBT is collaborative by design, and you partner with your therapist to tailor treatment to your individual needs. There are two experts in the room: The therapist is the expert on anxiety disorders and in providing treatment, but you are the expert on you—or your child. Treatment is more successful because of this collaboration.

CBT is designed to be short-term, and symptoms often begin shifting in a matter of weeks to months. Treatment ends when symptoms improve, and if symptoms are not showing any movement, you and your CBT therapist go back to the drawing board to figure out why and change course if needed. Your therapist sets an agenda for each session to help ensure that certain concepts are covered and helpful skills are taught.

Progress in CBT requires engagement and motivation. It's similar to what you could expect with an exercise program. If you work out with a trainer once a week but spend the remainder of the week on the couch devouring chips, you aren't likely to see much change. Similarly, the effort that goes into CBT—both within and outside of sessions—tends to determine the speed with which your symptoms will get better. Simply showing up isn't enough: You get out what you put in.

A CBT Play-by-Play

Psychoeducation

Early sessions of CBT prioritize learning about anxiety, tailored in a developmentally appropriate way depending on your age and insight. This is called *psychoeducation*. Many of the earlier chapters of this book map onto the psychoeducation content that you might learn about during CBT for anxiety.

Psychoeducation will emphasize that anxiety is a normal, natural emotion, and that experiencing it does not mean that you are defective or broken. Psychoeducation helps put anxiety disorders in perspective: What you're experiencing is an elevation in normal anxiety in which internal alarms are going off when there is no true threat. This feels awful but is not actually harmful. In effect, psychoeducation aims to make anxiety less scary, and to differentiate your emotions from your identity.

During Maddie's treatment, we identified the physical symptoms that she felt during her panic attacks and discussed how these symptoms were actually meant to keep her safe. While she initially balked at the notion that her panic wasn't going to kill her, understanding why her body was behaving in this way was transformative. Her parents joined the end of one of these psychoeducation sessions, and Maddie taught them about the fight-or-flight response. In this way, the entire family had a shared understanding of what was happening to her body, and why, during a panic attack. This made each future panic episode no less uncomfortable but much less terrifying.

This portion of treatment can also be helpful if you are struggling with uncomfortable physical sensations but don't see them as part of an anxiety disorder. Maddie's nausea and stomach distress made much more sense to her once she realized that when her fight-or-flight response kicked in, her digestion slowed down, which led her to feel a bit sick.

During this phase of treatment, you are introduced to the Three-Component Model and you practice identifying the feelings, thoughts, and behaviors that come up for you in response to anxiety-provoking situations. You look for patterns, noting the physical feelings that occur most regularly, unpacking the thoughts that are most frequent, and—most importantly—the behaviors in which you engage to cope.

I asked Maddie to fill out a bunch of Three-Component Model worksheets between our early sessions, which we pored over each week to uncover key patterns. The figure shows an example of her Three-Component Model worksheet:

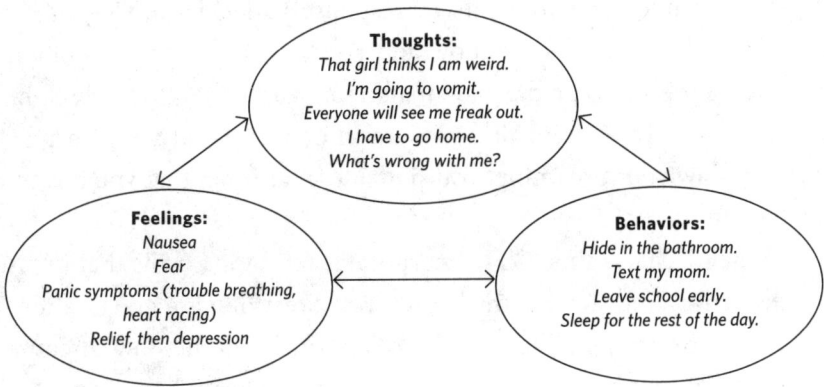

Maddie's Three-Component Model

You can see that when Maddie believed that a classmate was judging her, she felt sick to her stomach and worried that she was going to vomit. This fear fueled other panic symptoms, and she would hide in the bathroom so other kids wouldn't see her, frantically texting her parents until they agreed to pick her up. Maddie astutely noticed that she felt relief when her parents were on their way, but this was quickly followed by feelings of sadness and lots of nasty, negative self-talk. She'd get home, demoralized and exhausted, and crawl into bed and sleep for the rest of the day.

Key to all of this is learning how to *notice* your experience, which is also part of psychological flexibility. So mindfulness practices are typically introduced in this part of treatment as well. You practice noticing your thoughts, feelings, urges, and behaviors, without actively working to change them in the moment. Increased openness to your painful experiences often takes the power away from them. This is why psychoeducation is so important: Once you know your emotions and thoughts can't actually harm you, no matter how intense they feel, you can stop avoiding them—and start facing them with curiosity instead. Paradoxically, emotional acceptance is the doorway to healing.

Relaxation skills

Your body automatically shifts in response to feeling anxiety. Your breathing becomes more shallow and rapid to get oxygenated blood around your body to prepare you to fight or flee. Shallow, rapid breathing signals to your brain that you are in danger. So, if you can take steps to slow your breathing, you signal to your brain that you are actually safe.

To help achieve this, CBT incorporates relaxation skills that focus on deepening and slowing the breath. Box breathing is a great option. It involves breathing steadily to a count. Try it with me now: Breathe in slowly for four beats, hold your breath for four beats, breathe out for four beats, and hold your breath for another four beats. As you breathe, visualize drawing a square, or a box. Imagine a line being drawn upward as you breathe in for four beats, going left to right across the top of the box as you hold your breath for four beats. Now imagine the line being drawn downward as you exhale for four beats, and close the square by drawing the bottom line, right to left, as you hold for the final count of four beats.

Do this on repeat for several minutes at the very least, breathing as deeply and as slowly as possible. As I breathe, I like to imagine that my lungs are a balloon filling with air from the bottom up, expanding my belly first, then my ribs, and finally my upper chest. This helps to ensure that I am breathing low and slow.

Maddie was super skeptical of breathing techniques. She had tried them before and said "nothing worked." When we explored what it would mean if a breathing technique "worked," she meant that she expected it to make her anxiety go away entirely. When taking deep breaths didn't do that for her, she understandably dismissed them as an option.

This is a common and totally fair reaction. It's not just Maddie—deep breathing will not stop anxiety dead in its tracks for anyone. But what happens if we see these techniques as a way to turn the volume down on your anxiety, rather than shut it down completely?

For Maddie, resetting her expectations about relaxation skills helped tremendously. She learned that box breathing reassured her brain that she was safe and helped her get out of fight-or-flight mode so that *Maddie*—rather than *Maddie's anxiety*—could be in charge of her actions.

One round of box breathing isn't going to cut it. Maddie's homework between sessions was to set a timer for five minutes to practice box breathing, at least once a day. She started practicing this skill during moments of calm, which ultimately made it easier for her to access when she was anxious. As she got used to this skill, she started being able to use it to help get her brain and body back online as needed. She did box breathing right before a test—she was still anxious, but she was able to think more clearly. On mornings when anxiety was telling her she couldn't go to school, she did box breathing while taking a hot shower—which also helped to relax her muscles—and found this gave her a better shot at making it out the door. Anxiety was still there, but relaxation techniques helped turn the volume down.

Cognitive coping

This is the "C" part of CBT, and it's where the thoughts that you record on your Three-Component Model come into play. Cognitive coping strategies help you identify the thoughts that accompany your anxiety and examine their relationship to how you feel and what you do. You learn to challenge the common assumption that your thoughts are the truth, that they are always an accurate representation of your current and future experience. Instead, you work on seeing them for what they are: words and images in your head that don't have any power over your behavior unless you let them have power.

During CBT, you practice noticing your thoughts and then evaluate them in terms of how accurate or helpful they are to you. You also identify what would happen if your actions were totally governed by your thoughts. For example, if you buy into the thought "I am such a loser," you are going to act in ways that are consistent with being "a loser." You will see yourself as defective, fragile, and incapable of coping with your feelings and circumstances.

When Maddie had the thought "I'm going to vomit" and believed it to be the truth, she either fled to the bathroom or left school entirely. Similarly, thoughts like "No one likes me," "I'm a burden to my family," and "I'm never going to get better" fueled her feelings of anxiety and sadness and drove her to act in ways that increasingly isolated her, further compounding her depression and her fear.

You can't simply stop or effectively suppress your thoughts. However, you can change your relationship to your thoughts through learning different cognitive coping approaches.

COGNITIVE RESTRUCTURING. It helps to consider each thought as a hypothesis, or a guess. If a thought is a hypothesis, acting as if it is the truth is a bit silly. You owe it to yourself to consider the evidence that supports the thought, as well as the evidence against the thought.

To do so, some CBT approaches teach a technique called *cognitive restructuring*, or cognitive reappraisal. This process involves three steps. First, you identify an anxious thought and consider how truthful or helpful it actually is. Second, you do some detective work by examining the evidence for and against the thought. Finally, you come up with an alternative thought that is either more accurate or more helpful. Your therapist does this with you, and you practice it outside of your sessions until it becomes a skill that you can use independently moving forward.

When anxiety is driving the bus, we are all more prone to thinking errors, or "thinking traps." These are often shorthand judgments or ways of thinking that are anxiety-fueled, inaccurate, or unhelpful. For example, one common thinking trap is called mind reading, which is when you assume that you know what other people are thinking about you (and you usually assume it's not pretty).

This thinking trap runs rampant in folks with social anxiety. Maddie acknowledged that she was constantly mind reading and then behaving as if she knew what people around her were thinking. For example, she assumed that other kids were thinking that she was *devastatingly* uncool, and then she would slink away in shame. Another common thinking trap in anxiety-driven thoughts is catastrophizing, which is when you assume that the worst will happen ("My child will get kidnapped if I let him walk home by himself from the bus stop"). This thinking trap is closely related to jumping to conclusions, a thinking trap where you assume that you know what's going to happen—and your mind usually predicts a catastrophe. Maddie learned that she jumped to a number of catastrophic conclusions whenever she noticed feelings of panic or anxiety. Her worst-case scenario was that she would vomit or panic in front of her classmates, that it would go viral, and that she would be ridiculed and rejected forever.

Common Thinking Traps

Learning to identify thinking traps is the first step in cognitive coping. This is because you can only shift your thinking after you have identified a thought that needs some shifting. So start keeping an eye out for these types of thinking traps as you go through your daily life. Do you notice that you fall into some of these traps more often than others?

- Catastrophizing: Assuming that the "worst ever" outcome is going to happen.
- Jumping to conclusions: Rushing to judgment about a person/situation/thing without considering all the facts.
- Mind reading: Assuming you know what other people are thinking.
- *Should* statements: Thinking I *should* always be perfect, I *shouldn't* make mistakes.
- Perfectionistic thoughts: Setting expectations that are too high or saying things to yourself like "I am going to fail" or "I am not good enough unless I do everything perfectly."
- Labeling: Applying broad labels or judgments that ignore nuance and complexity, like "I'm a loser," "I'm bad at my job," or "Life is miserable."
- Ignoring the positive: Not considering the possible good things that could happen, focusing instead on the unwanted outcomes.
- Overgeneralizing: Assuming that because something happened once, it will always happen that way in the future.

Once you have identified a thinking trap, the next step is to evaluate the evidence for and against the thought, like a detective trying to solve a mystery. We used this approach on Maddie's thought "I am going to vomit in front of everyone." At first, she estimated that she believed this thought with about 80 percent certainty—meaning that she assumed there was an 80 percent chance that if she didn't leave class, she would lose it during chemistry. To be fair, if there were legitimately an 80 percent chance that I was about to vomit in public, I'd be sprinting to the bathroom, too. Maddie's behavior makes sense in this context.

But we acknowledged that this might be an overestimation. We had to figure out what evidence supported the conclusion that she would publicly vomit, and what evidence contradicted this conclusion. I asked Maddie, what does her past experience tell her about the likelihood that her fear will come true? What do the experiences of other people tell her about the likelihood that her fear will come true? Have there been times when she expected her fear to come true, but something else happened instead? What would she tell a friend who had the same fear? How might someone else look at this situation? Is this fear based on how she *feels,* or on actual circumstances? And importantly, even if her thought were true, how helpful or unhelpful is it for her to act on this thought?

These questions can be applied to many other thinking errors as well, and questions to help you challenge thinking traps can be found in the Resources section at the back of this book. Once you or your child have identified a thinking trap, you can evaluate it using these types of questions. You will likely come out on the other side with a more balanced, helpful, flexible thought.

Through this process, we recognized that there were two main pieces of evidence supporting Maddie's belief that she was going to vomit in front of everyone: (1) She had seen it happen to a peer, and (2) she felt nauseated. On the other hand, we were able to identify a number of factors that put this belief into question.

Maddie herself had never vomited in front of people, other than her parents, and only when she had a stomach bug. Even when she felt extremely nauseated and was having a full-fledged panic attack, she had never vomited. Across her fourteen years of life, we estimated that she had been in public settings thousands upon thousands of times; only once had she seen someone else vomit. We ultimately concluded that the likelihood that she would vomit in front of her peers was a low-probability event. At first, Maddie reestimated the probability at 30 percent.

"Really?" I asked. "Nearly a one-in-three chance?"

She gave her most exasperated teenage eye roll. "Fine, maybe ten percent."

The percentages themselves aren't the issue. The key is that Maddie was way more likely to resist anxiety's urges if she believed there was a low likelihood of her worst-case scenario coming true than if she was certain it was imminent. And resisting the urges to do what anxiety was telling her she needed to do—running to the bathroom, texting Mom for a pickup, leaving school—is what truly made an impact in her treatment. To this effect, cognitive restructuring helps you more accurately and effectively cope with your fears.

COGNITIVE DEFUSION. *Cognitive defusion* is another cognitive coping technique that helps you better manage your anxious thoughts. In order to understand cognitive defusion, it helps to first understand cognitive fusion. *Cognitive fusion* happens when you let your thoughts "hook" you, let them jerk you around, and allow them to drive your feelings and behaviors. For example, if you are struggling with an assignment and the thought "I can never do anything right" comes up, you have become "fused with" or "hooked by" this thought if you really buy into it and let it impact your actions. When you are hooked, you ruminate on the thought while you try to do the assignment, and it really gets in the way of your concentration. So you slam your laptop down and give up.

Maddie learned that she was getting really hooked by mind reading thinking traps. These thoughts involved themes that she was weird, ugly, or stupid, or that her peers were grossed out by her and wanted her to go away. Anyone would want to run and hide if these thoughts were true! They evoked not only anxiety but the feeling of shame for Maddie, and this painful-feelings pile-on made it more likely that she would hide herself away from a world that she felt was always judging her.

Maddie was so fused with thoughts that she was unlikable, unattractive, and unwanted that they had become part of how she saw herself. No matter how many times her parents or her friends told her how amazing she was, or that she was being ridiculous to assume that everyone thought so poorly about her, she couldn't stop herself from thinking and believing the opposite. And crucially, behaving as if these thoughts were the truth led her to isolate from others, which worsened her anxiety and depression.

Cognitive fusion is not an experience that is unique to anxiety disorders or depression; everyone gets hooked by unhelpful thoughts at times. Sometimes you get hooked by a negative prediction like "I'm going to fail" and can't move on. Sometimes you get hooked by a belief about yourself, like "I'm unlovable" or "I'm a horrible parent," and tumble down a rabbit hole of self-loathing. Sometimes you get hooked by a painful memory or image that gets "stuck" in your mind's eye. Sometimes you get hooked by physical pain or discomfort. Importantly, it's much easier to get hooked when you are in a vulnerable state—when you are upset, anxious, sad, or angry, or when you are sick, tired, stressed out, eating poorly, or not getting enough exercise.

In contrast to cognitive restructuring, the goal of cognitive defusion isn't to shift the thought. The focus is on creating distance between yourself and the thought. The thought is still there, but the goal is to create space between the thought itself and its impact on your feelings and behavior. Let's go back to the analogy of your painful thoughts as the beach ball in the swimming pool; cognitive defusion lets you swim in the pool alongside the beach ball, knowing that it will occasionally bump into you and disrupt your flow, but that you can simply acknowledge it and keep swimming your laps.

Maddie found a few defusion strategies helpful to counter the painful thoughts that she was unlikable, unwanted, or unattractive. The defusion strategy that we used the most often was one of the most straightforward: noticing the thought. Consider the different impact of the thought "Everyone hates me" versus "*I'm noticing* the thought that everyone hates me." Or "I'm so ugly" versus

"*I'm noticing* the thought that I'm so ugly." The first statements are declarative, as if they are facts, making it more likely that you will act as if you are universally despised or horrifying to look at. The second statements introduce nuance, an acknowledgment that your mind is giving you one way of seeing your situation, and that it's up to you to take it or leave it. It gives you space between yourself and your thought, making it more likely that you will choose a productive action.

Another defusion strategy is called naming the story. We created a title for the story that Maddie's mind was telling her about how she was unlikable, unattractive, and unwanted. She decided it would be called "Maddie Sucks." Whenever she noticed these types of thoughts arising, she would acknowledge to herself, "Here's the 'Maddie Sucks' story." Again, just enough space not to get totally hooked so that these thoughts drove her actions.

There are a ton of defusion strategies—they could fill an entire chapter. Your therapist may introduce a bunch of defusion strategies with you, using trial and error to see which are most effective and which you like the most. Some fall flat, and some are keepers. They are good tools to have in your coping toolbox, and like any new skill, they require practice to be effective.

During CBT for anxiety disorders, cognitive coping strategies are the means, but not the end. They will help you shift your relationship to your inner life, enabling you to do the most impactful work of treatment: exposure therapy.

Exposure therapy

Exposure treatments are based on the understanding that avoiding anxiety-provoking situations actually worsens anxiety over time. Exposure therapy reverses this dynamic by encouraging gradual engagement—*exposure*—with the things that you have been avoiding.

Exposure therapy is the key ingredient of CBT for anxiety disorders, and because of this, most cognitive behavioral treatments that address anxiety disorders spend at least half of their sessions on exposure practices. This is the change-maker. If you or your child are in anxiety disorder treatment that does *not* include exposure work, you are likely missing a key element. It's like baking chocolate chip cookies and leaving out the chocolate chips . . . nothing wrong with sugar, butter, and flour, but the chocolate is a defining ingredient.

Because exposure-based CBT for anxiety is still a specialized skill set, many excellent therapists do not provide this type of treatment. This is why it can be helpful to ask questions about the extent to which potential providers integrate exposure into their work before beginning therapy. The following questions may be useful to ask potential providers when seeking care for yourself or for your child when you are looking for exposure-based CBT.

Questions for Potential Providers

Here are some questions that may be helpful to ask potential providers to determine at the outset whether they will be a good fit for your needs:

- What can I expect to experience during a treatment session?
- Do you prefer to set an agenda or goals for sessions, or are sessions open-ended/patient-led?
- What kinds of skills or techniques do you teach in sessions?
- Do you integrate exposure therapy, or exposure with response prevention (ERP), in your work?
- If so, how? Do you practice exposures in sessions, assign exposure practice outside of sessions, or both?
- Do you assign homework or activities to practice between sessions?
- How do you assess and monitor progress in treatment? What do you generally recommend if things aren't improving?

Additional questions for parents seeking care for your child:

- How do you involve caregivers in a child's treatment? Do you meet with parents for separate sessions, or portions of sessions, or not at all?
- How are caregivers involved in exposure work?

The Flexibility Factor: Hold the Door Open

As you were reading through the play-by-play for CBT, I wonder if you found yourself thinking, "That would never work for me." "I've tried that already and it didn't help." Or, "Lady, you're dreaming—my kid would never go for that."

Pause. It makes sense if thoughts like this came up. It's easy to dismiss new things—and even easier if you are anxious, depressed, burned out, or otherwise demoralized by your symptoms and stressors. Try applying a simple defusion strategy here, reframing the thoughts as "I'm noticing the thought 'That would never work for me.'"

As you create a bit of space between yourself and your thoughts, can you also validate yourself here? Why does it make sense that you, in this moment, would have doubts? There could be many reasons. I'll go out on a limb and suggest that a likely contributor could be that the mental health system can be a spirit-crushing labyrinth. Trying to find good care can be as stressful as coping with your symptoms. Also, there are no guarantees with any treatment—and you should run from anyone who tells you otherwise. It makes sense that your mind would try to protect you from starting down a path that could lead to more disappointment.

Now, can you consider what you have already tried in an attempt to deal with your anxiety symptoms? I'm guessing that you've probably leaned into avoidance—opting out, tapping out, or maybe even tuning out by using substances or other unhealthy strategies to dull your pain. How have those strategies worked for you in the long term? Have they been successful in keeping the anxious thoughts and feelings from coming back? And what have those strategies cost you, in terms of time, money, opportunities, relationships, or joy? Has relying on those strategies taken you closer to or further away from the things you value?

As you reflect on these points, notice what comes up for you—annoyance, guilt, indignation, frustration, sorrow. If you're feeling some painful feelings, that's normal—*and* you can handle it.

The key question is—are you willing to try something new? Or, if you've tried something similar before, are you willing to try again? Can you hold space for your doubts and fears—let them hang out like the beach ball in the swimming pool—and also hold the door open for new ideas?

You may not be sure yet. And that's okay. I encourage you to read on and learn more about exposure therapy. It's so important for the treatment of anxiety disorders—and I believe in it so strongly—that we will spend the next chapter looking at how and why it works.

And if you are still reading, know that you have likely just practiced some psychological flexibility by walking through this thought exercise: You've noticed what's going on for you internally, held space for whatever thoughts and feelings come up, and you are still here, opening the door to learning something new that may help you and your family.

What Can You Take Home with You?

- CBT is different from many other therapies that you may have seen in media, read about, or even experienced yourself in the past. Because of this, it's helpful to know a bit about what to expect so you aren't surprised if, for example, your therapist shows up with an agenda for the session or has prepared reading material or worksheets for you.

- It's equally important to prepare your kid for CBT. It can be helpful to ask their therapist to share what a typical session is like, and to share any expectations that they have with you and your kid up front. It can be harder to get kids on board for treatment that may involve actively learning new material and skills, or that involves between-session practice, if they aren't prepared. For some kids, it can be helpful to frame CBT as a class they might take in school—it's a short-term period where you work on developing new knowledge and skills that can really help you in life.

CHAPTER 9

Unpacking Exposure Therapy

"I'm going to drop him. I'm going to drop him and he's going to die. I can't do this."

Marta sits at the desk in her bedroom with her baby in her arms, panicking. We are meeting via telehealth. She sought me out shortly after her son, Elias, was born and she started having crippling panic attacks. Marta's biggest fear was that she would have a panic attack while she was holding her son and that she would somehow hurt him.

By the time she started meeting with me, Marta only felt able to hold Elias if her husband was close by. She was so afraid of accidentally hurting her son that she began noticing panic symptoms every time she held him, even if her husband was within arm's reach. As a result, he ended up doing most of the hands-on work of feeding, changing, and snuggling their son, while she looked on, guilt-ridden, attached to a breast pump. She felt like she was failing her family in every way.

I ask Marta to tell me what she notices in her body in this moment. She pauses to mentally scan her body and reports back, shakily, through tears, "I feel like I am choking. I have that tightness in my chest and a lump in my throat, you know? Um . . . my heart is beating fast. I feel it in my chest and in my head. I feel dizzy, like I would fall over if I stood up. I feel tightness everywhere."

I remind her that everything she feels right now is her body doing what it is supposed to do when she's in danger, but just at the wrong time. I ask her what she notices about how she's holding Elias.

She pauses for a second, as if she is surprised by the notion. She looks down at her son in her arms. "I'm not squeezing," she responds. I agree that Elias seems perfectly safe and content. This is a big deal. One of Marta's fears was that if she had a panic attack while holding her son, she would crush him.

I ask her where her anxiety level is right now.

"About an eight," she says. We use a scale from 0 to 10 to rate how intensely she is experiencing her anxiety at any given moment. This scale is called *Subjective Units of Distress,* or *SUDS.* Marta's SUDS were at a 10 when her husband put Elias in her arms and left the room a few moments ago.

Noting this slight decrease in her anxiety, I ask her if she is willing to keep going. She nods. We spend the next fifteen minutes checking in with her thoughts and feelings and noticing her behaviors as she holds her son while panicking. She notices the way her feelings of panic shift over time, getting less overwhelming as she practices tolerating them, fully engaging with them. Elias is a pretty chill baby, but at one point he gets extra squirmy. Marta notices her SUDS increasing as she has to respond to adjust him in her arms. But she doesn't drop him. She doesn't crush him. She doesn't have a heart attack.

She also doesn't yell for her husband, although several times she notices the thought that she wants to call him. On my end, I resist the urge to respond to her husband's emails as they ping across my inbox in the middle of all this—as he sits anxiously in the next room wondering how she is doing. This is an exposure practice for him, too.

I ask her to mindfully describe Elias as she holds him. Through her panic, she describes the angel kiss on his left eyelid, the way his little hand is curled in a fist, that dagger of a fingernail on his pinky (how can something so delicate be so sharp?), and his long, dark eyelashes. I point out when she smiles at him through her tears and mimics his cooing sounds.

Another one of Marta's fears was that she would "traumatize" Elias if she held him while she was crying and panicking. In earlier sessions, we acknowledged that, yes, children do pick up on their parents' emotions and, yes, he is more likely to be upset when she is upset; we also acknowledged that the longer she avoided holding Elias independently, the more uncomfortable she would be with him, and he with her. We agreed that the damage caused by prolonged disconnection from his mother was likely to be way more problematic for Elias than anything else. Acknowledging these nuances helped build Marta's motivation to do this hard work.

After a while, Marta reported to me that her SUDS were around a 5. She was by no means relaxed but acknowledged that her heart rate had decreased, her breathing was less choppy, and she was no longer crying. She even was able to gingerly take one arm from around Elias to reach for a teething toy.

At some point, I float another idea. "What would it be like to stand up?" She looks at me like I asked her to organize a bank heist.

But she entertains the notion. It's not entirely novel. Over the past few weeks, we have practiced having her stand and hold Elias while her husband gradually stepped farther away. However, holding Elias and standing up, without the reassuring vigilance of her husband, was a whole new ball game. She notices her panic symptoms rising again simply from contemplating the move.

I gently circle back to some of the treatment goals she shared when we first started working together. Marta's panic symptoms made it unsustainable to rely on breastfeeding, and Elias would now only take a bottle. The forfeiture of her breastfeeding experience was a real source of sadness for Marta. But she wanted to be able to bottle-feed Elias without her husband in the room. She also wanted to be able to manage a diaper blowout independently. Her husband was struggling while trying to work remotely, and Marta felt ashamed to be so utterly dependent on him. And Marta wanted to experience those little moments of bonding with just her and Elias.

When she was pregnant, Marta had imagined herself bouncing her baby in her arms while she sang to him, like some blissed-out mama in a baby shampoo ad. But anxiety and fear had made this impossible. Giving birth to Elias during the COVID-19 lockdowns had already dashed so many of Marta's hopes for her baby's infancy. Panic disorder and postpartum depression had stolen even more. She hated the ever-present feelings of powerlessness, dependence, self-doubt, and fear.

Marta looks at me for reassurance. I acknowledge that of course there is risk, because there is *always* risk. And some risks are worth taking.

Marta stands up.

No Challenge, No Change

What are some of the top anxiety-busting activities that you can think of? Yoga. Smartphone distraction. Exercise. Alcohol. Long baths. Weekend getaways—without children.

These strategies definitely have their place in our broader coping tool kits. However, while these approaches may help us cope with mild anxiety, they are woefully inadequate to address anxiety disorders.

Prior to seeking treatment, Marta had tried a number of these strategies. Some of them did help her feel better in the moment. However, most took her even further away from Elias. They were Band-Aids that gave her momentary relief but ultimately fueled her anxiety by perpetuating avoidance.

Marta needed to do the opposite of avoidance. So we engaged in exposure therapy—sometimes called *exposure with response prevention (ERP)*—which is based on the understanding that when we perceive something as frightening, it is our natural instinct to try to avoid it. This is great, if the thing that is scaring us is actually a threat to our life or well-being. But what if it's not? What if it just *feels like* it is? The more we avoid the things that make us uncomfortable, the worse the discomfort becomes. That's what happened to Marta. The more she avoided holding Elias independently, the more impaired she became.

To take back her life, our work together centered on exposing her gradually to the very things that anxiety told her she wasn't able to do.

We started on the easier side; we practiced having her hold, change, dress, and feed Elias as her husband moved farther away from her. When she wasn't holding Elias, we also practiced tolerating uncomfortable panic sensations by having her intentionally hyperventilate or spin in place, which brought up physical feelings that mimicked panic symptoms. This helped teach her that these uncomfortable experiences were not, in fact, unsafe. Marta practiced during sessions with me, and between sessions as homework. Over a few weeks, she worked up to the session where she held Elias completely separated from her husband.

Exposure-based treatment was the most effective approach for Marta, as it is for many people. It is the "B" in CBT, as it involves changing your *behavior* in response to anxiety by doing the things that anxiety tells you that you can't do. It centers on actively pushing back against the urge to avoid. It can be wildly effective. It can also be really hard.

You engage in a form of exposure therapy all the time without recognizing it—for example, when you call out a response despite being unsure of the answer; when you ask someone out despite the fear of being rejected; when you walk into the party despite feeling nauseated; when you begin therapy despite fear of the unknown. Exposure means doing hard, uncomfortable things that are in line with your values. In essence, it's an exercise in psychological flexibility.

While the long-term aim of exposure-based treatment is to decrease anxiety symptoms, the goal of exposure work is *never* to get rid of anxiety. Anxiety serves an important function in all of our lives. Instead, you want to work toward improving your ability to cope effectively with anxiety. When your confidence increases, your overall anxiety decreases. The goal of exposure-based treatment is to get more comfortable doing uncomfortable things.

Why It Works

Why does facing our fears actually work?

Consider what it's like to get into the ocean on the first day of summer—no big deal if you are a Floridian, but if you live in New England, like I do, you can expect that first swim to be appallingly cold. Many of us get in the water through the painstaking process of *habituation*—by inching in until we get used to the cold. That first cold step in shocks your nerves and you have to resist the urge to retreat. But what happens when you stay in for a while? You get used to the feeling, and the water no longer feels cold.

That is, until you take the next step and experience a new wave of unpleasantness. Which you wait out. Gradually, step by step, you can fully immerse yourself in the water. You can have a grand old time playing in the waves and not notice the feeling of cold because your body has habituated to the temperature.

You see a similar process play out through exposure practices: When you face something challenging, anxiety decreases because you get used to—or habituate to—the feeling. We saw this, in part, during Marta's exposure. When her husband first shut the door and she was sitting in the room by herself holding Elias, she took a step into the freezing metaphorical ocean. Her anxiety spiked, her discomfort surged, and her emotions threatened to take over. She wanted to halt the exposure—which would have been a really effective way of easing her anxiety. But by this point in her treatment, she knew the drill. She understood that if she resisted the urge to avoid these scary feelings, they would start to decrease on their own. Her nervous system would get used to being in the situation and would temper over time. So she took another step, and we waited. When I asked her to progressively challenge herself, by holding Elias with only one arm, or by standing while holding him, it was a step deeper into the water and a new cold-shock that her system had to get used to.

Habituation happens all the time and in various ways. Think about what it's like to be in a room with a distinct scent. You are highly aware of the odor when you first enter, but over time you stop noticing the smell of the place. It's still there, but you are used to it. Or consider how, if you usually wear a watch on your left wrist and switch it to your right, this sensation initially feels strange, even bothersome.

Over time, however, you forget it's there because your nervous system has habituated to the new feeling.

We can see habituation happen within a single exposure practice. As part of my work with Maddie, we did exposures to target her fears that she would get uncomfortable in public places and wouldn't be able to escape. One way we practiced fighting back against this fear was by walking through a large bookstore together. Using the 0-to-10 SUDS rating scale, Maddie noted that her anxiety was at a 7 when we first arrived. After about ten minutes of wandering around, her anxiety decreased slightly to a 6. By the end of our forty-five-minute session, she reported SUDS at a 2. She habituated to her anxiety in that situation.

But there is more going on during exposure treatment than habituation, and exposures can be effective in decreasing anxiety symptoms over time, even if habituation doesn't occur. In other words, an exposure hasn't "failed" if you don't notice your anxiety decreasing. In fact, you can have a really effective exposure experience even if your anxiety stays high during the entire process—or even if it gets higher.

I worked with Cole, an eleven-year-old boy with social anxiety who had a hard time speaking with unfamiliar people. Cole's core fear was that he believed others would see him as "stupid" or "annoying." He also felt really uncomfortable when people were upset with him, and he was afraid of grown-ups speaking to him sharply.

As part of an exposure plan addressing these fears, Cole agreed to go into several stores, one after the other, and ask the cashier for change for a dollar. That meant that he would end up spending only a few minutes in each store, leaving little time for habituation. The verdict at the end of the practice was that his SUDS hadn't decreased; each time he interacted with a new person, his SUDS stayed at a 5 or 6 for the entire interaction. No habituation. In fact, his SUDS actually increased during the second-to-last interaction when the cashier didn't have change. This totally threw him off.

"It was *the worst!*" he moaned when he rejoined me on the sidewalk, dollar still in hand.

"The worst?" I reflected back to him. "How so? Did the cashier yell at you?"

"No."

"Anyone call you an idiot?"

"No."

"Did the rest of the customers pick you up and hurl you out of the door?"

"No."

"So what did you do when they said, no change?"

"I just said thanks and came outside."

"Got it. That can feel awkward, huh?"

"Yeah."

"Worst thing that has ever happened to you?"

Cole rolled his eyes at me. "Yes," he mumbled stubbornly. "The actual worst." He wouldn't give me this one.

But we both knew it wasn't the actual worst. It was awkward, and awkwardness is uncomfortable. And he survived. Even without feeling his anxiety decrease, he learned he could handle the feeling of discomfort. He learned that he was even able to pivot when the unexpected happened. It wasn't fun, but it also wasn't dangerous. And he learned he could cope. More to his credit, he was still willing to push himself to go into one more store and ask for change. This was the bonus round, as it helped him learn that he can recover from tough things, even when they get really hard.

None of this would have been possible without embracing the challenge of an exposure. When you try something scary, you are opening yourself up to the possibility that your worst-case scenario might come true: "I won't be able to escape the bookstore, the cashiers will be annoyed with me asking for change, I will drop my baby." More often than not, however, your worst-case scenario doesn't come true. And even if it does, you can handle it.

This principle is called *inhibitory learning*. It explains why learning something new that challenges your old beliefs is so critical for growth.

When your assumptions are violated, it introduces new information: "I thought I would flee the bookstore in a panic, but I didn't. I thought all the cashiers would be mean to me, but they weren't. I thought I would drop my baby if I held him while panicking, but I didn't." This new data gets integrated into your narrative about yourself, your world, and your capabilities. Instead of working desperately to avoid the possibility of experiencing anxiety, you learn that you can handle even the curveballs. And life is full of curveballs.

No Shame in Tiptoeing In

On the face of it, it seems so simple: If there is something that you are afraid of and that you are avoiding, you just need to *do the thing*. But simple doesn't always mean easy. If it were easy to face your fears, you would do it all the time, right? Me too. I would be at the front of the line for roller coasters, I'd be the one who volunteers to remove creepy-crawlies from the house, and I would try out that local Pilates studio that seems to exclusively cater to the fit and fabulous. But facing your fears is, by definition, terrifying. Remember that emotions evolved to feel intense in order to motivate the fight-or-flight response. The discomfort that you know you will feel by diving headfirst into the ocean can be enough to disincentivize even an avid swimmer.

Thank goodness for tiptoeing in. Getting into the ocean one step at a time, while painful, gets the job done. The same goes with exposure practices. The best treatment involves creating a hierarchy of anxiety-provoking situations, ranging from least anxiety-provoking to most. You begin exposure practices at the bottom and work your way up.

If you are seeking treatment for your phobia of dogs, for example, your therapist probably won't be recruiting a Great Dane for session one. Instead, you will collaborate on creating a *fear and avoidance hierarchy (FAH)*, which is a list of situations involving dogs that make you feel anxious and that you tend to avoid. Using our 0-to-10 SUDS scale, you rank these situations from least anxiety-provoking to most anxiety-provoking. For example, patting a Chihuahua who is on a leash might provoke moderate anxiety for you, whereas going to a dog park with a bunch of rambunctious canines is likely to be closer to the top of your fear hierarchy. This hierarchy is individualized and tailored to you, your circumstances, and your experience.

SAMPLE DOG PHOBIA FEAR AND AVOIDANCE HIERARCHY (FAH)

SUDS	Exposure Situation
10	Spending time alone in a small space with a large dog, off-leash
9	Going to an off-leash dog park
8	Patting an off-leash dog
7	Spending time in the home of a friend with a well-behaved dog, off-leash
6	Patting a large dog who is on a leash
5	Patting a small dog who is on a leash
4	Watching a live-action film of dogs
3	Looking at a photograph of a small dog
2	Watching a cartoon movie of a dog
1	Looking at a cartoon picture of a dog

Once you create the hierarchy, you start by dipping your toes in; you tackle situations lower on the hierarchy first. Your therapist will ask you to identify your SUDS before starting an exposure. They will typically help you identify the anxious thoughts that accompany your anxious feelings ("the dog will bite me; I will freak out and embarrass myself") and help you apply cognitive coping strategies before diving into the exposure. Throughout the exposure experience, your therapist will check in to see where your SUDS are at that moment. It can be helpful to graph SUDS over time.

But you can't just check exposure practices off your hierarchy like a grocery list. Repetition is key. Let's circle back to Maddie, who spent a session with me milling around the bookstore. For her homework, she agreed to spend thirty minutes at a local bookstore at least three times before our next session. I asked her to track her SUDS at the beginning and end of each practice. A week later, she had been to her local bookstore three times and noticed that it took less time for her SUDS to decrease each time she practiced.

"The last time I left a few minutes early," she confessed. "But not because I was scared," she qualified, hurriedly (Maddie was a people-pleaser . . . we worked on that, too). "I left because I was actually kind of . . . bored."

Chef's kiss to that. This is the outcome that you ultimately want—a situation that used to be anxiety-provoking becomes a nonissue, something that no longer takes up headspace. Repeated exposures continue to strengthen these "bravery muscles," teaching you that *you can handle this*—and similar situations. This growing confidence about your capabilities is ultimately what leads to the decrease in anxiety over time.

Get Your Form Right

Having proper form when you are exercising helps you get the most out of your workout, and the same goes for exposure practices. Not all exposures are created equal; if you want to make your exposure practice really count—and trust me, you do, because it means your treatment will go faster—get your form right.

Sometimes patients report to me that an exposure they practiced between sessions was a breeze, that they didn't feel the anxiety as expected. That's both great news and disappointing. I am obviously going to be pleased that it was easier than they anticipated, because I don't enjoy seeing my patients distressed. But I am also disappointed because I know that the learning was diluted.

The goal during an exposure is *not* to feel calm. The most effective exposures are ones in which you fully experience your anxiety and practice tolerating your distress in the moment. This is one of the ironies of effective CBT; you often feel *more anxious* during a therapy session, or at the beginning of therapy, than you did prior to initiating the process. Why? Because you are deliberately bringing on anxiety by facing the fears you have been avoiding. If you don't actually feel anxious or uncomfortable during an exposure, it's unlikely to be super helpful. This is because a goal of exposure practice is to reach a *comfortable level of discomfort*—not completely overwhelming but also not too easy. And there is a tremendous sense of pride in facing a true challenge.

Relatedly, it can be easy to fall into the trap of *white-knuckling* during an exposure. White-knuckling is a term for going through the motions of an exposure while at the same time trying to control or suppress the uncomfortable feelings that arise. You are figuratively gripping the handlebars as tightly as you can until the exposure ends. It is the difference between enduring your anxiety and coping with it. White-knuckling can seriously undermine how well exposure therapy works.

In order to practice coping with anxiety better, you need to experience it fully. You have to open yourself up to the challenge of facing your fear head-on, to see its ugliness in full view, and to stare it down. So, during exposure practices, you want to minimize distractions and do all that you can to reach that comfortable level of discomfort. In order to do this, it helps to bring mindfulness into exposure work.

People are often surprised when I suggest this, mostly because mindfulness is so often associated with relaxation. And exposures are decidedly not relaxing. While mindfulness can be a beneficial part of relaxation practices, feeling good in the moment isn't actually the goal of mindfulness. Instead, mindfulness exercises help to bring your full attention to your present-moment experience, whether pleasant or unpleasant—this is why it's the first step of psychological flexibility.

You can remain mindful during exposure by noticing and naming your experience in the moment: your thoughts, feelings, sensations, urges, and behaviors. When I asked Marta to tell me what she was noticing in her body during her panic attack as she held her baby, the aim was to practice mindfulness. When she named her urge to call out to her husband, she was being mindful of her thoughts and urges. When she checked in and reported her SUDS to me at various times, she was bringing mindful attention to her distress. When she described Elias in her arms, it helped her to fully experience the moment—both her fear *and* her joy.

Getting Rid of the Crutches

Another key tenet of effective exposure is to avoid the use of *safety behaviors*. A safety behavior is anything we tend to lean on to decrease our anxiety in the moment—a crutch that staves off the anxiety. We become dependent on it to function, and when that thing isn't present, the anxiety returns.

If you can only tolerate flying if your partner is next to you the whole time, dependence on your partner is the safety behavior. If you will only book a flight if you can score an aisle seat near the front of the plane, the position of your seat becomes a crutch. Same thing if you feel you must take an Ativan before each flight. Sure, you can fly, but anxiety dictates, "Only under these specific conditions. Otherwise, you're driving."

Safety behaviors may be a reason why your anxiety hasn't improved over time, even if you feel like you are doing all the right things. I worked with Olivia, a college student and a perfectionist who felt anxiety in all areas of her life. At the start of treatment, she struggled to understand how the relationship between anxiety and avoidance played out in her situation. "I am not avoiding anything," she protested. "I go to all my classes, I go out with friends and go to parties, but the anxiety isn't getting better."

Over the next few sessions, however, we uncovered all sorts of safety behaviors—some subtle, and some not so subtle—that were fueling Olivia's continued anxiety. She had a ton of anxiety around her schoolwork, and we learned that this was maintained through perfectionistic tendencies and routines.

Compared to her peers, she was devoting excessive time to studying, convinced that if she didn't study until she felt "right," she would fail the assignment. She also had a rigid bedtime routine that she felt ensured that she would get good sleep. She became really upset if her routine and sleep were disrupted, which they often were. And we realized that she was white-knuckling through pretty much every anxiety-provoking activity, effectively gritting her teeth to get through tough experiences through a combination of self-talk, "it's almost over, it's not that bad," or by distracting herself with her phone. She eventually shared that, yes, she was going out with friends, but only if alcohol was involved. Drinking tamped down the intensity of social anxiety for her, such that she started pregaming solo before she went out. Ultimately, Olivia realized how many safety behaviors she had put in place in order to curate conditions under which her anxiety was tolerable . . . but just *barely* tolerable. And the effort was exhausting.

Identifying safety behaviors is a vital part of effective exposure work. And getting rid of them is often an exposure itself. In Marta's case, reliance on her home's baby monitor was serving as a safety behavior. In planning for the session when she would hold her baby solo, both Marta and her husband initially felt reassured that he would be able to watch her from the other room using the video monitor so he could swoop in if Marta "needed him" during the session.

They immediately regretted bringing the video monitor up, because once I knew about it, I was a dog with a bone. A well-meaning, mildly irritating dog, but a dog with a bone, nonetheless. If, in the back of her mind, Marta knew that her husband was effectively supervising, her anxiety was kept in check. While that was reassuring in the moment, it ensured that she remained absolutely dependent on her husband. It was a challenging step to take, but ultimately, they agreed that access to the video monitor would get in the way of the exposure being maximally effective. They unplugged the monitor before our session.

With Olivia, we worked to remove the safety behaviors associated with study habits by planning study sessions that would end after a set time. This allowed her to test her fear that she would fail her assignments if she didn't study until she "felt ready." Spoiler: She didn't fail. We also knocked off the elements of her bedtime routine one at a time. This helped her confront her fear that not getting a full eight hours of sleep would mean she would "fall apart" the next day. She learned that she would be a bit tired but was ultimately fine. To get at her white-knuckling tendencies, we amped up mindfulness during exposures, which helped her learn that she could tolerate the feeling of distress. She also acknowledged that she couldn't effectively address her anxiety in social situations until she cut out drinking, so we started having her hang out in larger groups without alcohol. Through this process of gradually reducing her wide-ranging safety behaviors, she could address her core anxieties.

Safety Behaviors Versus Coping Strategies

A safety behavior helps you avoid hard things, while a coping strategy helps you do hard things. The key distinction between a safety behavior / safety signal and a coping strategy is its function—whether it helps you avoid more or engage more.

For example, say you are afraid to take the subway, but you feel you can do so if you are listening to your favorite podcast as a distraction. In this situation, the podcast is a safety behavior; it is a crutch on which you are dependent. If the podcast was unavailable, you would feel unable to ride the subway. In contrast, if your anxiety about riding the subway gets so high that you have the urge to bail entirely, but listening to a few minutes of your favorite podcast helps you reregulate—get to a comfortable level of discomfort—and continue on with your trip, listening to the podcast becomes an effective coping strategy, which you can turn off once you are a bit calmer.

The same behavior can be a coping strategy in one context and a safety behavior in another. Consider a kid who has been struggling with school avoidance. This week, his exposure task is to go into school and attend classes. But the anticipatory anxiety that this exposure suggestion brings up is too high for this kid, and he feels unable to do it. To help him meet this exposure goal, his dad agrees to go with him and will stay in the guidance counselor's office while his son is in class. At this juncture, his dad's presence is a coping strategy that enables the child to take the first steps to get into the school building. As he repeats this exposure and attends school for multiple days, however, his dad's continued presence can quickly become a safety behavior, because he feels he can *only go* if Dad is there. The next step would then be to get Dad out of the school building.

Don't get too bogged down trying to figure out whether a given behavior is a safety behavior or a coping strategy. A good rubric is to ask yourself whether you feel you can do a challenging task *only if* certain conditions are met. If that is the case, challenge yourself to get rid of those crutches.

Getting Ready to Get Ready

Patients sometimes ask whether they should wait until they *feel ready* before they try something this challenging. I believe that you can spend a lifetime waiting for motivation, inspiration, and courage that never comes. It takes a lot of bravery to do exposure work, and truly, you often won't feel ready. So how can you build motivation for this challenge?

Sometimes the motivation is already there, because anxiety has led to so much suffering that you are willing to try anything to get your life back. And sometimes motivation comes by taking an honest look at what anxiety is costing you. How would your life look different if anxiety weren't such a big player?

Acknowledging this gap can be painful for adults and kids. Many loving parents avoid discussing the true impact of anxiety with their kid. They shy away from pointing out how anxiety has eroded friendships, academic progress, or opportunities for joy. Parents do this because they don't want their kid to feel ashamed, sad, or more stressed. I get this. But it's one thing to gently help your kid recognize how anxiety affects their life and encourage them to imagine a different path; it's another to shame or blame them for their anxiety disorder. And while it may feel like you are protecting your kid when you help them avoid reflecting on their reality, you are suggesting to them that they lack the strength to handle hard feelings. Remember that one of the functions of sadness is to help us grow and change. Some amount of sadness can be motivating, and I've worked with many kids who are ready to take back their lives, having acknowledged what anxiety has stolen.

And let's face some other truths: You can be ready to take on the world in moments of calm, but your motivation can melt faster than an ice cube in hell when anxiety gets loud. In these instances, you may need something to sweeten the pot.

Enter positive reinforcement, which can be applied in many different ways. Positive reinforcement can look like telling your child that you are proud of them for being kind to a friend, giving a sticker each time a child practices a new skill, or putting down your phone and actively listening to your partner when they share with you about their tough day.

When it comes to combating anxiety, a rewards plan can be a vital tool, because even the most motivated of us can freeze up before doing something hard. Having the ability to remind yourself—or your kid— of the sweetener that will be doled out immediately after the challenging task can help nudge you in the right direction, and it is often more effective in the moment than remembering your long-term goals. Maddie was in her Billie Eilish era when we were working together, and her parents agreed to contribute toward concert tickets as part of her rewards plan. When she was having a full-fledged panic attack on the precipice of an exposure, the reminder that she was working toward those concert tickets could help get her over the hump in the moment.

The best rewards plan is developed in conjunction with your child, because identifying things that your child is motivated to work for is key. Rewards should be in line with your family's values and preferences, and rewards do not have to involve lots of money. Motivating rewards can range from things like getting to pick what the family eats for dinner, having at-home mani-pedis, or staying up thirty minutes later. It can be useful (and fun) to develop a menu of rewards and assign a point value to each item. Your child can earn points for engaging in exposures, which they can bank and use toward items as desired. In some cases, kids can also earn points for completing treatment activities that initially feel challenging, like practicing new coping skills or even just showing up to treatment.

You—not your kid—are ultimately in charge of any rewards plan, and you are not required to say yes to everything your kid wants to put on their rewards menu. In addition, if the rewards plan goes haywire, you can make changes. I have seen kids get super motivated by a rewards plan and rack up points faster than any of the adults were anticipating. If rewards are going to break the bank, it is totally okay for parents to say, "We need to come up with Rewards Plan 2.0 that acknowledges your hard work but is sustainable for the family." Your kid may protest, and that's okay. Modified rewards are still rewards.

Giving children specific verbal praise about their bravery during treatment can also boost motivation. Stick with praise that is focused on their effort and perseverance, rather than praise focused on their traits or inherent abilities. In other words, "I am so proud of you for trying out that exposure, I know that felt really hard," is going to be more impactful than a vague "You are so brave!" In the long run, warm, positive feedback and attention from a loved one beats any tangible reward.

Still Processing

Finally, I want to touch on a strategy that can help amplify what is learned during an exposure practice. Remember Cole, who I tasked with getting change for a dollar? Once we got back to my office, we wrapped up our session with some post-exposure processing. After some genuine praise for his accomplishments—he went into all five stores, despite the no-change curveball—we talked through some questions.

What did anxiety tell him was going to happen during the exposure practice? And was that prediction correct? How was he able to get through the exposure, despite it being so hard? How come he chose not to quit earlier—what kept him from flipping me off and storming back to the clinic? How did he decide he would go into the final store, even though he'd been caught off guard in the fourth store? And what does it say about him that he was able to complete this exposure? When he looks back on what he did, what will he be most proud of?

The purpose of this post-exposure processing was to help Cole more deeply consider what he had just accomplished and to integrate this experience into his understanding of what he is capable of and who he is as a person. Post-exposure processing is a valuable strategy to help the exposure experience sink in and create new learning in the brain. It offers an opportunity for reflection and helps make meaning out of the experience.

This is not to suggest that you play therapist by engaging your loved one in post-exposure processing after each challenge. (Good luck with even broaching the subject of "How did your exposure go?" with your teenager or partner.) But awareness of this strategy can help you stick the landing when the opportunity arises. Sometimes just floating the question "How were you able to work through that?" after an exposure can be enough to spur thinking. Even better, pair a post-exposure processing question with some genuine verbal feedback: "I was thinking today about how proud I am of you that you are sticking with your anxiety treatment. It can't be easy. How are you able to do it?" You may be completely ignored, but the wheels are likely to turn anyway.

The Flexibility Factor: Know What Matters

Exposure practice is psychological flexibility playing out in real time: You are mindfully accepting all your present-moment experience—fear, nausea, discomfort, self-doubt, irritability, worry—and choosing to act in values-guided ways. This means that whenever you or your kid take on the challenge to open up to discomfort—in ways big or small, in daily life or in treatment—you are building psychological flexibility.

Maddie was willing to participate in exposure therapy because having a "normal" teenage experience was important to her. She valued her autonomy and getting an education. She valued friendships and having fun. She wanted to go to concerts and get back to playing volleyball and to graduate on time with her class. Once Maddie identified what mattered most to her and how anxiety was getting in the way of these things, she was motivated to do the hard work of treatment. In addition, clarifying her values and goals created a road map for her treatment, and we focused most on exposures that involved reconnecting with friends and getting a handle on her schoolwork and attendance.

To do what matters, you have to know what matters. Start by figuring out what's most important to you. What goals do you have for yourself—as an individual and in your role as a parent—and what values are guiding those goals? Use this knowledge to prioritize meaningful exposures and to increase your motivation to tackle anxiety. Having clarified your personal values and your values as a parent, you will be better able to take an exposure-based approach to supporting your child's anxiety.

Exposure practice is the key component of effective psychological treatment for anxiety, and countless courageous kids and adults have reaped the benefits of this approach. But it's also vital for parents to consider how parenting anxiety intersects with child anxiety, and to challenge themselves to adopt an exposure mindset in the service of their child's treatment. We will explore this further in the next chapter.

What Can You Take Home with You?

- At the end of Chapter 7, I encouraged you to make a list of the values that you hold as a parent. Do the same thing now, but this time, keep it personal. There is a List of Common Personal Values in the Resources section at the back of this book that may be helpful. What are the top five to ten values that you hold most dear? Identifying your values helps you determine if and when anxiety is getting in the way and helps you pivot. This exercise helps kids, too.

- DIY exposures: You don't have to be in therapy for this approach to be helpful. Look for the low-hanging fruit: Are there things in your life that make you mildly uncomfortable and that you have been avoiding? Maybe you have been putting off a project or avoiding contact with someone. Maybe you want to get back to the gym or ask someone out. Can you intentionally lean into these things, despite the discomfort? Treat it like an experiment. Note your SUDS before you do the thing, and again afterward. Was it as bad as you expected? Probably not, but if so, you still survived.

- Remember love and limits. You are *not* a bad parent when you set an expectation that your kid will do something challenging. You can foster a love-and-limits exposure mindset for you and your family in daily life. Come up with a motto like "We can do hard things" and integrate it into conversations with your kids as much as possible. In the spirit of modeling, talk about when you leaned into something hard, "because I know I can do hard things." And combine it with positive reinforcement by using the exposure-mindset motto when you see your kids in action: "I knew you could do hard things!" Articulating this mindset and emphasizing it across their development makes it likely that an exposure mindset becomes a part of your kids' identity and will guide how they approach life's challenges.

CHAPTER 10

The Comfort Trap

Let me tell you about Bunnykins.

Bunnykins is a white stuffed animal bunny who wears a little pink tutu. Bunnykins joined our home when my daughter was four, courtesy of her grandmother. He is approximately six inches tall and was the bane of my existence for a time.

My daughter *loved* Bunnykins. He was an immediate bedfellow at night and accompanied her around the house during the day. Keeping tabs on a six-inch stuffy is no joke, and the question "Where's my bunny?" kicked off regular family-wide searches, typically at inopportune times. My husband and I were proactive; we scoured the internet and ordered an identical Backup Bunnykins from a dodgy website that looked like a prime source of identity theft. Backup Bunnykins arrived and was thrust deep in our closet, where he remains to this day.

Shortly thereafter, my daughter began asking to take Bunnykins with her to preschool each morning. My husband and I have differing views on who first capitulated to this request, but at some point, Bunnykins was shoved in the bottom of her backpack with instructions not to take him out, because he might get lost or distract the other kids. Or bother the teachers.

This directive was not heeded.

After a few weeks of preschool, Bunnykins began looking pretty shabby. His whiskers were trimmed on one side. An encounter with red chalk gave him a permanent case of pink eye. He was perpetually grubby after too many trips down the slide, and frequent soaks in detergent dislodged his tutu.

More importantly, the habit of bringing Bunnykins to school bred dependence on Bunnykins. We would be all ready to head to school when the question "Is Bunnykins in my backpack?" would arise, and if the answer was no, it would result in a tearful "I *need* Bunnykins!" After a frenzied search, punctuated by mild spousal verbal abuse, Bunnykins would inevitably emerge, and we would arrive late.

What was happening here? Why were grown adults frantically tearing apart the couch looking for a six-inch bunny in a tutu? Why were we mentally clocking "phone, keys, Bunnykins" before leaving the house? Why were we sheepishly reminding my daughter's after-school childcare to double-check her backpack, just in case Bunnykins got left behind (again)?

Of course, we were doing this because we didn't want our child to be upset, and because frankly, we didn't want to deal with the consequences of her being upset.

Taking steps to help others feel better is normal, and often these efforts are time-limited and not all that disruptive. However, it can be a very different story when anxiety is a major player in family life. In these circumstances, you may find yourself making all sorts of impactful changes to your behaviors and routines to try to minimize your loved ones' distress. This is called accommodation, and it often results in overparenting.

Parental accommodation specifically refers to changes that parents make to their behavior to minimize or decrease child distress. For example, you drop everything to respond immediately to anxious texts, you email teachers to get kids out of assignments, or you let your kid sleep in your bed. Parental accommodation can happen through specific behaviors like these, as well as through broader structural changes to family schedules or routines. This might look like taking time off from work so that your child can stay home from school when anxious, rearranging your schedule to sit in the car outside the movie theater while your kid is inside with their friends, or driving long distances to see family when your child is afraid of air travel.

Accommodation behaviors are widespread in parents of kids with anxiety disorders. The vast majority (95 to 98 percent) of parents of kids with anxiety disorders report accommodating their kids, and 61 percent of mothers of anxious kids report *daily* accommodation. Sadly, while these well-intentioned efforts to decrease your child's distress may be effective in the moment, parental accommodation ultimately makes things worse. Parents who accommodate more often tend to have children with more severe and debilitating anxiety who respond less well to treatment, and these parents end up more anxious, stressed, and depressed themselves. Accommodation often seems like the right thing to do in the moment, but it's bad news for all involved.

Understanding parental accommodation reframes everything. It is both a challenge and a huge opportunity for parents of anxious kids.

Understanding Accommodation

When my friend's daughter, Eleanore, was five, she was afraid of spiders. Totally developmentally normal, but it could occasionally get in the way of daily life. One day, Eleanore spotted an itty-bitty spider in her bedroom and lost her little mind. The spider was removed, but the damage was done. Eleanore declared she would no longer go into her room by herself. The bedtime routine was tear-soaked, with Eleanore fearing that spiders were lurking in the dark ready to attack. She sobbed and pleaded with her parents to stay with her as she slept.

My friend tried every tactic in the book to help calm Eleanore and extract herself from the bedroom, to no avail. Although outwardly calm, she was internally spiraling. Her own anxiety spiked as she tried to figure out how she would get Eleanore to bed, prevent Eleanore's wails from waking her eight-month-old, and finish the mountain of work she still had to do.

In a flash of inspiration, my friend grabbed a random shell from a recent beach trip and presented it to Eleanore. "Spiders hate seashells," she stated.

Genius. A confidently delivered explanation of how spiders absolutely can't be around seashells did the trick. Eleanore fell asleep solo, the clamshell resting on her nightstand.

An accommodation cycle begins with a situation that causes your child distress. In Eleanore's case, it was the spider. When you pick up on your child's distress, you feel your own flood of anxiety, which urges you to do *something*—an accommodation behavior—to reduce everyone's distress. That something was the seashell. The relief that both you and your child feel after parental accommodation happens is reinforcing—which means that both you and your kid are more likely to "need" the same accommodation when the same distressing situation happens again in the future.

The relief my friend and her daughter experienced did reinforce the presence of the spider-repelling seashell in the bedroom for a while. However, the accommodation was mild and effective, it was not burdensome to her family's life or routine, and Eleanore's anxiety about spiders wasn't very interfering. The seashell stayed on the nightstand for a few months, and Eleanore never noticed when it disappeared.

Sometimes parental accommodation looks like a clearly identifiable, distinct parent behavior, as in Eleanore's situation. Other times accommodations look like patterns of behavior. You may identify with the experience of "walking on eggshells" around your brooding teen. You add an extra bit of sweetness to your "How was your day?" inquiries, or you let their sass slide when ordinarily you would be all over it. One parent shared that they felt like they were placating a salty middle manager rather than a dependent. You accommodate to help out your teen, but also because you know that poking the bear might make your own evening worse.

We have limited data on how often parents accommodate when their kids don't have an anxiety disorder because parental accommodation is studied most often in families of kids who are struggling with a mental health diagnosis. However, one study found that nearly one in four parents report engaging in *daily* accommodation, even when their child does not have an emotional disorder.

This tracks for me. Parents across my personal and professional networks can all share stories of ways that we behave in response to—or in anticipation of—our child's distress. Some accommodation behaviors are just attentive parenting, like changing the channel when a disturbing news story comes on. Sometimes you accommodate when you just aren't sure how to respond. I was away overnight when my daughter was three, and that was the evening she decided to ask probing questions about death and dying. My husband short-circuited and blurted out, "You probably won't die, some people just never die," and then distracted her with something shiny. I was gone for thirty-six hours, and he told her she was immortal. The urge to ease our children's distress is that powerful.

Other accommodations are ones that you know are ridiculous and are embarrassed about, but that you do anyway. You rush back between home and school to get the forgotten assignment. You participate in elaborate bedtime rituals involving an absurd combination of colored lights, noise machines, and even some dance routines. You only buy *the one kind* of mac and cheese. You do extra loads of laundry so the uniform is ready for tomorrow's game (even though your kid is old enough to have done her own laundry and responsible enough to have thought ahead). You search for Bunnykins again and again.

How Do I Know If My Behavior Is an Accommodation?

Parental accommodation is pretty normal *and* is also highly associated with child anxiety. So how do you know if you are accommodating or supporting? How can you tell if you are helping or hurting?

This is one of those gray areas. It is not always clear at what point a parent behavior becomes accommodation, with all of the baggage that accommodation entails. And many accommodation behaviors in which parents engage, particularly when children are young, are developmentally appropriate. This is because when children are young, they need more support to regulate their emotions. Their world is new and unknown, and kids look to caregivers to give them information about how safe their world is until they develop the coping skills and the comfort necessary to take more risks. Sometimes accommodation is a short-term solution to a short-term issue. If your teen is spent before finals, it's not that big a deal if you agree that they can skip band practice after a fatigue-fueled meltdown when you know they will rally before the next practice. But critically, if anxiety is fueling the behavior, the outcomes may be different. Letting your teen skip an extracurricular on the rare occasion because they are fried is one thing; letting them regularly bail because of anxiety is another. As we know, avoidance fuels anxiety.

No one behavior is always an accommodation. Context matters. When determining whether a given parent behavior is an accommodation, Dr. Eli Lebowitz suggests that you ask yourself questions like these:

- Is my response helping my child to cope effectively with this situation, or is it allowing them to avoid more?
- Is my kid's reaction to this situation getting better over time, or worse despite my help?
- Does my behavior help my child take a step forward or backward, relative to how they have been coping recently?

Why We All Accommodate

Accommodation is a natural response

At the most basic, primitive level, the unpleasant feelings that you feel when your child is distressed motivate you to do whatever you can, as quickly as possible, to decrease their suffering. You inherited that excruciating drop in your stomach when you hear your kid scream from countless early ancestors, who leapt to their children's defense, encouraging the survival of our species. This instinctive, reflexive response persists today, and studies show how parents' heart rates still skyrocket when they listen to recordings of kids crying.

Overall, this reflex is profoundly beneficial, as it motivates adults to keep children safe. Nowadays, your kids are less likely to cry because a predator is approaching, but you feel the same unpleasant surge in your heart rate when they freak out because they forgot about an assignment due tomorrow—and this motivates you to drop everything and go buy poster board.

This drive also fuels healthy attachment. It's what yanks new parents out of dearly needed sleep when their newborn cries in the night. Soothing the child decreases everyone's distress and reinforces the parent-child call-and-response pattern. Predictably responding to kids' needs in early childhood provides the foundation for secure attachment, which is the cornerstone of healthy child development.

Accommodation can be reinforcing for you, too

Sometimes parents get something out of accommodating, too. Let's say you have a kid who has always been on the shy side, who prefers to avoid large gatherings, and who had a bumpy transition into middle school this fall. When your aunt suggests a family reunion at their place for Christmas, your child dissolves into a puddle and says all he wants is to stay home. To be honest, you hate the idea of traveling during the holiday, flights are insanely expensive, and your cousin's husband drives you bonkers. Staying home protects your kid from discomfort and also means you get the quiet Christmas that you wanted: win-win.

Sometimes your accommodation behaviors build connection with your kids, and parents eat that up. Let's say that your teenager has always been a bit nervous about getting behind the wheel. Driver's test passed, license in hand, she continues to ask you to take her to school in the mornings. On the one hand, you want her to be a confident, independent driver, and know that practice is key to her comfort. On the other, you really love your early-morning chats in the car with her, and she's so close to leaving the nest for good. Taking these points together, you are happy to keep driving. It's important to be mindful of your own motivations and the ways in which you may inadvertently benefit from accommodating your kid in order to evaluate the costs and benefits of continuing to do so.

You're embarrassed

You can find yourself accommodating because you feel too embarrassed to hold your ground, particularly in public. This is the origin of the child who tantrums in the grocery store and gets the candy. If your child is sobbing before their piano recital, you are more likely to agree that they don't have to perform if you are concerned that their distress is impacting the other students (and if you clock the disdainful glances of other parents).

It's easier

Often you will accommodate because it is just *easier* than dealing with the fallout of not accommodating. Sometimes you are just too tired, too stressed, too rushed, too burnt-out to take a stand. A father with whom I worked told me that whenever his teenage daughter said she was "too stressed out" on a given evening, he took over her household responsibilities—walking the dog, putting her dishes away, or taking out the trash. Although he felt resentment, taking on her tasks was often easier for him than getting into an argument and prolonging the tasks anyway. When your child is struggling with homework and tearfully asks for help, you may end up doing more of their work than you intended because it's faster and it's bedtime. Sometimes you'd rather just make separate meals than hear the complaining about dinner.

Child distress can have ripple effects throughout the family. Understandably, parents often share that part of their motivation for accommodating one child is to spare another. If they do not accommodate, their child's behavior may escalate to a point that it upsets siblings. In these instances, accommodation helps keep the peace in the short term.

When your child's distress reaction is very strong, you may accommodate because you are actively worried about the consequences of *not* accommodating. You may be worried that your kid will become aggressive, hurt themself or others, or destroy property. These are really tough circumstances for families who feel that they are held hostage by their child's emotion dysregulation. We will circle back to this issue a bit later.

You feel like you should

This one gets to the heart of cultural expectations around parenting. As we explored in great detail earlier, today's parents are bombarded with the message that being a "good parent" means sacrificing yourself on the altar of Intensive Parenting and prioritizing protecting your children from hard feelings. This is a recipe for parenting anxiety and for accommodation.

Remember Cole, my socially anxious patient whose exposure was to get change for a dollar at a number of stores? Prior to the exposures, his mother privately expressed her doubts to me: "What if he gets embarrassed?" She worried that allowing Cole to feel embarrassed in public situations, when she *could* just speak for him and prevent his discomfort, was a "bad parent" move. Her fears—in addition to Cole's—fueled the cycle of anxiety and accommodation.

The pull to accommodate because it feels like the "right" thing to do also impacts families without anxiety disorders. A friend of mine shared that she and her partner were desperate for a date night after the birth of their second child, but she struggled to commit to plans because her older child was having a hard time separating. She acknowledged the benefits to everyone if she had a child-free date night, and that it was important for her kids to get used to the new sitter, but she was concerned—was it even okay to leave the house while her elder child sobbed? Did that make her a bad mom?

These situations can also trigger parenting fears about how your behavior impacts your child's emotional health, and how your children will see it if you do not accommodate. Will your child think you don't care? Is an accommodation the thing they need in this moment to feel heard and validated? Sometimes your kids will really have your number on this one, and they go for the jugular: "If you really loved me, you wouldn't make me do this." Ouch.

You love your kids

Simply stated, we hate to see our loved ones upset. The parent-child connection motivates accommodation behaviors, even when it means you don't get what *you* want—or need. Leaving the new Marvel movie that you were psyched to see in theaters with your seven-year-old because he gets scared is a choice you make, sometimes counter to your own preferences, because you love your kid. A friend of mine whose child is nervous about drop-off classes is the only parent who waits in the parking lot for the duration of gymnastics, because he loves his kid. As you look at the ways in which accommodation can be problematic, it is important to remind yourself that, at its core, accommodation is a marker of parent-child connection and a sign of love.

The Comfort Trap

Accommodation is essentially parent-assisted avoidance, unintentionally fueling anxiety in the same way as avoidant behaviors that you engage in yourself.

The following figure should look familiar—you saw a similar one in Chapter 4. It all starts with an anxiety-provoking situation that causes an increase in your child's anxiety and distress. When you intervene by accommodating, the anxiety decreases, and your child experiences relief. Here is negative reinforcement at play once again, where the relief that you feel when something uncomfortable is removed increases the chance that anxiety will reoccur in the future.

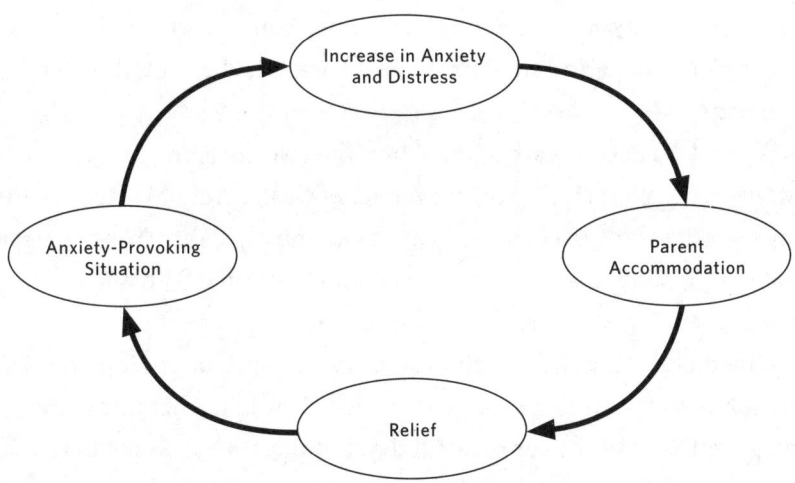

The Cycle of Accommodation

Let's say you sign your nine-year-old up for karate at the beginning of the school year. His cousin does karate, and he is *the coolest,* so your son wanted to try it, too.

On the first day of class, as you walk him up to the studio, he balks. Anxiety starts to prickle in your body. You try to understand—"What's wrong? What are you afraid of?" He is wide-eyed and keeps repeating, "I can't do this," tearing up as other families awkwardly shuffle past.

You try coaxing him into the studio, but he won't budge. "Why's that kid crying?" you hear another child ask.

You feel a surge of tension and desperation—how are you going to fix this? You cycle through your tool kit: You empathize and validate, you remind him of his cousin, you tell him that he is capable, you offer a toy store visit afterward. You say some things you know aren't helpful as your anxiety hooks you: You point out the younger kids who aren't having any issues, you tell him what a waste of money this is, you ask what's gotten into him.

He's crying harder now. You feel hot and tense as you notice the curious looks of passersby. The instructor comes to the door: "Will you be joining us today?" Your son shakes his head resolutely through tears.

Yikes, he is really having a hard time. You are irritated but also concerned. You hadn't anticipated pushback. Maybe something else is going on?

You take a deep breath and tell him fine, we are going home . . . but *you are going* next week. You see the relief wash across his face. By the time you two are back in the car, he is mostly calm. Your tension abates, too, but you are still perplexed and frustrated. What is so scary about karate? He can't freak out about new things like this.

The night before the second class, you remind him that he has karate tomorrow. This does *not* go over well. Through a herculean effort, you get him out of the car the next day, but this time is worse than last; he is sobbing and starting to hyperventilate, and all he can say is "Please don't make me do this" over and over. "Buddy, *you wanted* to do this!" you respond in exasperation.

You take him home, feeling defeated. Once again, your son calms fairly quickly, but when you are pulling into the driveway, he quietly says, "I don't know why I can't just do the things that I am supposed to do," and your heart breaks a little. This was something you thought he would enjoy, and you'd hoped that it would build his self-confidence. You worry that, instead, this experience is having the opposite effect.

"Maybe we just drop the whole karate thing," you suggest to your husband that evening. "It stinks to lose the money, but he is *so upset* and we don't want him to feel bad about himself." Your husband has a different view. His own parents would never have let him bail on anything like this, and he feels that it's important to teach your kids that when you make a commitment, you see it through. You agree in principle, but he hasn't experienced the scene at drop-off. How about he goes next week?

Karate is on everyone's mind in the days to come. Your son asks repeatedly about whether he has to go, and there are tears. On karate day, you get a text from your husband that your son is refusing to get out of the car. Not only that, but he's panicking, yelling and kicking the back seat. Your husband is mortified. He asks you what he should do, and you haven't the faintest idea. "Just come home."

That's the last time you try karate.

■ ■ ■

This situation, and situations like it, are incredibly common. Let's break it down to understand exactly how and why your well-meaning, totally understandable accommodation is actually worsening your child's anxiety.

First, it's important to acknowledge that everyone here is doing their best, and each person's behavior makes perfect sense given their feelings. When your son notices anxiety around karate, his alarm is going off: It means that he perceives something threatening about the situation. His urge to leave is therefore logical, based on the anxiety that he is feeling.

Your distress justifiably follows; your own anxiety increases, along with your concern for your son and your public embarrassment. Around the peak of his distress, you give in to anxiety in the moment. The decision to go home works wonderfully to decrease your son's anxiety, bringing it quickly from its peak back to baseline (see the following figure).

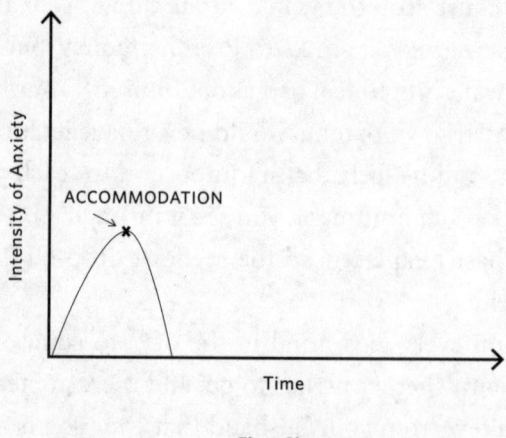

Anxiety Intensity and Accommodation During the First Karate Class

But while this was happening, other learning was quietly taking place. First, your son made the inevitable link between leaving karate and feeling relief. A new belief was forming, telling him that the only reason that he felt better was because he *didn't do karate*. Moreover, he lost the opportunity for new learning, by associating karate with positive things. He didn't have the chance to make a friend, to feel cool in his uniform, or to connect with his cousin about it afterward. Even if he hated the first class, seeing it through would have given him information about himself—he is a person who can do hard things, and he could deal with the class even if he didn't like it.

In addition, your son learned from your response. By giving in to his anxiety and taking him out of the situation, your son got the message that his anxiety alarm was accurate: that karate was indeed dangerous, and that he couldn't handle the class. This may not be your belief, and it absolutely wasn't your intention, but this is, sadly, the indirect message that comes with accommodation.

Taken together, this experience means that when your son goes to the second class, he feels even more anxious than the first time. His baseline anxiety intensity is higher and escalates faster. He expects to feel uncomfortable, and once he feels anxiety kicking in, it confirms his assumptions. His escalating behavior makes it more likely that you will feel distressed and be even more likely to accommodate by leaving the situation again. In addition, you are now second-guessing yourself: "Yikes, what is going on here? Maybe this is just too hard for him. Maybe it's wrong of me to have him keep trying."

What happens to your son's anxious distress after leaving the second class? It drops immediately, of course, and this negative reinforcement strengthens the link between avoidance and relief, meaning that the cycle is now even more likely to repeat itself (see the following figure).

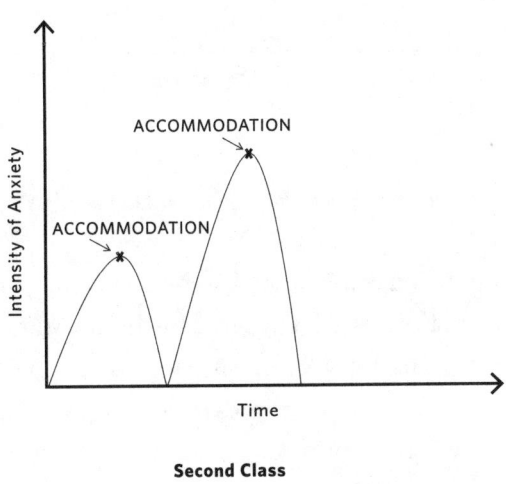

Anxiety Intensity and Accommodation During the Second Karate Class

Which is exactly what happens at the third class. A pattern has been established where karate → anxiety → avoidance → relief. And within this pattern, negative beliefs about the situation ("This is unsafe") and his ability to cope ("I can't handle this") have formed, which pushes your son's baseline anxiety higher. And the reflexive nature of the parent-child relationship means that the accommodation—leaving the class—has worsened anxiety for you *both* over time. You are now more anxious about karate because of your son's reaction. As a result, you are more likely to decide to leave again, because leaving was the coping strategy that decreased everyone's distress before (see the following figure).

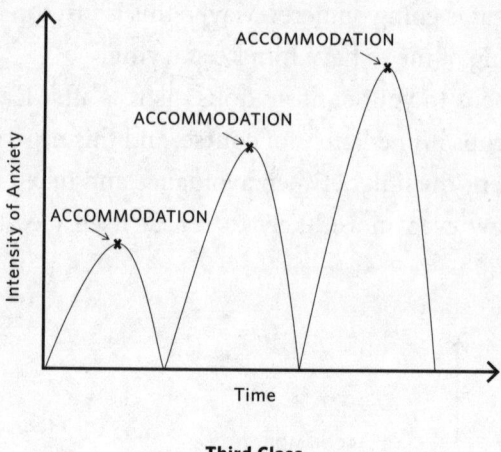

Anxiety Intensity and Accommodation During the Third Karate Class

What is your primary job here? On the one hand, you want to protect your son from the distress triggered by the situation, and from the distress caused by his burgeoning negative self-talk. On the other hand, you want to encourage his independence. A middle-path solution, in which these two truths can coexist, is not clear to you in the moment. So overparenting wins.

Sometimes the story ends here. Sometimes it's just that karate wasn't his thing. He tries basketball in the winter with no issue.

Unfortunately, the pattern can spread to other situations, particularly for a kid who is prone to anxiety to begin with. Accommodation can be like slapping a Band-Aid on a festering wound. Your son has to be picked up early from school during his class's Halloween parade. He becomes a regular visitor to the school nurse's office during gym class, and he refuses to go to school entirely on the morning of the holiday concert.

Sadly, your well-meaning, parent-assisted avoidance has fueled the issue. Unchecked accommodation can become a comfort trap, preventing natural exposure opportunities and calcifying a kid's negative beliefs about their ability to cope.

This happens because anxiety is an opportunist, and parental accommodation is like an escape hatch. If your kid can pull the lever whenever anxiety gets too intense and escape, it makes it harder for them to combat anxiety. Even the most dedicated, anxiety-fighting child will be hard-pressed to resist the relief they know will come if parents accommodate.

The key point here is that it is not helpful or fair to expect kids to independently fight back against anxiety if parental accommodation is playing a part in their anxiety cycle. Without attention dedicated to reducing parental accommodation, anxious kids are set up to struggle harder, for longer.

The Good News

Here is where there is good news, and lots of it.

Over the last decade, cognitive behavioral treatments have emerged in which therapists treat child anxiety by working directly with parents to reduce accommodation. This process parallels the practice of exposure therapy but puts parents in the driver's seat. Remarkably, these parent-based approaches lead to improvements in child anxiety *without needing to directly involve the child in therapy*. And this parent-based treatment is just as effective in reducing child anxiety symptoms as individual CBT delivered directly to the child.

Working to reduce or change parental accommodation is an incredibly powerful tool. Not only does it help treat child anxiety, but it can reduce your own anxiety around your child's distress while building confidence in managing your child's symptoms and improving your family's health. This is excellent news for parents. If your child is in their own individual therapy, it means there are things that you can do to help optimize their treatment. If your kid refuses to go to therapy, you can still take steps to help address their anxiety.

Even if you or your kids aren't dealing with an anxiety disorder right now, this is worth attending to. We live in a culture where parental accommodation seems synonymous with "good parenting," which means that you may feel like a pariah if you encourage your kid to persist in something that is uncomfortable. But good parenting feels bad sometimes, and your willingness to tolerate your own discomfort while reducing accommodation is a powerful catalyst for change. You can do hard things, and so can your kids.

The Flexibility Factor: Pick Your Battles

Psychological flexibility is key when shifting accommodation patterns. Decreasing accommodation is best attempted after thoughtfully clarifying your values, thinking through the factors that make success more likely, and remaining open to experiencing your own discomfort.

By understanding accommodation's role in anxiety, you have the knowledge to flexibly choose which behaviors you will accommodate and which you will not, in line with your goals and values. In previous chapters, I recommended that you take some time to clarify the top values you hold for yourself and the values you hold in your role as a parent. That effort also pays off here, where your values help guide your decisions about which behaviors are "worth" accommodating and which are not.

Let's assume that you deeply value community service, and you have a kid who tends to be socially anxious, particularly in unfamiliar situations. If volunteer work is a way you live out this value, and it's important to you that your children cultivate this as well, you can choose to bring your anxious kid to a service activity with you, even if you expect that she might be uncomfortable. You accept that this may mean some awkward interactions with other volunteers, and some serious pouting, but you understand that facilitating her avoidance is going to worsen, not improve, her social anxiety. So you make a choice, and you prepare as well as you can to cope with the consequences of that choice, using your value system to guide your priorities.

The values that you hold for yourself—as a person, not just a parent—can be helpful here as well. Say you value your physical health, but you have let exercise go recently because of your child's separation anxiety. You have options here. You can accommodate them and exercise at home. But becoming wedded to the old stationary bike in the basement reinforces your kid's separation anxiety, and it may not totally refuel your tank. If exercise matters a lot to you, you could choose to start reducing accommodation by taking short runs around the neighborhood. In other words, clarifying your values helps you pick your battles. You will be better able to tolerate your child's distress, and your own discomfort, if you are doing what matters to *you* as you work to reduce accommodation.

Finally, modeling your own distress tolerance in the face of your child's distress nurtures their psychological flexibility. Consider the powerful message that you send if you acknowledge to your child that you are both uncomfortable in this moment, and that despite that discomfort, you are committed to this choice. Your example shows your child that hard emotions are safe and can be worth experiencing if they are in the service of something larger. Modeling this framework provides your child with key building blocks for resilience.

What Can You Take Home with You?

- Begin to notice your internal reaction when your child is anxious or distressed. What thoughts and feelings come up for you? Where do you feel your distress most in your body? What urges do you notice—what do you want to do to cope with this feeling?
- Start tracking the ways you respond when your child is anxious or distressed, and what it ultimately means for your kid. What is your go-to coping strategy? And most importantly, is your strategy making things better or worse for your child over time?
- Introduce the idea of accommodation to your child. It can help to share stories from your own life about times when your

anxiety was accommodated in ways that, unfortunately, made things harder for longer. In calm moments, point out to your child how your accommodation makes things easier for them in the moment, but you wonder how helpful it is in the long term. Starting this conversation lays the foundation for future changes you might make to accommodation behaviors.

- Challenge yourself to resist accommodation in low-stakes situations and get curious about the outcome. For how long was your child distressed after you didn't accommodate? Did your worst-case scenario actually come to pass? Was it harder or easier for you to tolerate your discomfort than you expected?

CHAPTER 11

Ripping Off the Band-Aid

I hope I've persuaded you that reducing parental accommodation is an effective tool for addressing child anxiety, and that it facilitates the exposure process, giving kids the space and opportunity to fight back against anxiety rather than being "rescued" from distress by their parents. So why isn't this strategy being shouted from the rooftops? How come it isn't all over social media? Why do we hear the word "accommodation" and still think of an education plan or a ramp in a subway station?

In part, I think it's because parental accommodation can be a loaded topic. For clinicians, it's often the elephant in the room; it's uncomfortable to point out the parent behaviors that, sadly, may be maintaining or worsening child anxiety. Clinicians working with these families understand that parents already feel a ton of pressure to do the "right" thing, that they are deeply invested in helping their child, and that they probably feel overstretched when they finally get to treatment. In this context, addressing accommodation might make parents feel blamed and judged. No one wants that.

For parents, it can be tough to learn about accommodation, and defensiveness is a valid reaction. "So you're saying it's my fault" can sometimes be the response.

But no, it's not your fault! Responding to your child's distress is the most natural thing in the world. It is also reinforced culturally, through the message of Intensive Parenting, that parents are solely responsible for their children's outcomes and that "good" parents respond to children's emotions with attentiveness. There is a ton of pressure—from both internal and external forces—for well-meaning parents to accommodate anxiety.

But in an era where parents are used to assuming complete responsibility for their child's well-being, they sometimes feel a deep sense of guilt when they learn about accommodation. Many tell me, fighting back tears, "I wish I had known this earlier." They believe that understanding these patterns sooner might have prevented a lot of suffering for their child. I get that, and it's heartbreaking. But research into the links between parental accommodation and anxiety have only been around for a little over a decade. It can take a while for research findings to percolate into the mainstream. And beating yourself up about what you didn't know is pretty unhelpful.

Even for those of us who study this for a living, the urge to accommodate when our kids are in distress is still incredibly strong. Pushing back on accommodation doesn't feel good for the parent, and none of us are immune to parental guilt and self-doubt. Not even yours truly.

A few years ago, my daughter developed a mild habit of dramatizing her bumps and bruises. She'd get a scrape or take a tumble and if she thought no one was looking, she could rally without a hitch, but if there was an audience, the waterworks would turn on. Not uncommon for kids at that age, but my husband and I wanted to make sure we weren't inadvertently reinforcing this pattern. We understood that if the adults in her life dropped everything and came running to obsess over a paper cut, she was likely to be the kid who sobbed over a paper cut. We didn't want that for her, and so we decided to pay attention to our reactions.

Around this time, my daughter and I joined another mom and her daughter for an afternoon at a local beach with the dogs. The girls were collecting baby crabs, and as we were packing up to head home, one of the baby crabs pinched my daughter's thumb. No blood, but real tears. Once I realized she was physically fine, in the spirit of psychological flexibility, I reconnected with my values and made a choice in my response: I acknowledged the hurt warmly, validated the surprise and the pain, and used a supportive statement. But I did not drop everything (literally, we were packing up the beach chairs and corralling the wet dogs) to croon over the pinch. Then the other mom looked at my daughter and lovingly asked, "Do you need a hug?" and embraced her.

It was like the fairy godmother had swooped in to comfort her, while the hill-witch wrestled a beach chair.

My daughter's sweet friend, distressed by her distress, started crying, too. The girls held one another and sobbed. Then the deeply feeling and soaking wet retrievers got involved, which made the crying girls collapse into giggles, the pinch totally forgotten. It ended up being a super-sweet moment.

I thought a lot about my actions afterward. I worried that in my effort to encourage self-soothing, I wasn't warm enough. I worried that the other mother, who I like very much, thought I was an insensitive parent, and maybe a crappy child psychologist to boot. At the same time, I liked the fact that when I didn't drop everything, my daughter had the chance to learn that she can also be comforted by friends. I liked that I acted in accordance with the priorities that I had set for my kid at that time in her life. I like that as she's grown, she is soothing herself more independently and even shows off the bruises on her shins as a testament to how she is crushing it in soccer, though it's unclear how much my actions that day impacted this trajectory. I think it was the right move for my kid at that moment. But who really knows?

While this example doesn't have to do with anxiety per se, I bring it up to illustrate how tricky this stuff is, to highlight how vulnerable it can make you feel. I also share it to show you that shifting your response to your child's anxiety or distress will not feel good in the moment, and that second-guessing your parenting choices is part of the journey. Discomfort and self-doubt are going to be unwelcome companions as you work to reduce accommodation.

So let's set you up for success and explore what reducing accommodation might look like. You acknowledge that embarking on accommodation reduction is like ripping off a Band-Aid; you know it needs to happen, but you know it will be painful. I'm here to tell you that you can do it—your child, and your own mental health, are worth it.

Accommodation Reduction 101

Set realistic expectations

Imagine a world in which your kid has grown up getting a cookie to eat before dinner each night. At some point, you rethink this choice and decide that it's probably not healthy for him to fill up on sweets before he tackles the broccoli. So you set the expectation that, starting tonight, no cookie before dinner.

How is your kid likely to react? Pretty poorly. Because something that he is used to, that he likes, and that makes him feel good in the moment is no longer available. Even if he is old enough to understand the links between eating habits and health, in that moment he doesn't care *at all*. He wants a cookie, and he is mad as a hornet that you will no longer give it to him.

"It's not fair for your kid to suffer because you changed your mind," some folks might protest. "You can't just switch things up on him like that."

Sure you can. You don't have to be a jerk about it, but if you, as a parent, have learned that something is problematic for your kid in the long term, you absolutely can—and should—shift your behavior accordingly.

What you can't do is expect your kid to be happy about it.

Whether it's a cookie moratorium or a shift in parental accommodation, it's helpful to be realistic about how your kid is likely to respond. If you are unprepared for a bad reaction, you may be more likely to give up entirely. Then you are back to square one. Moreover, now your kid has learned that if they pitch a big enough fit, you will back down. (We will discuss this dynamic in more detail in Chapter 13.) Reducing accommodation is going to increase child (and parent) anxiety in the short term, but this discomfort opens the door to fighting anxiety more effectively.

Reframing "I Can't"

I encourage you to consider what you mean if you are thinking, "I can't switch things up on my kid." Are you physically incapable of reducing the accommodation? If not, what is your concern, at the core?

I would wager that rather than asserting that you "just can't" make this change, the more accurate statement is probably "I am dreading how bad it will feel when my kid has a tough reaction to me reducing accommodation."

That is totally fair. Making a big shift in your behavior, so that your kid is experiencing a new and unwelcome situation, can be hard. *And* you can handle it. Think of all the hard things, big and small, that you have helped your children through—getting their shots, being placed in a classroom without their best friends, getting cut from the team or the school play. You have helped them cope with all sorts of frustrations, disappointments, losses, and grief. You have tolerated their distress, and your own. I know you can rise to the challenge of reducing accommodation.

When you remove the accommodations that your kid is used to and comfortable with, anxiety is going to get loud. Just like making sure that they eat their vegetables, kids don't have to be happy about it for it to be the right thing for you to do.

Start low and go slow

It can be tempting to make grand plans to stop *all* accommodation in its tracks. But pulling the rug out from under your kid is unlikely to be successful because, in an effort to lean away from the left side of the parenting dialectic, you end up leaning too far to the right. Over-parenting can become undersupport rapidly, and neither end of that dialectic will help your kid's anxiety.

For example, if you have a child with separation anxiety, starting to reduce accommodation by dropping him off at Grandma's while you take a weekend trip is an unwise place to start. Without prior practice in separation exposures, he is more likely to be super distressed, and Grandma is more likely to call you in the middle of the night to let you know what a hard time he is having. And *you* are more likely to struggle to resist the pull of your child's distress without prior practice. So you'll probably end up bailing on your weekend plans and rushing home in the middle of the night, "rescuing" him from his anxiety when you had promised that you would stick to your plan. This not only reinforces his belief that he can't cope without you but suggests to him that you won't do what you say you will do.

Instead, start with some low-hanging fruit. Begin reducing accommodation by tackling a mildly anxiety-provoking situation. For example, you could set the expectation that you are going to walk down the driveway and get the mail while your child stays inside the house. Work up to walking around the block while he stays home. The momentum that you and he build by tackling these smaller challenges first can help increase confidence to address larger ones.

Create a road map

Recall that when starting exposure-based treatment, we begin by developing a fear and avoidance hierarchy (FAH). This is a list of situations that are causing problems in the child's life, ranked from least anxiety-provoking to most anxiety-provoking, and it serves as a road map for the exposures that will be focused on in treatment. It can be helpful to take a similar approach to reducing accommodation.

This starts with noticing your own behaviors in response to your child's distress: Are there things that you are doing—that you wouldn't ordinarily do—because of your child's anxiety? Maybe you always attend playdates or parties with your kid, while other parents of children his age drop off and come back. Maybe you've started sleeping in his room. Alternatively, are there things that you are *not* doing—that you ordinarily would do—because of your child's anxiety? Maybe you decline dinner invitations from friends because he is afraid when you are away from him at bedtime.

Do you change your family's routine because of your child's anxiety? Maybe you have made job choices based on the ability to work from home, where he feels that you are safe. Maybe you promise to avoid a certain busy road because he is afraid that you will get in a car crash, even though it's less convenient.

Do you provide your child with certain things because of his anxiety? Maybe you caved and got him a smartphone so that he can track your location. Or maybe you got him a pet because he insisted it would help him feel better. As far as you can tell, Squeakachu the Hamster has done nothing to reduce your son's anxiety, but it has quickly become a thorn in your side. And now your son is insisting that *two* hamsters are actually what he needs to feel better.

Once you have a sense of what these behaviors are, consider ways you could shift them. Then list those behaviors from least anxiety-provoking for your child to most anxiety-provoking. You can absolutely do this collaboratively with your kid—in fact, the more buy-in, the better. See the following page for a sample accommodation reduction hierarchy that targets common separation anxiety challenges.

SAMPLE ACCOMMODATION
REDUCTION HIERARCHY

SUDS	Accommodation Reduction Practice
10	Parent goes away for one overnight, responds to a maximum of one communication (such as a text), child stays with Grandma
9	Parent goes out in the evening, does not respond to any nonemergency communication, child stays with babysitter
8	Parent sleeps in their own room, child in his own
7	Parent goes out in the evening, Grandma babysits
6	Parent goes for a fifteen-minute walk in the neighborhood, responds to a maximum of one communication (such as a text), child stays home alone
5	Parent goes inside a local restaurant to pick up takeout, child waits in the car outside the restaurant
4	Parent goes out during the daytime on a weekend, child stays with Grandma
3	Parent takes the "busy road" to the office (rather than the longer, less congested route)
2	Parent works from the office, rather than home, while child is at school
1	Parent goes outside to get the mail while child stays inside

By clearly identifying accommodation behaviors and creating concrete goals to reduce them, you outline a path for meaningful change with your kid. Charting accommodation reduction situations from least to most anxiety-provoking also helps to break down the challenge into manageable steps. Now you have a sense of exactly where the low-hanging fruit is, and you can start there. (And I hope it goes without saying, but don't get another hamster.)

Don't cancel positive reinforcement

Positive reinforcement has gotten a bit of a bad rap in recent years. A quick social media search will invariably bring up content sounding the alarm about this approach. The warnings go something like this: If you use positive reinforcement—in the form of verbal praise, tangible rewards, or access to preferred activities—to motivate behavior, your child will lose their intrinsic, internal motivation. Instead, they will become "approval junkies" who will only pursue behaviors that will be rewarded or that are pleasing to others.

Awash in this narrative, concerned parents may worry that if they praise or reward their child, they are molding them into consummate people-pleasers and eroding their self-confidence. Or they worry that their child will be overly motivated by material rewards. Even worse, this narrative suggests to parents that their child will feel that love and approval are contingent upon "good" behavior. This has all led to the notion that verbal praise and rewards are bad for your kid. I even had one parent tell me, "I know you're not supposed to tell your kid that you are proud of them, but I did in this instance," fully anticipating a wrist slap.

I find this unbearably sad. It's also so unnecessary, particularly in the context of child anxiety. The evidence to date simply can't support the rebranding of positive reinforcement strategies as All Bad. In fact, applying praise and rewards thoughtfully can really help move the needle in the fight against anxiety. It's not going to ruin your kid.

My colleague Dr. Julia Martin Burch and I did a deep dive into this topic, since we are increasingly seeing these beliefs as a challenge for parents and kids in anxiety treatment. Rewards can be problematic under specific conditions: For example, a reward is most likely to be a long-term issue if it is given *regardless* of the quality of the effort or if the task was even completed—I'm looking at you, participation trophies. In contrast, when you are working to develop behaviors that can become self-reinforcing over time—things like exercising or trying a new food—or when you are encouraging behaviors that aren't naturally enjoyable, like cleaning their room, thoughtful and measured positive reinforcement can be really useful. Exposure work falls into both of these categories.

There are a number of reasons why integrating positive reinforcement is helpful. First, remember that kids' brains are still developing.

It is simply harder for children to appreciate the long-term toll that their anxiety disorder is taking. While this awareness often builds as they grow, the pace of brain development makes it riskier to rely exclusively on internal motivation to help kids—particularly young kids—meet the challenge of exposure work. This is why we are more likely to use rewards plans for school-aged kids in treatment. But if needed, it can be a useful tool at any age.

Another important reason not to cancel positive reinforcement is that anxiety is not self-correcting. This means that once anxiety-driven avoidance becomes a habit, it is unlikely to change without a nudge. If a kid is intrinsically motivated to change their behaviors around anxiety, that's great, but if they are struggling, there is good evidence that the advantages of applying measured positive reinforcement outweigh the negatives. Building the motivation to do hard things often takes a little grease.

This is another instance where the cultural norms of modern parenting contradict what we know actually works for child anxiety treatment. Listening to the influencers and forgoing positive reinforcement removes a vital tool from your parenting toolbox when you are trying to help your kid, and it just isn't supported by the data.

I'm Gonna Need a Professional: SPACE Treatment

Reducing parental accommodation is a daunting task. Even if you feel that you understand the fundamentals, having an objective partner to help you to do so is ideal if your child is struggling with a clinical anxiety disorder.

As I mentioned in the last chapter, we now have psychological treatments for child anxiety disorders in which the therapist works only with the parents to reduce accommodation behaviors. Doing so opens up the opportunity for kids to practice exposures that they couldn't tackle if accommodation remains in place, and child anxiety decreases. This treatment is called SPACE, which stands for Supportive Parenting for Anxious Childhood Emotions, and clinicians around the world are being trained to deliver this treatment. My colleagues and I recommend SPACE-based approaches to address child anxiety and OCD, either as a stand-alone treatment for parents or in addition to individual treatment for the anxious child.

You can search for providers who deliver SPACE treatment close to you through this website: www.spacetreatment.net. In addition, the creator of SPACE, Dr. Eli Lebowitz, has written a terrific book for parents to independently implement a SPACE-based approach to child anxiety and OCD, which I highly recommend. It's called *Breaking Free of Child Anxiety and OCD: A Scientifically Proven Program for Parents*.

The Flexibility Factor: Get Real with Yourself

Your kid is likely to struggle when you reduce or remove an accommodation that they are used to. What is that going to be like for *you*?

Use your mindfulness skills to notice what you experience when your child is pulling hard for accommodation—when they are upset and look to you to "fix" it. What painful thoughts and feelings come up for you? Where do you feel distress in your body? What thoughts take up the most headspace? Get particularly curious if you reach a point where you snap—you decide to reverse course and give in to your kid's anxiety—and reinstate the accommodation. What thoughts or feelings did you have right before that moment? Use a Three-Component Model worksheet to collect data on these experiences.

With your data in hand, you can develop a coping plan to manage your distress when you are reducing an accommodation and your kid is struggling with the change. What are some of your go-to coping techniques? Do you text a friend for support in the moment? Do you have deep breathing techniques that you like? Maybe you take a shower or run the stairs.

A personalized, values-consistent coping plan that's based on what you noticed about your distress reaction may be even more impactful. For example, say you notice that your shoulders get so tense that they end up scraping your earlobes. Do you have a heating pad that you can apply directly to your shoulders? If you notice that you are overwhelmed with thoughts of guilt and self-doubt, like "I am the worst parent" or "My kid is going to hate me forever," come up with a values-consistent coping thought that counters these thinking traps directly. Maybe something like "My kid will continue to love me because I give him what he needs, not just what he wants." Or keep it simple and to the point: "I am a good parent." Write these thoughts down on a card that you can keep in your pocket or stick to the fridge—somewhere easily accessible during tough moments. Tying these coping thoughts to your values—the ones you hold as a parent and as a person—can help you follow through with reducing accommodation by taking a psychologically flexible approach to tolerating distress.

What Can You Take Home with You?

- Reducing unnecessary accommodation may be beneficial for kids, even in the absence of a clinical anxiety disorder, or if there is only mild interference. Reducing accommodation can promote your child's independence and can help inoculate them against future challenges. It will still mean exposing kids to some discomfort, but coping with discomfort builds bravery muscles.

- Introduce any plans to reduce accommodation to your kid. Be direct and set clear expectations. For example, "Starting next week, I'm not going to wait in the lobby during your gymnastics class. I will be back before the end of class. I know you can handle it." Have realistic expectations about how your kid will receive this information. It can be really easy to get pulled into a fruitless negotiation with your kid, so set an intention to be direct and brief.

- If your child is struggling with a clinical anxiety disorder, partner with a therapist to guide and support you in reducing accommodation whenever possible.
- Please don't cancel positive reinforcement, particularly when it comes to treating child anxiety. That's shooting yourself in the foot. Instead, partner with your kid to come up with a list of potential rewards that can help motivate them during bravery challenges. These rewards should be consistent with your family's values and preferences—they shouldn't break the bank or give your kid access to something that you don't feel is right for your family.

CHAPTER 12

Charging the Batteries

Wouldn't it be incredible if your kid was totally fine with less accommodation, if they were just cool with you no longer responding to their anxiety in the way they think they *need* you to?

Any parent knows this is wishful thinking. In the short term, reducing accommodation can be taxing for you, for your kids, and for the parent-child relationship. Kids can struggle to understand the long-term benefit of what you are trying to achieve. Before you embark on this journey, it's important to shore up connection, energy, and support.

What are you like when your internal battery is fully charged? If I have slept well, exercised, and had a bit of restorative downtime, and I am also connecting regularly with family and friends, I am a *delight*. When challenges come up, facing those stressors with a charged battery means that I have an energy reserve that will help me cope better. On the contrary, I'm less effective when my battery isn't charged because I have fewer internal resources to call upon. It's rumored that I am *not* a delight in these moments.

You and your kid each have a battery. When things are tough, when anxiety or stress or other challenges present themselves, your respective batteries will naturally be drained. Parents and kids who seek anxiety treatment are pretty fried at baseline. The parent-child relationship is often frayed, too. As a family, you and your kids will likely have a harder time coping with the short-term stress of doing exposures and/or reducing accommodation if you don't charge your respective batteries first.

While having a charged battery does include healthy behaviors like quality sleep, nutrition, medication compliance, and movement, we will focus on strategies to improve communication and increase support within the parent-child relationship. In this way, reducing accommodation feels like a partnership, and things will likely go more smoothly.

Validation Remains Valid

Validation is key to this. We introduced validation in Chapter 2, but it's worth revisiting here. You probably hear mostly about validating someone's emotions, but you can also validate thoughts, opinions, beliefs, or desires. You can validate how challenging something is; you can validate effort, effective behaviors, and hard work. You can validate how a person's history or experience affects how they perceive a particular moment and how they react. You validate through your words and through your actions, your tone, and your body language—so keep an eye on your nonverbal cues.

Validation helps your kids emotionally regulate at the same time that it strengthens your parent-child relationship. It's not just an anti-anxiety tool. You can use genuine and thoughtful validation when communicating with your children about the range of their experience, regardless of whether it's anxiety-laden.

I was reminded of this recently when my kid burst into tears after school over some friendship stuff. At first, my Mama Bear instinct got loud: "Who was mean to you?" She was so sad, getting more upset with my questions. Once I got the basics, I just validated. "Oh, honey, that hurts, I am so sorry." I was so tempted to get all the details of what had happened, to solve whatever problem was brewing among these girls. But once I validated, she just crumpled against me, and I held her as she cried. Like all emotional waves, her distress receded with a bit of time. We watched TV for a little while. It felt good to comfort her, and she seemed to need it. Validation was helpful for her and bolstered our connection.

With time and patience, you can get better at validating, and your child can get better at receiving validation. The result is a stronger and more trusting parent-child relationship that is better able to withstand stressors.

A Basic Truth: Attention Is Gold

Here is a fundamental truth about human behavior: Attention—in whatever form—is reinforcing. This means that whatever behavior gets attention will be repeated in the future.

If you thank your kid for clearing his plate after dinner, he is more likely to do so again. If you tell your partner that you like the shirt they are wearing today, you will probably see the shirt again. If you stay glued to your kid's side when they are having a panic attack, they will probably have more panic attacks and feel they need you to cope. Your attention gives oxygen to whatever behavior it alights upon, fueling that behavior.

When anxiety is a player within a family system, parents often find that they are more likely to interact with their anxious kid when something is wrong, rather than when things are going well. You may spend a lot of time checking in, processing worries, problem-solving, providing reassurance, and arguing with your kid.

In contrast, if your kid is having a "good" day, if they seem relaxed or happy, or if they don't appear nervous in a situation that typically provokes anxiety, you may find yourself "letting sleeping dogs lie," trying not to draw your kid's attention to the fact that things seem good. The thinking goes something like this: "If I point out that they seem comfortable right now, will they remember they are supposed to be anxious?"

But that's not how it works. If your kid with social and separation anxiety disorders plays with his cousins without you, it is still beneficial to whisper to him when he comes back, "You did such a good job of playing with your cousins by yourself!" Even if he then starts cling-ing to you for dear life, you have still used your attention to reinforce his brave behavior. He is more likely to branch off from you and chat with other kids in the future.

The same principle applies in reverse. You only have so many op-portunities to interact with your kid during the day. What information is it sending when the majority of your interactions involve attending to their anxiety-driven behaviors? What does it do for your kid if you don't acknowledge that he actually spent time with other kids, away from you, at all, but when he comes out and clings to you, you spend the rest of the evening trying to process with him *why* he is afraid and insisting that there is nothing to be scared of? All of this parental in-teraction is, unwittingly, reinforcing his anxiety: The more anxiety he displays, the more time and attention he receives from you, and the less opportunity he has to talk to others.

We don't need to express approval of a behavior to reinforce it. Simply paying attention to it is enough to reinforce the behavior. Re-member back to your own childhood when your sibling decided it was hilarious to poke you in the back, over and over. When you turned around and yelled, "Stop!" they knew you weren't pleased. But you also reinforced their behavior. Any attention—regardless of the *tone* of the attention—reinforces behavior simply by giving it oxygen. Poke, poke, poke.

By devoting inordinate attention to your kid when anxiety is driv-ing the bus, rather than when it's taking a back seat, you teach them that anxiety is the most important factor to pay attention to in chal-lenging moments. Your attention then teaches your kid to believe that feelings are facts, that feeling alarmed means that there must be dan-ger here. Prioritizing anxious thoughts and feelings quickly becomes a habit, and avoidance gets an easy foothold, further ratcheting up anxiety.

Parental attention is an incredibly powerful tool. Use it wisely to shore up the parent-child relationship and to help shift accommoda-tion patterns. Let's explore how to do so.

Water the flowers

Think back to when your kid was a toddler and hadn't yet learned about hitting. Your little one whacks her brother, he wails in response, and you say, "No hitting!" She dissolves into giggles, and you worry that you've birthed an adorable psychopath. Unfortunately, if this is the only intervention used to quell hitting, it's going to be an uphill battle. Why? Because attention is reinforcing.

Yes, it is important to give your child information about what they should not do, and with hitting, something along the lines of "We don't hit because hitting hurts" is great. Timing is central, though, because if she only gets this information about hitting right after she's whacked someone, that attention may actually be reinforcing the hitting behavior. This is why talking about a behavior *before* it happens, during a neutral time, and setting expectations about what you will do in response, such as saying "If you hit, playtime is over," is helpful.

Reinforcing *positive-opposite behaviors* to hitting is going to make your efforts even more effective. A positive-opposite behavior is the active opposite of a given behavior. The positive-opposite of throwing might be playing gently with your toys. The positive-opposite of being rude might be using respectful language. The positive-opposite of procrastinating by scrolling on social media might be turning off your phone.

A positive-opposite behavior is incompatible with the original behavior: You can't play gently with your toy and chuck it at the same time. Sometimes the positive-opposite behavior is a first step on the way to a positive behavior shift; turning off my phone doesn't necessarily mean I am going to make a significant dent in my work, but it makes it more likely.

What is the positive-opposite behavior that you want to see your Wreck-It Ralph toddler display here? *Not hitting.* Sure, but that's the passive *absence* of the hitting behavior. Also, saying "Great job *not hitting* your brother" isn't super helpful, and honestly, it reads a little passive-aggressive. It doesn't give your kid information about what they should strive for; it only provides nonspecific information about what they should avoid.

So how can you reinforce an active, alternative behavior, rather than just the absence of a behavior? What behaviors do you want to see more of instead—behaviors that are incompatible with hitting?

Keeping your hands to yourself. Using gentle hands. Either of these behaviors is an active, positive-opposite of hitting.

Once you identify the positive-opposite behavior, you can watch for it and provide praise to reinforce it in your kid. In this way, reinforcing a positive-opposite behavior is "catching" your child acting positively. You are hyperaware of their behavior, and you are proactively deploying your attention to reinforce positive-opposite behavior *before* the unwanted behavior happens. So, when your toddler is playing with her brother and there is no hitting, you should be all over that. Identify what she is doing and praise it: "Great job keeping your hands to yourself!" "I love how gently you are playing with your brother!"

Apply the same approach to anxiety. Think about some behaviors you can observe when your kid is anxious. For example, if your kid struggles with social anxiety, you might see them declining invitations to hang out with friends, remaining glued to their phone during social gatherings, or avoiding eye contact during conversations. Rather than chastising them when you see these behaviors, it's more effective to "catch" them doing the positive-opposite.

You could tell them, "I'm proud of you for agreeing to hang out with your friend tonight; I know that's not always easy." Or, "Thanks for putting your phone away." You could also say, "I noticed that you made really good eye contact with your teacher today during our meeting." As with our hitting example, this type of feedback gives your kid information about standards and expectations. And because this feedback is more specific than "Good job," it gives them something concrete to strive for in the future. Even if your teen scoffs at your efforts to praise them, they're taking it in. Your input really does matter.

Do you know the old saying "Water the flowers, not the weeds"?

It's a useful metaphor here: Pay more attention to brave, resilient behaviors (the flowers) and pay less attention to the anxiety-driven behaviors (the weeds). Start this process by first identifying the anxiety-driven behaviors that you hope to see less of in your kid, and second, figuring out some positive-opposite behaviors you want to look for. Then pounce whenever you see them—give verbal praise, watering the flowers that you want to grow.

Here are some common child behaviors that are often associated with anxiety, along with some suggestions for the positive-opposite behavior that you might look for chances to reinforce.

COMMON ANXIETY-DRIVEN BEHAVIORS AND THEIR POSITIVE-OPPOSITES

Anxiety-Driven Behavior	Positive-Opposite Behaviors
Texting repeatedly for reassurance	Texting once only, waiting for a response before texting again, coping with hard things independently
Excessive length of time spent picking out clothing before school	Getting dressed quickly, wearing the first outfit chosen
Clinging to Mom	Playing independently
Isolating from family or friends	Spending time outside your room, going out with friends
Fleeing from a feared animal (insects, dogs)	Staying in the same room as the spider, getting closer to the dog
Yelling, tantruming	Keeping a calm body, calm voice
Only eating certain specific foods	Trying new food items, showing openness and flexibility to trying new things
Excessive test preparation	Balancing studying and sleep, going to bed at a reasonable hour before a test, making time for yourself

Like validation, praising the positive-opposite both helps your kid and supports your relationship with them. Pointing out positive-opposite behaviors means you have the chance to give warm, meaningful praise and attention to your kid. It helps to charge their battery, particularly during anxiety-fueled seasons of life when positive feedback is often scarce. This isn't just showering your kid with praise and affection for the hell of it; your attention to specific behaviors actually helps shape your kid's response to their own anxiety. It feels good for you to specifically praise your kid for something meaningful, and it feels good for your kid to receive this feedback.

Don't water the weeds

So what should you do in response to the anxiety-driven behaviors you want to see less of, the ones that are taking up too much space in your kid's life?

Are you about to tell me to ignore my kid when they are anxious?

No. And yes.

Stay with me.

No one is suggesting for you to simply bail when your kid is having a panic attack. That is undersupport in a nutshell, and it's not good for child anxiety. Instead, you want to shift your attention away from anxiety-driven behaviors and then direct your attention back to your child when brave, resilient behaviors show up. This is one of those distinctions that is too nuanced for memeification, and as a result, there is a lot of confusion and misunderstanding around it.

I wonder if this situation sounds familiar: Your child is really anxious about something. They are worrying out loud, maybe crying; they are irritable and visibly agitated. You try to help, cycling through one problem-solving approach after another, asking questions to try to clarify the issue, suggesting potential solutions to the problem, reminding them about coping skills that they could use in this moment. But nothing seems to move the needle. Your kid rejects one suggestion after another, becoming increasingly irritable, while you become more and more frustrated, demoralized, and agitated. And because of the culture in which you are parenting, directing your attention anywhere else seems like the "bad parent" choice.

But the "good parent" choice isn't helping either. Not only that, it is likely reinforcing anxiety by giving it oxygen—by watering the weeds. This is why your dedicated attention implicitly tells your kid that this emotional experience is a *big deal* that they can't work through on their own. This breeds dependence on you, and it doesn't give your kid the opportunity to work through the challenge themself. It's also a bit of a "squeaky wheel gets the grease" situation, insofar as your anxious kid is getting a ton of your time and attention, which means that the needs of the rest of the family must wait.

Your well-meaning attention is inadvertently watering the weeds of panic, worry, agitation, inflexibility, and dependence. Honestly, it's dousing them in Miracle-Gro, and our Intensive Parenting culture applauds you for doing so. Here is another serious mismatch between how modern parents believe "good parents" should act in situations like this and what anxious kids actually need to break the cycle of anxiety.

So what is the alternative? How can we find a middle path, a psychologically flexible approach between overattentiveness to our child's distress in the moment and too little support when they are struggling?

Step 1. Establish expectations.

Go back to your hitting toddler for a second and recall that it was important to give information about hitting behavior outside the hitting context: talking to your toddler about how hitting hurts, why we don't hit, during a time when hitting is not happening. Similarly, it is important to set expectations with your kid about how you will respond to their anxiety at a moment when anxiety isn't the focus. This means communicating with your kid during moments of calm about your intention to react differently in the future and to explain your reasons for doing so. You might even revisit a recent episode in which your attention didn't end up helping, and explain how it actually may be making their anxiety worse in the long term. It then might look like setting the expectation that, in similar situations in the future, you will offer a hug and one suggestion for coping, and then take some space so they have the chance to work things through without you breathing down their neck.

Step 2. Follow through with active ignoring.

Fast-forward to the next time anxiety gets loud. Now that you have explained how you will respond, it's up to you to follow through: Validate the emotion, offer a hug (even if it is rejected), and suggest one concrete coping strategy (maybe to use a mindfulness strategy or take a brief break). Then remove your attention by giving your child space. You could physically leave the room, or you could divert your attention elsewhere by reading a magazine or checking your email while your kid works through some hard feelings. You are removing your attention from the anxiety, *but you are not ignoring your child*.

Quite the opposite, in fact. Your attention has shifted, but now you are looking for the next opportunity to reinforce what you want to see. You are totally tuned in, but kind of sneakily, because at the same time, you are resisting the urge to reengage with their anxiety. You then check back after a few minutes and "water the flowers," paying attention to any positive-opposite behaviors that you see. You might point out that your kid handled really tough feelings independently, praise the way they practiced a coping skill, or highlight how they kept their body safe and calm.

This process is called *active ignoring*. It's *active* because while you are shifting your attention away from the behaviors that need to decrease, you are actually laser-focused on your child but in a way that is less obvious. You are instead quietly monitoring their actions and quickly shifting your attention back to them when any behaviors you want to see more of show up. Active ignoring is an incredibly useful part of the effort to reduce parental accommodation.

As another example, imagine your young child is afraid of dogs. Whenever she encounters a dog while on a walk in the neighborhood, she cries, clings to you, or even tries to climb you like a ladder. In response, you scoop her up in your arms, reassure her that the dog can't get her, and hustle home as soon as possible.

How could you start to shift your response here?

First, you communicate your intention to respond differently in advance, so your kid isn't caught off guard. Then you follow through. You might no longer pick her up if a dog approaches. Instead of providing excessive soothing or reassurance, you could use a supportive statement—acknowledge that it feels scary for her *and* that you are confident she can handle being around this friendly dog. You could model bravery around the dog by patting the dog yourself. You could stay with the dog until your kid calms, actively ignoring crying or whining, and instead praising her any time she shows even the slightest inclination toward coping with her own anxiety: as her body becomes calmer, when she looks toward the dog, and especially if she gets closer to the dog or pats it. In this way, you are using your attention and actions to shape your child's brave behavior.

One-on-One Time

When parents are struggling, or have a kid who is struggling, they often find that they simply aren't spending as much quality time together. In these circumstances, if you were to lay out all the parent-child interactions taking place in your day and rate them as either positive or negative, you would likely find that the number of negative interactions is far greater. This makes sense, because the stress of coping with anxiety can sap the joy from your interactions. The parent-child bond can become strained, focused on problems, or characterized by tiptoeing around one another to avoid provoking a negative reaction. The relationship needs a little TLC.

It's not dissimilar to a marriage, where intimacy and connection don't just happen naturally, particularly when it feels like the house is on fire. You have to work at intimacy by deliberately making time for it. In the same way, when anxiety is an unwelcome third wheel in the parent-child relationship, you have to intentionally look for opportunities to connect. You can help by setting aside time for some high-quality one-on-one time with your kid. Like, actually make time for it. Schedule it, set an alarm, and make it happen a few times a week.

I know that adding anything to your parenting life is a huge ask. I wouldn't recommend one-on-one time if it weren't backed by research and if I hadn't seen it produce results. Importantly, the time commitment here does not need to be extensive. Indeed, five minutes of high-quality one-on-one time absolutely beats an hour of poor-quality bonding, in terms of how restorative it is to parent and child alike.

Ideally, one-on-one time is deliberate. You tell your kid that you'd like to have more quality time together and then come up with a plan to make it happen. Start a project together, like a puzzle, a garden, or a Lego build. Cook something. Play mini golf. Draw together. See a play or a musical. Go for a walk or a bike ride. Take an exercise class together. Give the dog a bath—a stinky, soggy experience is always a bonding one.

There are steps you can take to make it more likely that one-on-one time will be a battery-charging exercise. First, it helps to give kids the choice of the daily one-on-one activity that you do together. And resist the urge to "manage" the activity. For example, if your kid wants to play catch, this isn't the time to give corrective feedback about their pitching technique. If they want to bake something, resist the urge to micromanage cracking an egg. If they want to go for a walk with you, follow their lead in how much they want to talk, and resist peppering them with questions. Just be together.

Commit to communicating warmly during this time. Let your kid know how much you love being with them. Point out when they say something kind, smart, funny, or thoughtful. Tell them how much they matter to you. And you can use your attention to genuinely water the flowers. If anxiety or worries elbow into these situations, you can briefly validate and then gently shift the topic to keep it light.

During one-on-one time, you really want to avoid the QCCs: questions, commands, and criticisms. QCCs often increase the likelihood that a positive interaction will go south. So, if you're feeling grumpy, snarky, or like a volcano about to explode, try to reset before one-on-one time begins. If you are having a rough day, postpone and try again when you are in a better frame of mind. Seriously, this should be time that you both enjoy.

Dos and Don'ts of One-on-One Time

Do:
- Set an intention to remain mindful during one-on-one time
- Validate
- Use verbal praise to reinforce positive-opposite behaviors
- Follow your child's lead
- Express warmth and positive regard for your child with your words, your tone, or physical touch
- Actively ignore behaviors you don't want to see (rudeness, irritability)
- If anxiety comes up, validate and gently shift the topic

Don't:
- Ask questions
- Give commands
- Criticize
- Fall into the invalidation trap by jumping into problem-solving mode or dismissing concerns outright if anxiety-related topics come up

You can create positive one-on-one time without your kid being fully aware by harnessing your psychological flexibility. During a time when you know you will naturally be alone with them, you can commit to flooding the interaction with the best ingredients of one-on-one time for a brief period. Say your kid is setting the table while you get dinner ready. Here's your moment! You could thank them for setting the table, you could reflect on how they have grown in recent months, you could steal a hug as they pass by with the forks. For this brief time, you could commit to watering the flowers and not the weeds.

You may have a kid who is pretty shut down or a parent-child relationship that feels very frayed. In these situations, you might worry that pushing for one-on-one time might feel punishing for your kid—or simply unnatural or forced. So you can start off by building in time when you are "together, separately," meaning that you are neutrally occupying the same space as your kid, but not necessarily doing the same thing. You could be reading a book while your kid is watching TV; you could be cooking while they are doing homework at the kitchen table. During these times, keep an eye out for opportunities to have warm communication, and limit QCCs. You want to be sure that the foundation for spending more quality time together is free from negativity. Once these "together, separately" interactions become easier, you can start working on building in time when you are doing something together, like watching TV, going for a run, or going to see a play.

Putting It All Together

I worked with Emma, a teenage girl struggling with generalized anxiety disorder, whose family sought treatment once their nighttime routine went completely off the rails. Emma worried about anything and everything, and as darkness fell each night, her fears poured out: "What if Mom gets in a car accident? What if I get laughed at in school tomorrow? What if I fail my history exam? What if I get cancer?" Her parents were spending hours with her in the evening working through her fears, lying in bed with her, trapped in conversations that led down countless rabbit holes of worry, which often escalated. Everyone was exhausted, strung out, and utterly depleted.

First and foremost, we had to come to a shared understanding about what was going on. Her parents were doing their best to help Emma by processing her worries each night. But this accommodation was actually propelling her anxiety disorder, and they needed to make some changes. Her parents initially balked at the recommendation to decrease the time they were spending absorbing Emma's worries. This was particularly uncomfortable for her mom, who shared that she had an anxiety disorder herself. She struggled to see how a good parent could do anything other than attend to their child's worries and distress when the child wanted to talk.

Here's what I told them about worries. Broadly speaking, talking through your kid's concerns with them is good practice if it helps the child to reframe concerns more realistically or come up with solutions. However, anxiety disorders can change this equation. Paradoxically, if you pay a ton of attention to your kid's debilitating worries—processing the same concerns over and over again, providing reassurance on repeat—the worries don't actually get better. Instead, rumination breeds more distress, kids become dependent on this "processing process," and the worries can get bigger, broader, and hungrier. It also prevents independent exposure practice.

At the core of most worries is uncertainty. In order for uncertainty to be less crippling, Emma needed to practice *tolerating* uncertainty rather than trying to avoid it. She needed to make room for the fact that she couldn't actually know whether her mom was going to get in a car accident, or whether she would fail her history exam. Emma was having so much trouble tolerating uncertainty, in part, because she hadn't had the opportunity to learn to cope with it independently.

I sometimes tell a story from my own childhood where this concept was starkly impressed on me by my mother. I was about ten years old, and my family went to an amusement park one summer night with friends. Our group was waiting in line to go on a massive Ferris wheel, and I got nervous. Looking for reassurance, I asked my mom,

"What if it breaks while we are on it and collapses?" She thought for a moment and said, "Well, I guess we'd all die and there wouldn't be anything we could do about it." The unadorned truth of this was shocking. But she was right, and hearing it was ultimately helpful.

She didn't massage my fears by telling me there was no way the Ferris wheel would break, or by reassuring me that every amusement park employee was a highly trained engineer and therefore nothing could possibly go wrong. She laid out the reality of the situation, and she allowed me the space to cope with it. I had to tolerate the uncertainty and make a choice of how to act. I went on the Ferris wheel and lived to tell the tale. And for the record, my mom is a wonderfully warm, attentive, loving parent, and the fact that I felt *more* anxious once she laid some hard Ferris wheel truths out for me didn't make me love her any less.

Once Emma's parents fully understood the cycle of worry and reassurance-seeking, reducing their attention to worries at night made sense; they saw it as a needed intervention, rather than neglect of her distress. They began to understand that while their loving, undivided attention at night helped their daughter feel safer in the moment, it wasn't doing her any favors in the long run.

We also learned that the flowers weren't getting much water. Outside their nighttime worry-fests, her parents had limited and perfunctory interactions with Emma. So no one's batteries were charged, which only contributed to the tearful fights and sleepless nights.

To effectively address her anxiety, we needed a multipronged approach. First, Emma's parents worked to shift the ratio of positive to negative interactions, creating space for high-quality one-on-one time to strengthen the parent-child relationship. They worked on improving their validation skills, with Emma and with one another. They also decreased invalidation by limiting how often they minimized concerns ("There is no reason to be worried") or jumped immediately to problem-solving ("Why don't you just check with your teacher first thing tomorrow?"). They began practicing an active ignoring approach, shining an encouraging light when they saw Emma coping better, and shifting their focus when they noticed behaviors driven by anxiety. These tools both increased support for their daughter and strengthened their relationship with her.

With their batteries charged, their efforts to tackle accommodation were enhanced. Emma's parents started using a timer to gradually decrease the amount of time spent processing worries each night. But first, they needed to establish expectations about this change with Emma. We planned their conversation ahead of time in one of our sessions. It went something like this: They told her they had noticed that they were spending a long time every night talking through her worries, and that while the same topics kept coming up, the worries didn't seem to be getting better. They believed that this pattern wasn't helping and was actually making her worries worse.

They then acknowledged that their job as her parents was to help her in the best way they knew how, even if it didn't always feel good. They told her that, starting that night, they would set a timer for twenty minutes at bedtime, and when the timer went off, they would say good night and leave the room—even if they were in the middle of a conversation.

Then they followed through. They stuck to the plan. When the timer went off, they said good night and left the room. They did not get sucked into any arguments or humor any negotiations.

I know that it did not feel good for them to leave the room. It didn't feel good the next night either. But with steadfastness, and with time, they gradually pulled back from the nighttime downloads completely, confident that they were being "good parents" by limiting how much power Emma's anxiety would have in the family. They balanced less engagement during worry-centric times with more positive interactions outside the nighttime routine. High-quality time together and clear communication helped support Emma through the stress of accommodation reduction and charged everyone's batteries.

Emma rose to the challenge. Because she could no longer rely on her parents to be her lifeline once they decreased their overinvolvement in her nighttime routine, she had to start applying the coping skills that she was learning in therapy. This independent practice was key for her treatment success.

The Flexibility Factor: Anticipate the Painful-Feelings Pile-On

Most parents with whom I work understand, intellectually, that emotions themselves aren't harmful for their kid. They get the value of active ignoring. But in the moment, when your kid is really struggling with big emotions, you're not thinking rationally. Thanks, amygdala hijack.

It is really hard not to give negative emotions oxygen, especially when you're steeped in an Intensive Parenting culture. You will inevitably find yourself looking at your situation through the lens of other parents who you fear would condemn you for leaving your child alone in their room when they are having an unpleasant feeling.

If you are vulnerable to the messages of Intensive Parenting when you are calm, you will be even more vulnerable to them when you are doing anything other than facilitating emotional avoidance in your kid. If (when) guilt and self-doubt rear their heads, start by noticing your thoughts and feelings . . . before you act. In this pause, remember that feelings are not facts, and that not all thoughts are truth. Feeling uncomfortable when you actively ignore does not mean that you are doing the wrong thing for your kid. And thoughts like "I'm not sure I'm handling this right" or "I'm the worst parent" should be held lightly, because they may or may not be true (although I seriously doubt that you are the *worst parent*). Openness to these thoughts and feelings during child anxiety treatment—even anticipating that they will come up—can help you cope more effectively.

These thoughts and feelings are normal reactions to shifts in how you are responding to your child's anxiety. This is a perfect opportunity for self-validation and for reconnecting with your values before you take action.

What Can You Take Home with You?

- Under what circumstances does your kid get most of your attention these days? Is most of your attention going to your child when things are going poorly—when your child is worried or panicking, when you are lecturing them, or when they are yelling at you? If you find that most of your interactions with your kid center on hard things, look for opportunities to shift the balance toward more positive interactions.

- Building in more positive parent-child interactions is one of those treatment recommendations that can be easy to dismiss. Like your doctor telling you to sleep better, eat better, or get more exercise, you don't doubt the benefits, but these recommendations feel so basic and foundational that they often get ignored. Don't fall into that trap here. I know that parents most want discrete coping skills to address anxiety, but you are handicapping your kid and yourself in fighting anxiety if you are doing it without charging everyone's batteries first.

CHAPTER 13

When the Sh*t Hits the Fan

It's all well and good to *talk* about doing hard things. But what happens in the moment when you and your child are facing down anxiety and their fight-or-flight response goes into overdrive? How do you manage a situation where your child is—perhaps literally—kicking and screaming in an effort to make everyone give in to old anxiety-driven patterns of avoidance?

This is the moment that parents dread most, and for good reason. Once you've committed to setting limits, you open yourself up to the very real possibility that your kid will push back, hard. In fact, folks in my field are so confident that this will happen that we have a term for it: *extinction burst*. It sounds like an explosive Paleolithic experience. What it means is that when something in your environment changes such that your old behavior doesn't get you the result you are used to, you double down on the old behavior to see if you can get the expected result. If you don't get it at that point, you have to behave differently. We've all been there.

You expect that when you push the call button outside an elevator bay, the elevator will arrive shortly in response to your call. So what do you do when you have pushed the call button, but the elevator doesn't arrive as expected? You push the button again . . . and again . . . and *again*, harder and faster, as if your button-pushing rage will jolt the lazy elevator to attention. But what happens if the elevator still doesn't show up? You aren't going to stand there forever; you eventually take the stairs. The next time you have to take that elevator, you remember what you've learned about its slowness. This time, you maybe press the call button twice, but you give up faster and decide to take the stairs sooner. The next time, you probably head straight for the stairs.

Extinction bursts are adaptive because they're often effective. If you need a response to your email, you email again and again and again until you hear back from the irritated recipient. Kids plead incessantly until their beleaguered parent caves to their demands for dessert or a smartphone. And in heated situations, anxiety hijacks the distress of devoted parents and distraught kids, providing oxygen for the extinction burst.

This is when the wheels come off the bus. During anxiety-fueled extinction bursts, you are likely to see any of the behaviors that are part of the fight-or-flight response—crying, clinging, becoming nonresponsive, running away, negotiating, or pleading. It may also involve yelling, tantruming, slamming doors, deliberately making a mess, or saying hurtful things. These behaviors have "worked" for kids in the past—people around them have likely given in to anxiety's demands when they engaged in those behaviors. This means that when the environment shifts, you can expect these behaviors to get bigger and louder for a time as part of the extinction burst.

When anxiety signaled a true threat, it would have been helpful for the fight-or-flight response to make our early human ancestors go ballistic—it might have even saved their lives. Amygdala hijack is in full force when an extinction burst is happening, so the emotion center of the brain is in charge and the rational prefrontal cortex can't get a word in. This response is normal. It's predictable. *It will also be time-limited, as long as you stick to the limits that you set.*

In this chapter, we will look closely at how extinction bursts play out in anxiety-producing situations and why it's so important that parents tap into psychological flexibility and follow through with the plan. I'll show you how to increase the likelihood that you'll succeed in riding out extinction bursts and offer concrete coping strategies to help you persevere in the toughest moments. When you, as a parent, commit to tolerating your own distress in response to your kid's distress, you can break the cycle of anxiety.

In Defense of Limit-Setting

Before we dive in, let's first challenge the assumption that setting limits is bad for kids. There is a powerful narrative circulating in the parenting ether that parents should not cause their children any distress. These fears are driven, in part, by the recognition that adverse childhood events involving trauma or chronic stress can have profound impacts on health and development. But there is a surprisingly slippery slope between wanting to protect your children from actual trauma and assuming that you are the author of trauma if your actions upset your children. Clinicians in my field hear from parents who are really hesitant to set limits that might upset their kids out of a fear that their children will be permanently damaged by the intensity of their feelings. It doesn't help that kids naturally are going to push back against limits; you are going to be hard-pressed to encounter a kid who is thrilled for the adults in their life to set expectations for their behavior. In this context, it can be tough for you to have confidence that you are doing the "right" thing.

However, getting what we want is different than getting what we need, and kids need limits to help them learn. Even though it drives parents bananas when kids test the limits, it's a natural and important process through which they learn where the limits are—based on the boundary that you set and maintain. Boundaries and expectations help kids feel safe, creating predictability and certainty in an unpredictable and uncertain world.

On the other hand, when you set a limit and then don't follow through, you teach your kid that you don't really mean what you say, not only creating more uncertainty and unpredictability but opening the door for escalating pushback in the future.

> Kids need the adults in their lives to be compassionate and firm guardians and teachers. It's okay for you to set reasonable limits—it's beneficial!—and it's okay for your kids to be mad about it.

The Cycle Disruptor

In the last chapter, I introduced Emma, who struggled with debilitating worries at bedtime. Recall that she had become dependent on her parents to help manage her worries by lying in bed with her each evening as she downloaded all of her fears. This process gave her slight relief in the moment but slapped a Band-Aid on the problem that didn't help in the healing. It was an accommodation that they had to get rid of. So we started by having her parents set a limit on how much time they would dedicate to processing her worries by setting a timer. When the timer went off, her parents would say good night and leave her room, even if Emma was midworry. I shared how this treatment was successful. But we had to get through an extinction burst first.

Even though Emma was on board with the plan to gradually get her parents out of her room, we prepared together for an extinction burst, just in case. And it was a good thing, because when the timer went off in the middle of a spiraling stream of consciousness about whether she would get into college, anxiety got loud. Emma protested. She cried. She pulled on her mother's arm to try to get her to stay in the room. She told her parents she hated them. She threatened to never go back to therapy. She asked how they could possibly leave her alone when she clearly needed them.

Emma's mom told me later that she cried, too. She questioned whether she was doing the right thing. And she was a total champ. She stuck with the plan, giving the single supportive statement that we had agreed on: "This is really hard. I love you, and I know that you can handle this." She did not respond to the crying, the protesting, the pulling, or the harsh words said in the heat of her daughter's fight-or-flight moment.

Once out of the room, she and Emma's dad were an amazing team. They did not respond to the door-slamming, the sound of books being thrown to the floor, the shouting for them to come back, and the sobbing as their exhausted daughter at last cried herself to sleep. Everyone was fried. But the next night, when the timer went off, things went a little better. There was protest and some name-calling, but Emma's response was a bit diminished. The third night, there was minor grumbling that probably included some choice words about me, but that was about it.

As awful as it felt in the moment, Emma's parents showed incredible psychological flexibility—they set a values-consistent limit around their daughter's anxiety and they followed through, even in the hardest moments. With her parents out of her room at bedtime, Emma was initially more anxious and distressed. But crucially, without them by her side, she could fully practice the needed exposure to uncertainty. She could exercise the mindfulness, self-validation, and coping skills that she was learning in treatment. She learned that the metaphorical elevator wasn't going to come, no matter how many times she pushed the call button, and she got better at taking the stairs. In doing so, she was developing her own psychological flexibility and building resilience.

The Art of Staying Steadfast

In this case, the extinction burst burned itself out fairly quickly because Emma's parents held firm, tolerating their distress rather than giving in to the urge to rush back into their daughter's bedroom and soothe her, which would have kept the cycle of anxiety going strong. But what happens when the limit isn't held?

In Chapter 11, we discussed how a kid who has always been given a cookie before dinner is going to be pretty unhappy if his parents decide there will be no more pre-dinner cookie. He's going to increase behaviors that have gotten results in the past. We can imagine him pouting and crying and throwing things. It could get pretty unpleasant.

Let's say that his parents feel that their kid's cookie escalation is more than they bargained for, and they cave in: "Fine, you can have your cookie tonight, but starting tomorrow, you won't get one!" The kid calms down in the moment, but now he has learned that he needs to escalate his behavior and become *that* much more oppositional when his parents set a limit. That means that his response to tomorrow's cookie moratorium is going to be *that* much more intense, making it more likely that his parents will cave again. The cycle will then continue, amplified.

Limits around cookies are one thing; setting limits around anxiety is another. When you don't hold firm in the face of an extinction burst, you not only give in to avoidance, but you are reinforcing the escalation of unwanted behaviors that show up as part of the fight-or-flight response—more crying, more panicking, more slamming doors, more threats. It makes it that much harder for you to hold firm in the compassionate limit-setting that your child needs in order to tackle their anxiety disorder.

I worked with a family whose six-year-old son, Charlie, had a vomit phobia. Charlie's fear of getting sick motivated his family members to take all sorts of steps to ensure that his food wasn't "contaminated." One way the family accommodated his anxiety was by using a disinfectant to wipe down the groceries before they came into the home. Treating his anxiety meant we needed to pull back on the grocery decontamination, which opened the door for Charlie to learn that he could eat "possibly contaminated" items and not actually vomit.

This was a particularly tough ask for Charlie's mom. She did the majority of the shopping and so was on the front lines of managing her son's distress. Acknowledging this challenge, we piloted a plan where his dad took over the grocery duty and navigated Charlie's anxiety while unpacking the groceries. Charlie's dad rode the wave of the extinction burst for nearly three weeks of grocery shopping, and Charlie was making excellent progress in eating these foods at home. (No vomiting, either.)

Then Charlie's dad had to go out of town, and anxiety, ever the opportunist, saw an opening with his mom back in charge. Charlie pushed back harder than any of us expected, and his mom felt overwhelmed by his distress. He had a tantrum the likes of which she hadn't seen since he was a toddler, and it freaked her out. She ended up repacking the groceries that she had put away and disinfecting them outside the home, and then she took an extra anxiety-appeasing step by disinfecting the pantry and refrigerator where any "contaminated" item had been placed. This was, unfortunately, a big setback. It meant that the family had an even more challenging uphill battle with an even bigger extinction burst to overcome as their treatment continued.

No one could fault Charlie's mother for how things unfolded; we can all see ourselves in her shoes. The extinction burst opens up the very real possibility that overwhelmed parents feel compelled to return to anxiety-maintaining patterns. This is particularly likely if parents are struggling with their own anxiety.

The extinction burst is never fun, but it is surmountable with some thoughtful preparation. Let's talk about a few ways that you can set yourself up for success as you face extinction bursts.

Only set limits if you can follow through

It's more problematic to backtrack on a limit you've set than to never set a limit in the first place. So only set limits with your kid if you are prepared to follow through. Knowing your kid, your partner, and yourself, you should consider the worst possible extinction burst and honestly evaluate your ability to cope. And it's important to advocate for what you need to see it through.

I worked with Casey, an eleven-year-old with generalized anxiety disorder and social anxiety disorder whose well-meaning parents were firmly ensnared in patterns of accommodation. There were two main areas of accommodation we wanted to pull back on in order to allow Casey to practice more independent coping: speaking for herself in public and completing her homework without her parents' input. I suggested that the family tackle the first one by having Casey order for herself at a restaurant as part of her homework between sessions. At first, Casey and her parents seemed on board, and they agreed that when the server asked their daughter for her order, no one would jump in to provide it. She would either order for herself or not get dinner. We thought we were set, but her dad wisely asked us to circle back before the end of the session. He had social anxiety himself, and he guessed he would struggle to tolerate the awkward pause when the server asked for his daughter's order if no response came; he wasn't sure he could resist jumping in and undermining the exposure opportunity.

I was so, *so* glad that Casey's dad raised this, and I told him so. We put the restaurant exposure on the back burner temporarily and returned to the drawing board. Since we also wanted to pull back her parents' involvement in homework, we agreed to start with a plan where her parents would no longer sit with her as she did her work and would spend no more than five minutes per day answering homework-related questions.

We acknowledged that an extinction burst was possible, but both parents felt that they could hold the limit, since any pushback from Casey would happen in the privacy of their own home, where her father's social anxiety wouldn't be a factor. As treatment progressed and both Casey and her parents gained confidence in fighting back against anxiety, her dad was better able to tolerate exposures in public, and we revisited the restaurant exposure successfully. Her father's ability to be self-reflective about the likelihood of his follow-through was key to the success of Casey's treatment.

Are you with me?

It's vitally important for anyone involved in a child's care to be aligned, because it is so much harder to follow through with limit-setting if there isn't a united front. I got my own introduction to the importance of being on the same page early in my parenting journey. When my daughter was six months old, we decided to sleep-train. Well, *I* decided to sleep-train, once she started waking up every forty-five minutes and not napping. My husband, who has been wrapped around my daughter's little finger since the moment she was born, was initially not on board. And I was too tired to mount a solid argument to get us on the same page.

This was a problem. I worried that on that first night of sleep-training, I wouldn't be able to resist the pulls of her cries, my own discomfort, and my husband's urging that we ditch the plan. I needed backup.

I called my mom, who came and spent a few days with us. She held my hand and talked me through the extinction burst, reminding me that my daughter was safe and loved, and that this was short-term pain for long-term gain. Her calm, supportive presence helped me follow through. My mom's presence also effectively tempered my husband's reaction. Instead of mounting an obnoxiously rational argument in front of his mother-in-law, he only managed to grumble, "I don't think this is going to work," before shuffling out of earshot of his baby girl's cries. Three days later, he good-naturedly conceded that he had been wrong about sleep-training for our kid. We sent my mom back home and all enjoyed our sleep.

Getting on the same page may be helpful with sleep-training but is absolutely crucial in the treatment of anxiety disorders. This is because anxiety will find any vulnerability and exploit it. When child distress increases in the face of a limit, everyone else's distress is also going to skyrocket—this is anxiety's foothold. In these moments, it's easy to doubt yourself, to doubt others, and to ultimately give in and "rescue" your kid in the middle of an extinction burst, fueling the cycle of anxiety.

It's rare that everyone in a family is fully aligned in their views of the best way to respond to child anxiety. This means that you will be well-served by having honest conversations with anyone who may be a part of the extinction burst—parents, stepparents, grandparents, childcare providers, even siblings. You want to know ahead of time that everyone's willing to lock in and hold firm. This is also the time to examine and counter any negative beliefs about anxiety, to dispel myths about its harmfulness. Proactively plan for how everyone can support one another, and the child, during extinction bursts. Getting on the same page minimizes the likelihood that you will set a limit that you can't maintain.

Call in your ride-or-dies

My experience with sleep-training highlights the importance of planning ahead for the support you need to be successful. When you know that giving in to your child's distress will only embolden anxiety, the best thing you can do is shore yourself up by calling in your support system. My mom's presence was a game changer.

In a two-caregiver household, where both parties are solidly committed to making changes, parents can lean on each other for support. I often suggest that they come up with ways they can signal to each other if they are having a hard time in the moment. They might establish a code word that either parent can use if they are reaching their limit and need to take a break. Or they come up with a shared motto or coping thought to remind each other of their values. My personal favorite: "Good parenting feels bad sometimes." We build in self-care or rewards for managing extinction bursts by actively scheduling time for each parent to exercise, take a long shower, or do something else to refill their tank. One couple got their favorite dessert from a local bakery as a parenting reward and devoured the whole thing in one sitting after a particularly rough extinction burst.

You can also call on people beyond your nuclear family. Sharing what you are going through with a trusted friend or family member and asking for their support can be super helpful. I have worked with parents who have asked a friend to be "on call" with supportive texts during an extinction burst or to send their best memes and gifs to lighten the mood. It's always heartening to see how friends show up for one another in times like this—they often just need to be asked.

Self-care for the caregivers

Confession: I *hate* the term "self-care," particularly as it is applied to parenting. When you feel like you are drowning with responsibilities and demands, guilt and frustration, the last thing you need is for someone to opine about how you should take better care of yourself. When someone points out my lack of self-care during a stressful time, I catch myself thinking, "Great, here's another way that I am failing myself and my family."

But truly, we are all better able to tolerate distress when our physical and emotional needs are met. So we need to talk about self-care. For parents shepherding their children through anxiety treatment, this means paying attention to your sleep, wellness, nutrition, and movement. It's making wise decisions about when and how to begin challenging parts of treatment so you increase the likelihood of success. For example, if the fire alarm in your house randomly goes off the night before you planned to start reducing a major accommodation, push the plan back a day so that you begin feeling rested. Maybe wait until you and your child are both over your colds before plowing forward with an exposure plan that is likely to create a lot of distress.

Self-care also includes setting boundaries that increase your overall coping capacity. In her book *Real Self-Care,* Pooja Lakshmin argues that setting healthy boundaries is the key to quality self-care. More of this, please! What can you take off your plate? Do you *need* to help plan your cousin's baby shower the same week as you are working to get your school-refusing kid back into class? Can you talk with your partner about how they can support you in taking time to restore by going to the gym, seeing a friend, or taking a nap? Sure, your mother will be disappointed if you cancel your weekend visit, but if the sleeping arrangements at her house mean that your anxious child will lose the progress that he is just starting to make in sleeping independently, setting a boundary might be worth the passive-aggressive blowback.

Riding Out Chaos Like a Boss

What can you do in the middle of an extinction burst when your child is crying, yelling, pleading, panicking, and all you want to do is to give in to anxiety and *just make it stop*?

First, you need some self-validation. This stinks. Of course you feel anxious and distressed when your kid is anxious and distressed, because you are a loving and devoted parent. *And* you can tolerate this distress.

While there is no easy way to avoid the painful thoughts and feelings, there are some techniques that can help you get through tough moments. These are called distress tolerance skills, and they help you regulate your emotions and avoid acting on unhelpful urges. There are any number of ways to tolerate distress in the moment, and it's a bit of a choose-your-own-adventure situation. Some people take deep breaths or do some box breathing. Some listen to music or a comedy routine. I follow a few Instagram accounts of mood-boosting golden retriever puppies. Truly, it's doing whatever you need to do in the moment to ride the wave of emotion and keep your cool.

A handful of skills that CBT therapists teach in treatment, with kids and with adults, are worth adding to your tool kit. You can learn these skills and share and practice them with your kids.

Intense physical sensations

Several distress tolerance techniques involve safely bringing on intense physical sensations, which harness your body chemistry to shift your attention to physical feelings and temporarily away from emotional distress.

Ice diving

Your sympathetic nervous system kicks into high gear when you experience strong emotions—your heart rate increases, your blood vessels expand, and your breathing becomes more rapid and shallow. To rein in this system, quickly bringing down your heart rate can help you become calm more rapidly and think more clearly. One way to do this is to use a technique called ice diving, in which you use cold water to trick your body into activating an ancient adaptation that will rapidly slow your heart rate. When mammals—including humans—are submerged in cold water, their heart rate plummets. This is called the mammalian dive reflex, and it increases the chance of survival in cold water by preserving energy. It's also super helpful when you are panicking or are otherwise very stressed.

And you don't even need to do a full cold plunge to achieve it. To mimic being submerged in cold water, get a large bowl full of ice water, hold your breath, and plunge your face beneath the surface for at least thirty seconds. You want to mimic the experience of being submerged under water as much as possible, so it's important that you bend at the waist so you are facing down, and that you hold your breath for at least thirty seconds—longer if possible. In response, your heart rate will naturally decrease as this ancient reflex is triggered. It's pretty remarkable.

Ice diving in a bowl of cold water is ideal, but in a pinch, holding ice packs over your eyes, temples, and upper cheeks while you bend at the waist and hold your breath for at least thirty seconds can mimic this experience. I often recommend that families buy the kind of ice packs that crack to release the cold sensation, which can be kept easily accessible in backpacks, purses, or gym bags for use in a pinch. Note that this technique is *not* recommended for those who have a heart condition or for those who are taking a beta blocker.

Intense exercise

What does it feel like to be in a full-out sprint, pushing your body as intensely as possible? It's really hard to think about or feel anything else, other than your physical exertion, and it's therefore a helpful coping strategy for tough moments. Using intense exercise as a distress tolerance strategy typically takes only a few minutes and can usually be achieved from wherever you are in the moment—gym equipment not required. Some tried-and-true options are to do high-knee lifts or to run in place, do as many jumping jacks as you can, or run the stairs until you are totally out of breath. I heard from a colleague about a teenager who would get dysregulated when he had to stop playing videogames. He coped by rapidly doing push-ups to help him reconstitute and move on to homework—an excellent and effective coping strategy in the moment.

The key here is that the exercise needs to be intense enough to really get your heart rate up and tax your body so that painful thoughts and feelings can't compete for your attention. Gentle yoga or stretching isn't going to cut it as a distress tolerance skill—this calls for some intense cardio. As a bonus, intense exercise also helps to release the muscle tension that builds during emotional storms, helping you feel calmer afterward.

Other strong physical sensations

You can use your other senses to bring on intense sensations that help refocus your attention and tolerate your distress. Mindfully eating something with a strong sensation or taste can be very grounding—think a sour lemon or spicy cinnamon candy, a powerful mint, candy with a fizzing or popping sensation, or something cold like a Popsicle. You can hold an ice cube, using your sense of touch to safely bring on an intense physical feeling. Or you can smell something heavily scented, like a candle or perfume. The intensity of these physical sensations draws your attention away from your spiraling emotional experience, helping you to reset and take values-based actions.

ABC categories

When your thoughts are spiraling, using ABC categories is a technique to focus your attention, anchor your thoughts in the moment, and pass the time as you are working through your distress. It's simple, engaging, and modifiable. First, pick a category, any category. Some crowd-pleasers are animals, foods, countries, celebrities, and cities. Next, think of an item within the category that starts with each letter of the alphabet, and progress through each letter sequentially. If you pick countries, you would start with the letter *A* (Armenia) before progressing to *B* (Brazil), and so on.

ABC categories can be done in many different ways. You can say the words silently in your head, write down your answers, say them out loud with a partner or in a group, or think of just one answer for each letter or as many responses for each letter as you can. In addition to being a terrific grounding strategy when emotions are high, it can also be a helpful coping strategy when your mind is spinning, or if you are struggling to fall asleep. Bonus: It's also an excellent car game if you're stuck in traffic.

5-4-3-2-1

The 5-4-3-2-1 technique can help ground you by prompting you to notice your surroundings through your senses. Here's how it works: Pause as you read this and engage with your environment. Notice five things that you can *see*, four things that you can *feel* or *touch*, three things that you can *hear*, two things that you can *smell*, and one thing that you can *taste*. As you notice things in your external world, try to also nonjudgmentally notice the thoughts and feelings that arise when you do this exercise.

Let's practice: Notice five things that you can see—not just the objects themselves, but the way the light reflects off of them; notice their texture, their shape. Next, notice four things that you can touch or feel with your hands, your feet, your entire body. Consider the sensation of your clothes against your skin, the temperature of the room, any sensations inside your body, the position of your body in space. Use your hands to feel textures or temperatures of objects close to you. Then bring your attention to what you can hear, and try to identify three things: the sounds inside and outside your room, the hum of household items, music or footsteps or cars going by, birds or insects, the sound of your own breathing, and yes—even the sound of your kid having a hard time in another room. Now take a deep breath and see if you can identify two distinct scents. If it's hard to distinguish, hold your clothing or your hair up to your nose and notice the scent, light a candle, or make coffee or tea and breathe in the aroma. Finally, notice the taste in your mouth, or mindfully eat or drink something and notice the sensations.

Like ABC categories, this practice has many helpful variations. The 5-4-3-2-1 strategy can also be done using a single sense. For example, anchoring yourself with rainbow colors, look around your environment and find five things that are red, four things that are orange, three things that are yellow, two things that are green, and one thing that is blue. Another option is to notice five things that are rectangular, four things that are circular, three things that are square, two things that are triangular, and one thing that's a wild card shape. Seriously, any permutation of 5-4-3-2-1 that helps anchor you is a winner. What else can you come up with?

Breathing techniques

Dozens of breathing techniques can be used as distress tolerance skills. The box breathing technique I described earlier—visualizing a box being drawn as you count your breath—just happens to be my go-to.

I called on this one when I was riding the subway home in New

York City one rush hour in February, and the train got stuck. Everyone was crammed in like sardines, I was overheating in my winter parka, and I felt like I was going to pass out. I was pressed up against a woman toting stinky takeaway on one side and a guy coughing shamelessly into my face on the other. There was literally nothing I could do to take the edge off but to breathe. Box breathing helped me ride out my discomfort without losing it in public.

■ ■ ■

Remember that distress tolerance techniques are a means to an end. If you rely solely on ice diving, ABC categories, or box breathing to treat your anxiety, you aren't going to get anywhere. In fact, these things could become safety behaviors, crutches on which you are dependent, and do little to help you to truly combat anxiety. These techniques are meant to help you to ride the wave of distress until it decreases *just enough* that you can do the actual anxiety-busting thing: facing your fears, practicing exposures, reducing accommodation, and riding out an extinction burst. When used in this way, distress tolerance skills increase your psychological flexibility and set you up for success.

Safety First

In the face of anxiety and distress, kids may act in ways that are truly unsafe. Some kids turn to self-injury, physical aggression, destruction of property, or suicidality. In these circumstances, parents can be understandably afraid that their child will hurt themself or someone else if they set limits.

I met with seventeen-year-old Rachel and her parents for an initial evaluation to assess her severe anxiety, panic, and depression. Rachel's parents reported that she would scream, throw objects, and threaten suicide when she was anxious or upset. This was understandably terrifying for everyone. To cope, her parents had desperately tried to ensure that Rachel experienced *zero* stress at home. They brought her meals to her room and cleared her plates. They made sure everyone was silent while she slept. They stopped allowing visitors to the house. But while home became a sanctuary of comfort, everywhere else was full of stressors that Rachel felt less and less able to handle. By the time we met, Rachel was homebound with no structure, expectations, or contact with anyone outside her family.

Rachel's parents cared so deeply about her that they had upended their world to try to help. Of course, the zero-stress goal was an impossible endeavor, and by the time we met, even the slightest inconvenience sent her into a panic-fueled, high-risk meltdown. Her parents were held hostage to the fear that Rachel would get so upset that she would hurt herself. And Rachel's anxiety, depression, and suicidality had only worsened despite the family's extraordinary efforts.

These situations are really tricky. While anxiety disorders may be fueling the distress in these circumstances, anxiety is no longer the top problem. Without confidence that a child has some level of control over their behaviors, and without a solid safety plan in place, most clinicians would not recommend starting with anxiety-based treatment that involves exposure work or accommodation reduction—not because it wouldn't ultimately be helpful for the child's anxiety, but because the child doesn't yet have the skills to cope safely with tough feelings during an extinction burst. The priority becomes getting those risky behaviors under control to ensure the safety of the child and those around them. This was the case for Rachel.

It's often recommended that kids in these circumstances get treatment targeting emotion dysregulation, aggression, or self-injurious or suicidal behaviors *before* focusing on their anxiety through exposure-based treatment. Sometimes this involves participating in treatment at a higher level of care, like completing a day treatment, residential, or inpatient treatment program. Dialectical behavior therapy (DBT) is the recommended psychological treatment approach for those struggling with self-harm or suicidal behaviors. Rachel and her family needed to take this approach first before anxiety work could be helpful and safe.

It can be really frustrating for families who know that their child's issues are rooted in anxiety to be told that their child needs to get another type of treatment first. But prioritizing anxiety disorder treatment over safety and behavioral control is like trying to lift heavy weights when you have never done any strength training. Anxiety disorder treatment is going to be so much more helpful when fears that your child will hurt themself or someone else are no longer top of mind. Thorough diagnostic assessment is always the best way to clarify the best treatment plan for your child and your family, helping you to prioritize the most pressing symptoms and to increase the likelihood of treatment success.

The Flexibility Factor: Roll Back Without Backing Down

Sometimes an exposure pushes anxiety higher than expected. If distress gets so high that you risk capitulating to anxiety's demands, it can be reasonable to modify in the moment.

Between the two poles of either giving in to anxiety entirely by quitting the exposure or rigidly digging your heels in by forcing the exposure to continue, you can find a psychologically flexible, middle-path approach, one that allows you to balance responding sensitively to your child by setting limits as you'd intended. CBT therapists call this approach to tough exposures "rolling back without backing down." It means that you shift the exposure slightly so that you roll back the intensity of the demand, rather than backing down entirely and letting anxiety win the day.

Let's return to Charlie, who struggled with the "contaminated" groceries. Recall that his mom felt overwhelmed when Charlie's distress spiked following a grocery trip, so she removed all the groceries from the house and sanitized them. What's a middle-path approach between leaving all of Charlie's "contaminated" groceries in the kitchen and taking them outside to decontaminate them? Maybe removing the items from the fridge but leaving the ones in the pantry. Or letting Charlie choose five items that he wanted to be removed and cleaned, keeping the rest. Either of these options remains a challenge for anxiety and allows for a learning opportunity, albeit a less complete one.

In these situations, it can be helpful to validate and present alternative exposure options as a choice. For example, you might say, "I can tell that you are really overwhelmed, and I know that we can still find a way to fight back against anxiety. I will not let anxiety win by taking all of the groceries out of the house, but we can do one of two things instead," and then offer the choice. In this way, we model psychologically flexible, compassionate support that meets our child where they are, while maintaining limits around anxiety.

What Can You Take Home with You?

- Setting limits disrupts the cycle of anxiety, and while your kid may not be pleased, it can be one of the best things you can do as a parent to help them. But don't set a limit if you can't follow through. You will only embolden anxiety, create more unpredictability and uncertainty, and teach your kid that you don't mean what you say.

- Building in self-care can seem impossible, especially if you don't have the luxury of being able to call upon a partner, friend, or family member to help lighten the load. But if there is even the smallest way to take the edge off during a challenging season, it's absolutely worth exploring. Before you write it off entirely, please give yourself the grace of considering if there is *anything* that you can do or take off your plate to help you refuel.

- Distress tolerance skills can help kids *and* adults. Just make sure that you and your child understand what these skills will and won't achieve. Remember that they turn the volume down on strong emotions, helping you ride out the emotional storm, so that you don't do something that makes your situation worse. But don't expect distress tolerance skills to get rid of painful thoughts and feelings entirely. It's the feelings that prompt change, and you are capable of coping.

CHAPTER 14

Finding Your Way

"I don't even know where to start."

My friend Sarah had called looking for guidance. She and I have been close since high school and have always kept in touch. From what she was sharing, it sounded like her daughter was struggling with a clinical anxiety disorder and would benefit from exposure-based CBT. Sarah lives in an area of the country where I don't have any direct referrals, meaning that she was unfortunately tasked with navigating her local healthcare system to try to find accessible, affordable, quality care for her child with few leads. It was, understandably, overwhelming. And she had questions.

First, there were facts that she simply didn't know and that required some digging. She didn't know what mental health benefits she had through her insurance. She also wasn't sure how to assess her local providers. Was it worth seeing a therapist who didn't take insurance if they provided the exposure-based CBT her daughter needed? Sarah's oldest child had seen a play therapist years ago, and while it was helpful, she thought that her middle daughter needed a more structured approach to address her anxiety.

On top of all that, Sarah was worried that her daughter would resist treatment. She also wasn't sure whether her daughter would need medication, or if therapy would be sufficient. And Sarah worried about logistics; she felt like she couldn't possibly fit in therapy for her daughter while also juggling her many other responsibilities as a working parent with three kids.

Sarah's questions are common ones, but that doesn't make them any easier to answer.

The mental health landscape in the United States is extremely challenging. There are a dizzying number of decisions to make, and many of the variables are constrained by affordability and insurance coverage, the availability of the provider, and logistical and geographic barriers to accessing treatment.

There's no one-size-fits-all guidance to crack the healthcare code. But it helps to anchor yourself with greater knowledge about a few elements of the treatment-seeking process. You now know that CBT that incorporates exposure work is the most recommended approach for anxiety in kids and adults. Learning a bit more about the ways that you might access it and some alternatives if it's not the right fit is a really good place to start.

In this chapter, we'll look at the different types of CBT and touch on frontline psychiatric medication recommendations for anxiety as well. We will also consider evidence-based alternatives to traditional CBT. The goal is to provide you with a road map for seeking care and navigating a confusing—and often inequitable—healthcare system. There is help, if you know what you're looking for and where to look.

You've Got Options

Like most forms of psychotherapy, CBT was initially developed for individual outpatient therapy, meaning therapy involving a patient and a therapist, taking place once a week for sessions of forty-five to sixty minutes. It's been adapted over time, retaining the core content but shifting the treatment format or delivery mechanism, providing alternatives for individuals and families seeking anxiety disorder treatment that fits their lifestyles and needs. Here are some of the options.

Group-based CBT

CBT for anxiety can be effectively delivered through group therapy. This approach provides the chance for people to learn from and support one another. This can be particularly useful for folks with social anxiety, providing a safe and validating space to practice engaging in social situations. During the COVID-19 pandemic, the clinic where I work shifted our group-based treatment into a virtual format. For kids who were struggling with their anxiety in literal isolation, the opportunity to connect with peers who were also struggling, to practice skills, and to support one another in taking charge of their mental health was a lifeline.

Intensive CBT

Intensive treatment approaches deliver more treatment, more quickly, through longer or more frequent sessions, or both. These programs are called intensive outpatient programs, or IOPs. This intensive approach can function as a bit of a jump start, putting you on the right path to addressing your anxiety.

Intensive CBT can be a good fit for people who can devote a concentrated period of time to their mental health. For kids, this could be during holiday or summer vacations. For adults, intensive CBT makes sense when you have a clear goal and where time is a factor. For example, if you want to address your fear of flying so you can take your kids to Disney World over spring break, an intensive treatment might be great. It can be particularly helpful for folks without local access to CBT. Many families who attend treatment in the clinic that I help direct outside of Boston relocate temporarily for treatment and receive a year's worth of CBT in just a few weeks through our intensive treatment approach.

Behavioral parent training

CBT for child anxiety can also be delivered through a behavioral parent training approach. This means that while the child is the patient, the therapist works primarily with the parents. Parents explore their responses to their child's anxiety, learn coping strategies to manage their own anxiety and distress, and get guidance to shift their behavior in response to their child's anxiety.

Behavioral parent training approaches are most often recommended for children younger than eight, or for kids who are struggling to participate in their own treatment. Behavioral parent training can be very helpful even if a kid has their own therapist, and this approach is even more vital if kids are unable to engage in their own treatment.

Telehealth and CBT

While the internet has many sins for which to answer, increased accessibility to mental healthcare is not one of them. Through various platforms and formats, greater internet access and technological literacy has expanded healthcare options, allowing patients and families to access needed support, often at a reduced cost and regardless of geography.

Some technology-based approaches involve the delivery of CBT with little to no therapist involvement. These approaches are self-paced and are sort of like playing a videogame or taking an online class. Other approaches leverage smartphone technology to deliver treatment content. Thousands of behavioral health apps are available for download. But these apps aren't required to show that they work before they are released to consumers, so it is truly a mixed bag—I can't say that I have found a fully virtual program that I could confidently recommend as a substitute for involvement with a therapist to treat clinically interfering anxiety disorders. Virtual reality and artificial intelligence technologies are poised to alter the landscape, but we have a ways to go.

I do have a lot of confidence in CBT delivered via telehealth formats that use videoconferencing-based methods. Virtual platforms like Zoom allow patients and therapists to meet together, remotely and in real time, to do the kind of work they would do if they were together, in person, in the therapist's office. By and large, research does *not* find meaningful differences in treatment outcomes for children or adults receiving treatment remotely versus in person. Telehealth-based approaches often facilitate more parent participation in their child's treatment. And as telehealth-based therapies become more common, you are no longer restricted to finding a clinician in your area. In fact, more therapists are getting licensed in multiple states, so you may be able to meet virtually with a provider from a different state who provides excellent care for you or your kid. So while telehealth may not be a perfect fit for everyone, it can be a solid, evidence-based option for accessing quality care. One caveat is that younger kids, or kids who struggle with sustained attention or concentration, may have more trouble participating in fully virtual CBT. In these cases, I typically recommend in-person or behavioral parent training approaches.

You Can Bring a Horse to Water, But . . .

What if your kid refuses to go to therapy? Or what if they attend but won't participate in a meaningful way?

If this is your experience, you are not alone. When you have found a therapist, often after spending tons of time and energy in the search, it's natural to feel frustrated when you don't see your kid making good use of the treatment that they so desperately need. It's one of the most maddening examples of the universal experience that we have as parents, where we have all of the responsibility and none of the power.

Engagement can be a barrier for many families who are seeking treatment for their child's anxiety. It's a different calculus than with adults. The majority of adults seeking treatment for anxiety disorders are invested in getting care; anxiety is impacting their life negatively and they want to do something about it.

For young people with anxiety disorders, treatment-seeking is often driven by parents, and kids can be resistant to therapy for a variety of reasons. Kids are still developing emotional awareness, and they may have limited insight into the ways that anxiety is affecting them. Kids are more likely to experience anxiety through physical complaints—like stomachaches or headaches—and may balk at the notion that their distress is due to anxiety. They also don't have the foresight to see how their life could continue to be disrupted if the disorder goes untreated. Kids who are avoiding school, fun activities, or friends because of anxiety can't fully grasp the milestones that they will miss, and don't see how this can derail their development over time. They may also have learned some reinforcing coping strategies to handle their anxiety, and they are reluctant to change. A child who is coping with anxiety by insisting that Mom sleep with him every night is not going to be up for starting a treatment that he knows is geared—at least in part—to getting Mom back to her own bed. So they may not be motivated to participate in therapy.

Or consider a kid with anxiety-driven school refusal. For this kid, school is a scary place where they are vulnerable to any number of stressful or frightening experiences—judgment from peers, inability to leave when they want to, separation from parents, unpredictable situations, and academic pressures. In contrast, home is their "safe space." Not only is home free of school's demands, but it's full of cozy and pleasant elements, like a warm bed, comfy couch, streaming services, pantry access, videogames, and snuggles with the cat. So many kids with anxiety-driven school refusal aren't all that motivated to get back to school.

While these kids may understand on some level that staying home from school isn't doing them any favors, the more they avoid school the harder it is to go back. It is pretty common to encounter parents who are seeking treatment for their school-refusing kid and for the kid to have *zero willingness* to meet with the therapist: They know that the goal of the adults in their life is to get them out of their bubble and back into school, which is terrifying. (If you're looking for more information on school refusal behaviors, check out the Appendix at the back of this book.)

I hate to break it to you, but therapists also can't "make" a child engage in treatment, particularly in treatment like CBT that is active and skills based. Rarely do I meet a kid who is psyched to be in therapy, but even a little buy-in is helpful. If a kid comes to treatment with the acknowledgment that their anxiety symptoms are messing things up for them—making it harder for them to enjoy the things that they love, taking up too much headspace, dictating what they can and can't do—and if they are somewhat open to exploring different ways to make things better, that is a great starting place.

For the (understandably) hesitant child starting therapy, therapists work to first and foremost develop trust. Therapeutic alliance—meaning the strength of the relationship between the patient and the therapist—plays a large role in treatment outcome, regardless of the type of therapy. If your kid does not like or does not trust their therapist, it doesn't matter how "good" that therapist is; treatment gains are going to be hard to come by. So when a kid is more hesitant, therapists may spend more sessions building trust and rapport early on. Along the way, we work to build motivation for change. We can help improve emotional awareness and identification for a child who doesn't view their struggles as anxiety. In partnership with parents, we can work to establish incentives to help encourage participation.

I hold out hope that CBT can and will be a good approach for everyone with anxiety at some point in their life. So I don't want to burn the CBT bridge early by "forcing" a kid—or a young adult who is meeting with me only at the urging of their parents—into CBT when they aren't willing. Then their narrative becomes "I tried CBT years ago and it didn't work for me," rather than "I tried CBT when I was younger, but it wasn't the right time."

And there are other options. CBT for anxiety disorders can—and sometimes should—be combined with or preceded by other approaches, like psychiatric medication, supportive therapy, peer mentorship, or social skills training, to name a few. This needs to be determined on a case-by-case basis.

Your Alternatives

Medication-based approaches

As a clinical psychologist, I don't prescribe medication. But it's often a helpful part of treatment for anxiety disorders, and so I want to touch on the ones that are most commonly prescribed: antidepressant medications called selective serotonin reuptake inhibitors (SSRIs), and anti-anxiety medications called benzodiazepines. If you are looking for more information about psychiatric medications from somebody who went to medical school, start with your primary care provider or your child's pediatrician. They will be able to answer your questions or refer you to a psychiatrist or psychiatric nurse practitioner with specialized expertise in the medication-based treatment of anxiety.

We know that for kids with anxiety, antidepressant medication is about as effective as participating in weekly CBT. This is good news, because it means that if you don't have access to CBT or other psychotherapy, or your kid is struggling to engage in therapy, they may get some symptom relief by taking antidepressant medications. You may recognize the names of fluoxetine (Prozac), sertraline (Zoloft), or escitalopram (Lexapro), among others. At a very basic level, these SSRIs work by blocking the reuptake of serotonin in the spaces between neurons, increasing the amount of serotonin hanging out in the brain, which is helpful for improving anxiety and mood symptoms. And yes, antidepressant medications can be helpful for anxiety disorders, not just depression.

In the United States, the Food and Drug Administration (FDA) has approved the use of SSRIs for the treatment of anxiety disorders and depression in adults and in children as young as seven (and sertraline/ Zoloft is approved for the treatment of OCD in kids as young as six). Compared to other types of antidepressant medications, SSRIs are reasonably well-tolerated by many people and are non-habit-forming. It typically takes a few weeks of using the medication daily to begin to feel the beneficial effects. As with all medications, there can be side effects for both kids and adults: stomach distress, headaches, weight gain, sleep disturbances, and sexual dysfunction, among others.

There is a potential risk of increased suicidal thinking in children and adolescents who take SSRIs. While the risk is quite low, it is crucial that young people have regular follow-up appointments with their prescriber when starting SSRIs. For the vast majority of young people who take these medications, we don't see suicidal thinking increase, and patients find that the benefits outweigh the risks and side effects. And we know that untreated anxiety disorders and depression often lead to increases in suicidal thoughts and urges. Taken together, the pros and cons of taking medication should be carefully evaluated with the prescriber.

Parents often have valid hesitations about initiating any type of medication regimen with their child. This is why, even though the literature supports CBT with SSRIs as the "best" approach to the treatment of anxiety in young people, many providers recommend starting with CBT-only first to see if symptoms can be improved without the use of medication. Happily, this is often the case, particularly for anxiety disorders of mild to moderate severity. If the anxiety symptoms are so severe that the child is struggling to benefit from CBT because they are too anxious, I am more likely to recommend adding medication.

Sometimes kids don't want anything to do with therapy but are eager to swallow a pill once a day. If that's what helps this kid get their life back, it's worth considering.

Sometimes it's the opposite, and kids who are in therapy have fears about adding medications. During my postdoctoral fellowship, I worked with Declan, a bright eighteen-year-old senior in high school who was highly engaged in treatment but whose anxiety symptoms were really overwhelming. Declan was super motivated, showing up for his session each week, eager to learn. He was trying *so hard* to shift his behaviors and lean into the exposure work, but the physical symptoms of his anxiety were just so high that he reported extraordinary distress in trying to face his fears and couldn't fully make use of the stuff he was learning in treatment. Part of this was because he wanted to do it all by himself. This perfectionism impacted his life in many other ways as well, and he felt like taking medication meant that he wasn't strong enough. When he felt anxiety increase, he also noticed his thoughts telling him "You *have* to do this by yourself," which only increased his anxiety. Declan also reported fears that taking an SSRI would change his personality. "Isn't it, like, a happy pill?" he asked me. He was afraid to lose himself.

As much as his parents and I supported his hard work and independence, we also saw that he was really struggling and that his progress was slow. Part of our work together involved dispelling the myths that he believed about taking medication and shifting his beliefs around what it meant to be strong. Declan did eventually begin an SSRI as he continued in CBT, and within a few weeks we began to see benefits. He reflected that he didn't feel like a different person—on the contrary, he felt more like himself. Taking a medication didn't make anxiety go away, but it turned the dial down on the intensity so that he could do the things that actually help anxiety diminish over time— exposure practices. Ultimately that meant that he could wrap up with both treatment and medication more quickly and get back to living his fantastic young life.

A word about benzodiazepines, which are often prescribed for anxiety: These are medications like alprazolam (Xanax), clonazepam (Klonopin), or lorazepam (Ativan). Unlike SSRIs, benzodiazepines decrease the experience of anxiety quickly—they are a solid Band-Aid approach. However, this means that benzodiazepines are more likely to lead to dependence, misuse, and abuse, so they should not be prescribed in the context of a substance abuse history or for people who are prone to abusing prescription medications. It's important to note that they have an increased mortality risk if they are misused in combination with opiates. They can also interfere with how well CBT works because they reduce the physical feelings of anxiety in the moment, undermining the fundamental goal of exposure—which is to learn that you can tolerate an anxiety-provoking situation *despite* your feelings of anxiety. So they should be a temporary solution, and their administration should be monitored closely.

ACT and DBT

During your search for anxiety disorder treatment, you may come across the terms *acceptance and commitment therapy* (ACT) and *dialectical behavior therapy* (DBT). These are both versions of CBT that can be extremely helpful in addressing anxiety disorders. I integrate a lot of ACT- and DBT-based techniques and theory into my clinical work, and this book is influenced by these approaches as well.

ACT is used to address a range of concerns: treating anxiety and depression, managing chronic pain, and coping with life's stressors. At its core, ACT prioritizes the development of psychological flexibility (one of the many reasons why I love it), integrates exposures through what it terms "committed action," and prioritizes mindfulness. ACT works about as well as traditional CBT in treating anxiety disorders and is a terrific option, particularly for older kids and adolescents as well as adults.

DBT was initially developed to help people who were experiencing chronic suicidality and self-harm, and many of the strategies in DBT can be applied to good effect for anxiety disorders as well. But typically we wouldn't recommend DBT for the treatment of primary anxiety disorders unless the patient was also struggling with other issues, like emotion regulation difficulties, challenges in relationships with others, identity instability, or self-harm and suicidality.

How Do I Find a Therapist?

Start by asking your primary care physician for referral recommendations. If you are looking for care for your kid, reach out to their pediatrician and their school's guidance or counseling office. See if local hospitals or community health centers have outpatient behavioral health clinics. Ask your friends, family, and neighbors if they have recommendations for good providers. Or inquire on community-centered online forums.

There are some good online resources as well, which I have listed here and in the Resources section at the back of this book. Consider geography; whether the therapist holds sessions in person, online, or both; whether they accept your insurance; and the type of therapy that they provide.

- Association for Behavioral and Cognitive Therapies (ABCT): www.abct.org. This organization is all about CBT. It has terrific educational information and a Find a Therapist service to help you locate a provider who is more likely to be trained in the approaches outlined in this book.
- Anxiety and Depressive Disorders Association of America (ADAA): www.adaa.org. This organization is a great resource for best-practice information for the treatment of anxiety and related disorders, with a Find a Therapist directory that lists members who have expertise in treating these conditions.
- Supportive Parenting for Anxious Childhood Emotions (SPACE) treatment: www.spacetreatment.net. This website is dedicated to the parent-based treatment for child anxiety that I have referenced throughout. You can find more information about SPACE treatment, and there is a directory of providers who have received training in this approach.
- Society of Clinical Child and Adolescent Psychology. The division of the American Psychological Association dedicated spe-

cifically to mental health in kids has created a website to promote evidence-based therapies for kids. They have a ton of great resources, as well as a Find a Therapist tool. Visit them at www.effectivechildtherapy.org.

- The American Psychological Association's Therapist Locator: www.locator.apa.org.
- The National Register of Health Service Psychologists: www .findapsychologist.org.
- Psychology Today's Find a Therapist tool: www.psychology today.com.

Some Troublesome Truths

One of the hard truths about finding evidence-based anxiety disorder treatment is how few providers are trained to offer this type of care. And let's face it: It's a challenge in the United States to find *any* mental healthcare, given widespread shortages in mental health professionals. A 2009 study showed that 18 percent of counties in the United States had unmet needs for mental health providers, and a 2023 study showed that nearly 20 percent of counties in the United States do not have a single psychiatrist. For adults, finding a provider who can offer CBT has been cited as one of the greatest challenges in addressing anxiety disorders.

Despite the landmark 2008 Medical Health Parity and Addiction Equity Act, which aimed to address discrepancies in insurance coverage for behavioral health conditions and to prevent insurance companies from imposing excessive limits on behavioral health benefits, things haven't gotten much better. Out-of-network usage continues to be many times higher for behavioral health treatment than for medical treatment, and in-network reimbursement levels are much lower for behavioral health providers than for medical providers.

This system massively disincentivizes behavioral health clinicians from partnering with insurance companies, and more and more are leaving insurance networks altogether. Kids and families are caught in the middle.

Cost is, of course, a major barrier to accessing mental healthcare, even for those with adequate insurance coverage. Children from low-income households are more likely to experience mental health concerns but less likely to receive the care that they need. In addition to cost, such families also report more systematic and logistical barriers to accessing care—things like inflexible work schedules, transportation issues, or childcare conflicts.

This state of affairs only amplifies inequality, as ethnic minority families are more likely to have lower incomes. But money is only part of the inequity equation: Regardless of socioeconomic status, white children are more likely to access mental healthcare than their Black and Latinx counterparts, and Latinx youth with anxiety and depression are the most likely racial/ethnic group to have unmet healthcare needs. This is a vicious cycle and a huge public health issue.

Steps for Working with Insurance Companies

It's really important to understand your unique health insurance coverage situation before connecting with a therapist. You want to determine what your options are for in-network and out-of-network coverage, and what each is likely to cost you. See the following broad guidelines that can help point you in the right direction.

I can't stress this enough: Take notes during each call that you have with an insurance representative or your human resources department. Note the date, the time, the name of the person with whom you spoke, and the details of your conversation. This stuff gets tricky and confusing, and you will thank yourself later for having a paper trail.

First, what's your insurance coverage situation?

- Review your healthcare plan to determine your behavioral healthcare benefits. Your plan description should include information on what is covered under behavioral health services or for mental health disorders. Call your human resources department or the insurance company itself to understand what your plan offers. Not all healthcare plans provide coverage for behavioral health or mental healthcare.

- If you do have behavioral health coverage, determine if there are any limits on what they will cover. For example, some plans will cover a certain number of treatment sessions but then need proof that ongoing care is "medically necessary." If this is the case, get clarity from your insurance company on what their criteria are for "medically necessary" and how this needs to be demonstrated. Confirm if you have a deductible that you need to pay prior to insurance coverage kicking in, and what it is. Figure out what your copay is for behavioral health sessions, because it may be different from your copay for seeing your primary care provider.

What's the deal with out-of-network providers?

- Out-of-network providers aren't contracted with your insurance company, so they don't receive payment through the insurance company. You pay your therapist the full fee at the time of session, and they give you a superbill, which you submit to your insurance company with a claim form to request reimbursement for whatever portion of the cost your plan will reimburse. Your insurance company processes the claim and mails you a check for reimbursement.

- Before you go this route, figure out if your plan reimburses for out-of-network providers, and at what rate. This helps you determine what percentage of the session cost you will get back.

Typically, insurance companies will reimburse 50 to 80 percent of the cost of each session. For a $200 session, that means you may get back $160, bringing the cost per session to $40. If your copay would have been $30 for a provider who takes insurance, this might make out-of-network care a possibility. Ask whether prior authorization is needed to use out-of-network benefits, and if there is a maximum coverage limit.

What if I don't have behavioral health benefits or insurance coverage?

- Get in touch with your state's mental health agency to get a list of providers who offer sliding-scale fees. This means providers who charge based on patients' income, offering lower fees to families with lower income.
- Inquire about behavioral healthcare options at a community health center.
- Contact the National Alliance on Mental Illness (NAMI) to inquire about referrals.
- Check with your employer to see if they offer therapeutic support through an employee assistance program (EAP).
- Explore online therapy platforms that may have sliding-scale fees.

Room for Hope

In the meantime, I encourage you not to dismiss providers who don't accept insurance before doing some digging. Start by calling your insurance company and clarifying your out-of-network coverage and reimbursement rates. Most providers who do not accept insurance will still provide you with documentation (a superbill) that you can submit to your insurance company for reimbursement as an out-of-network provider. Depending on your coverage, you may be reimbursed for part of the out-of-pocket cost for therapy. Many folks find that a significant proportion of each session is reimbursable, making short-term CBT accessible.

In addition, many larger practices that don't take insurance do have sliding-scale fees, where the amount you pay for sessions is based on your annual income, number of household dependents, and so on. Scholarship funding may also be available to support the cost of care, particularly within larger organizations.

Another option is to look for CBT that is delivered as part of a training clinic for doctoral students in clinical psychology. Treatment delivered by these student clinicians is often available at a reduced fee, compared with fees for seeing a psychologist who already has their doctorate, and licensed clinical psychologists supervise the students' clinical work, so you actually have two professionals involved in your care.

My friend Sarah had success by pursuing this avenue. She found a clinic that trained doctoral students and offered treatment at a reduced rate, and her daughter connected immediately with her graduate student clinician. The clinic wasn't close—they couldn't get there for weekly in-person appointments—but it offered a telehealth option as well as a virtual skills and support group for parents of anxious kids. Virtual therapy made it easier for Sarah to participate in treatment sessions as needed while juggling work and the needs of her other two children. And the short-term nature of CBT meant that her daughter's symptoms improved within a few months, which made the cost manageable for Sarah and her family.

It's a challenging landscape for sure, and one that does nothing to improve the stress and anxiety of already overburdened parents. But there are reasons to be optimistic. More and more clinicians are learning how to deliver CBT that integrates the approaches highlighted in this book, meaning more opportunities for quality care for families in need.

But crucially, I want you to know that research consistently shows that one of the very best protections a kid can have is a stable relationship with at least one safe, steady, nurturing adult. This means that *you* are your child's best protection and greatest strength, just by being there and loving them. When I feel overwhelmed by the system-based soul-crushers that make me worry for my kid, this is my North Star. Let it be yours as well.

The Flexibility Factor: You Are Enough

You're doing your best, but a nagging inner voice is constantly berating you: "You missed her basketball game last week, you're ordering too much takeout, you haven't spent enough money, your house is a mess, you're letting him have too much screen time, you're not emotionally regulated enough to be a good model."

Next time you find yourself in one of these parent-guilt spirals, pause. Notice what thoughts and feelings are coming up for you. Are there any potential thinking traps in there? Things like "I'm the worst parent" or "This is all my fault" or "I am not doing enough for my kid"? Remind yourself that feelings aren't facts, and thoughts aren't necessarily the truth.

Validate yourself that all caring parents are vulnerable to these thoughts and feelings. This is the sharp end of parenting.

But consider this: How are you likely to behave if you fuse with the thought "I'm not enough" and get hooked? If you let this thought drag you around and dictate how you behave? I'd probably ping-pong between overparenting or wallowing in parental self-loathing. I might fall into an internet vortex to try to fix whatever I think I am doing wrong, or volunteer for *all the things* when I don't have the bandwidth, or buy stuff my kid doesn't need, all in the service of trying to make myself feel like I am enough. Or I could get increasingly self-focused and grumpy and not take care of myself. My daughter would have either a hyped-up, overstretched mom trying to win at parenting, or an irritable, sluggish mom who is throwing herself a pity party. Neither of these outcomes is good for me, and it's certainly not good for her.

Any of this sound familiar?

Guilt can be a helpful emotion when it encourages you to shift behavior that needs to be shifted, but it's decidedly not helpful when it's leading you to rake yourself over the coals in deference to unattainable parenting ideals. So get curious about what might be driving your parenting guilt. How much of it is driven by your perception of how other people might think you should be parenting in this situation? Or are you giving your kid exactly what they need to be resilient: a steady, nurturing adult presence that combines love and limits?

Getting hooked by Intensive Parenting–fueled guilt helps no one. It's burnout-inducing and demoralizing, particularly if you're already threadbare. Instead, can you hold these thoughts and feelings lightly? Let them be the beach ball in the pool, knowing that they will bump into you from time to time but they don't have to dictate your experience. Your relationship with your kid is what counts the most. You are enough.

What Can You Take Home with You?

- Consider therapy that is delivered through less conventional formats. You may assume that once-weekly, in-person, individual therapy is your only good option, but CBT can be delivered through different structures and formats, and often kids do just as well, or better, with these options. I've worked with many families who were skeptical about group treatments, virtual treatments, intensive treatments, or parent-only treatments, but who ultimately got so much out of them. So I encourage you to be open-minded.

- Finding a therapist who is accessible, affordable, and qualified and who you actually like can feel like looking for a needle in a haystack. It will likely be a more streamlined and successful process once you first get clarity about your financial picture by figuring out what options you have under your insurance plan. Depending on your policy's reimbursement rates, out-of-network options may ultimately be more affordable than you were expecting, opening more doors. So get a cup of coffee to fuel you when you're put on hold and call your insurance company. Don't forget to take notes.

CONCLUSION

How the Struggle Becomes Strength

My daughter began asking to take Irish step dance when she was three. My husband and I took her to a brewery one afternoon around St. Patrick's Day (quality parenting choice, right there) where she saw some Irish step dancers. She was mesmerized. I eventually signed her up, and like the kid trying karate class in Chapter 10, she balked on the first day. She started crying and refused to enter the classroom.

"I've seen this movie before," I thought, recalling all the kids I had cared for whose anxiety first found a foothold in situations just like these. "No, ma'am."

I got my exposure pants on. "This feels hard because it's new." I validated her while she clung to me, and rounded it out with a supportive statement: "And I know you can do this." Then, I set an expectation: "You can go in when you want, but we aren't leaving until the end of class." I stood up, actively ignored her clinging and crying, giving praise when I saw her peek into the class or do anything that showed she was warming up to the idea. She stayed at the door the whole time and cried. I stood with her. And then we left.

Sure, I'd seen this movie before . . . but not in my family. Honestly, it really threw me.

Not because I hadn't anticipated it. My kid had never been the first one down the slide, so based on her temperament, I expected that we might be in this situation at some point. And not because I didn't feel prepared practically—I knew what to do in the moment, and what to do moving forward.

We went back every week until she started participating in the class. When she was calm, outside of class, we talked. We talked about how her big feelings were normal and wouldn't hurt her. We talked about how she could do hard things. She helped come up with a rewards plan. And we started off small, agreeing that she would earn that first reward if she went into the class for one minute, and then build from there. It took a week or two before she plucked up the courage to actually go in. But she did, and she stayed, and she's been loving it ever since.

It all looks neat and easy, doesn't it? The headline could be *Child psychologist expertly guides kid in "love and limits" approach, aces anxiety.*

Hold your applause. If you rewind the tape, you'll see it was anything but seamless. I had not anticipated how much I would question myself during those few weeks.

When she didn't go into class the second week, I started noticing some doubts. Rationally, I knew I might have to give this exposure plan a few weeks to work—that's absolutely what I would tell anyone else who was in the same boat. But when it's your own kid, you second-guess everything.

So I did what any modern parent does when they have doubts. I explored online, and the social media algorithms found me immediately. I was bombarded by the Intensive Parenting narrative, which told me that I was on track to scar my kid for life. The content I was served up urged me to prioritize attachment (translation: *You'll no longer be her safe space if you keep taking her to class, your relationship is doomed*), always follow my child's lead (translation: *You're traumatizing her by taking her to class before she's "ready"*), and to never use tangible rewards (translation: *She'll think your love is conditional, you're raising a people-pleaser who'll end up in an abusive relationship*).

I'd been able to see this type of content before and not get sucked in. But in a moment when I was questioning how best to help my struggling kid, these messages amplified my uncertainty. I noticed that I was losing confidence in myself as a parent *and* as a child psychologist. I worried I was about to fail my kid.

My husband was a stabilizing force. "Meredith, you deal with this stuff all the time," he said when I questioned myself out loud. "No way she's quitting. That's not what you'd tell a patient, right?"

Right.

You Know Better

I had the benefit of six years of graduate training and a husband who knew better to steer me away from accommodating. In no way did it feel like an expert move on my part. All of which is to say, it is extraordinarily hard to parent when your kid is struggling with anxiety. It's even harder when they are struggling with an actual anxiety disorder, particularly if it's been controlling the family dynamic for a long time, or if you're contending with an anxiety disorder of your own.

But having read this book, you now know *so much* more. You now know that feelings aren't facts, and that thoughts aren't the truth. You now know that anxiety is painful but not harmful, and that feeling uncomfortable is *not* synonymous with being unsafe. You know that wondering "Am I doing the right thing?" doesn't necessarily mean you are doing the wrong thing. You know that painful thoughts and feelings can bump into you, and now you can let them come and go without wasting your energy suppressing them. You know that behaviors are what really make a difference.

I hope that you can also notice when self-doubt, guilt, and anxiety rear up and then choose whether you get hooked. Harnessing your psychological flexibility, you can now pause, notice, and decide to act in ways that bring you closer to your values.

Because now you know that avoidance fuels anxiety, and that accommodation is a comfort trap. You know that either overparenting or undersupporting your kid is bad news for their anxiety. And you know that contemporary parenting culture too often sanctifies overparenting as "good parenting," and that anxiety has exploited this opportunity to set up shop in today's kids. You can resist the judgment of other parents when you know better, grounded in the awareness that good parenting in the face of anxiety is always compassionate but not always intensive.

And you know that resilience comes from facing fears head-on, with openness to discomfort, because that is how bravery muscles are built.

Turn Insight into Action

Knowing all these things is half the battle. I know that exercise is good for me, too, but understanding this and actually exercising are two very different things. To realize the benefits of exercise, I have to exercise. And that's harder. But it becomes self-reinforcing once I do it.

Same thing with the concepts and strategies in this book. For the benefits to be realized, you have to put them into practice. And once you do, they start building on one another. As you become stronger and more flexible, life opens up. I hope you can pocket the following four final suggestions as you move forward.

Avoid avoidance

Look for opportunities to push back against the urge to avoid. Do more things that feel uncomfortable or downright hard. Model this for your kids. Talk to your kids regularly about the link between avoidance and anxiety. Point this relationship out when you see it in movies, in books, in the behavior of others—and in yourself. Keep validating and use supportive statements. Check yourself before swooping in to rescue your kids from painful feelings. Praise and reward your kids for doing things that get them out of their comfort zone, that build their independence, and that give them new information about their amazing capabilities. As uncomfortable as it can be for both kids and parents, embracing discomfort when it matters empowers lasting growth.

Practice psychological flexibility

Like mindfulness, psychological flexibility can be practiced anytime, anywhere. Regularly practice pausing, noticing what you are experiencing in the moment, and then acting in line with your values. You can practice this in moments of contentment and in moments of pain. Acting according to your values might simply mean you choose to continue what you are doing in the moment. But the practice of pausing to notice what's going on for you internally and then deliberately taking committed action helps you apply this skill during emotional storms, when you need it most.

Get more help if you need it

If anxiety is interfering in your life and causing distress, please don't hesitate to seek help. Anxiety disorders often respond well and quickly to good treatment. This means that anxiety disorders do not have to be a chronic condition, a permanent label, or a fixed identity. Yes, the healthcare system is an inequitable quagmire. But the hurdles of finding care just can't hold a candle to the distress and disability, missed opportunities, and untapped potential that can come from under-treated anxiety disorders. And despite all of the healthcare system's flaws, good people are working hard to increase access to assessment and treatment. There are more and more options to receive CBT for anxiety through a variety of treatment formats, structures, and organizations. And effective anxiety treatment can be truly transformative.

Reframe your thinking about what counts as "good" parenting

Cultural standards of what makes a "good" parent are always shifting. Today's good parent may look like one of hell's emissaries a generation from now. But we know that a love-and-limits parenting style—

marked by warmth, encouragement, and good communication, as well as clear expectations and boundaries—is good for kids. We also know that the abiding presence of a caring adult is one of the most impactful buffers against adversity that a kid can have, providing more protection than the latest high-end stroller, a fully organic diet, or a free ride to the college of their choice. You are enough.

■ ■ ■

In a world oversaturated with parenting opinions and advice, it is so important for you to have solid knowledge about anxiety. I never want you to be in the position of acting as your kid's therapist. But you also shouldn't feel powerless.

A cognitive behavioral approach to anxiety disorders isn't secret knowledge. This stuff is practical and useful and becomes clearer the more you apply these strategies. You don't have to be a therapist to challenge the misconception that what feels uncomfortable is also unsafe, or to move away from culturally sanctioned parenting methods when they aren't helping your kids. By aligning with your values and making compassionate, measured choices to counter anxiety, you can break the cycle and shape your child's resilience. What a powerful foundation to build for your kids.

ACKNOWLEDGMENTS

This project has had the uncommon good fortune to be shaped by two extraordinary editors. To Amanda Cook and Libby Burton, thank you both for the editorial wisdom and encouragement that helped bring this work into its final form. Your keen insights took *Parenting Anxiety* to the next level, and I am so grateful for your partnership. My deepest thanks to my agent, Zoë Pagnamenta, whose steady guidance, expertise, and unwavering advocacy for this project made all the difference.

I owe so much to the Crown team for believing in this work and helping it find its way into the world. Thank you to Gillian Blake for your early enthusiasm and for your advocacy throughout the process. To Katie Berry, I am so grateful for your professionalism, for your attention to detail, and for making each step feel manageable and clear. Deep appreciation to Andrea Lau and Rabiya Gupta for your beautiful and intuitive work on the interior layout and cover design, and for your responsiveness and patience throughout the decision-making process. Thank you as well to Natalie Blachere and Jessica Heim in production for the care and coordination that you brought to every detail. This book has benefited from the stewardship of an exceptional publicity and marketing team. Special thanks to Tammy Blake and Kimberly Lew for bringing your experience and strategic vision to this book. A special thanks also to Sally Holloway, Samantha Jackson, and my UK publishing team.

This book is grounded in decades of research and clinical practice led by pioneering behavioral health professionals. Their work has shaped our understanding of how anxiety develops, how it functions, and how it can be treated. I offer this book in gratitude and in service to this legacy—and to help carry this knowledge to the parents and kids who need it most. Thank you from the bottom of my heart to my academic mentors—with particular gratitude to Drs. Donna Pincus, Jonathan Comer, and R. Kathryn McHugh for their outstanding and enduring mentorship—and to the most talented and hilarious cohort of graduate student clinicians to ever earn a doctorate: Drs. Aubrey Carpenter, Gretchen Reynolds, Kate Bentley, Kristin Szuhany, Lauren Rutter, and Michelle Bourgeois.

Treating anxious kids and families is a skill set and an art form. I am so fortunate to practice with some of the very best. To the clinicians in the Child Division at McLean Hospital, and at the McLean Anxiety Mastery Program in particular, thank you for embodying this work every day with extraordinary skill and unwavering compassion. You provide the type of care that every parent wants for their kids.

To my brilliant work-wife, Dr. Julia Martin Burch, who shares a passion for this subject with me: You are simply the best. Thank you for every voice note, every animated conversation, and every moment you reminded me that this message matters. Your friendship has made this book infinitely richer, and I can't wait for the chapters still to come.

Many thanks to Drs. Anne Pezalla and Alice Davidson for your pioneering scholarship on gentle parenting. Our conversations have been enriching and energizing, and I look forward to future collaborations.

I am incredibly grateful to Emily Muller, who helped me wade through design questions I never dreamed I'd be asking. Your advice—especially in the moments I felt most uncertain—was invaluable.

To my ride-or-dies—Diana, Caroline, Laura, Liz, and Sarah—whose support has been as unwavering as it is generous: Thank you for cheering me on, for sticking around when I went quiet, and for reminding me of who I am outside of deadlines. Your loyalty and love through this long process has been a gift I will never forget.

To my parents, who have always been my most enthusiastic supporters, gratitude just doesn't cut it. Your encouragement, your interest, and your ability to find joy in each milestone—even when I was too exhausted to celebrate—meant the world. I carry your love for me, and for our family, in every word on these pages.

Thank you to my in-laws, who were friends before they were family, for your genuine encouragement and practical help throughout this process. Special thanks to my glitter-fabulous sister-in-law, Jenna, for lighting the path with your insight into the author's world. Thank you for reminding me that creativity and fun can (and should) go hand in hand.

To my husband, who is forever pushing himself to the bleeding edge of his capabilities, and who helped me to find mine, there are no words, but I will try. Thank you for encouraging me in this project, for reminding me why I started it, and for making room in our life for this book to exist. I can't wait to get our weekends back. You are my greatest teammate, the truest friend, and the most extraordinary father.

And to my daughter—my heart walking outside of my body, my greatest joy, my deepest love—you are all I ever wanted and more than I could have ever hoped for. Thank you for being the brightest light in every long day. You are the best thing I've ever had a hand in creating, and being your parent is the deepest privilege of my life. I love you to the moon and back.

Decoding Diagnoses

Self-diagnosis is rarely a useful endeavor (I'm looking at you, WebMD). However, having some knowledge of the different anxiety disorders and the conditions that often go along with them can be helpful when you are pursuing assessment and treatment.

In this section, we demystify the process of assessment and diagnosis for anxiety disorders and review the major anxiety disorders and commonly co-occurring conditions. Throughout, I reference the diagnostic criteria as described in the *Diagnostic and Statistical Manual of Mental Disorders,* 5th Edition, Text Revision (DSM-5-TR), the most comprehensive technical resource used by professionals to diagnose mental health conditions.

Why Diagnoses Matter

When you go to your primary care doctor with a fever, sore throat, congestion, and headache, your symptoms could be caused by lots of things. Your doctor will likely order a test that confirms a diagnosis of an influenza virus. "Flu" then becomes a shorthand that allows providers to communicate quickly and clearly about your condition. This in turn helps determine treatment. As a viral illness, the flu won't get better with antibiotics. So having the right diagnosis facilitates communication and informs the right treatment.

The same principle applies to mental health. There are many overlapping symptoms among mental health conditions. For example, difficulty with concentration is a symptom of both generalized anxiety disorder and attention deficit/hyperactivity disorder (ADHD). The treatment for these conditions, however, is very different, and treating the wrong condition means that the true concern is neglected and can get worse during treatment. On top of that, side effects of some medications prescribed to treat ADHD can increase anxiety, so if an anxious child with inattention difficulties is misidentified as having ADHD and treated with ADHD medications, their anxiety is likely to worsen. Accurate diagnosis is key. And if the results of an assessment indicate that you or your child does *not* meet full diagnostic criteria for a mental health condition, this information is helpful, too.

Psychological Assessments

Mental health assessment is like putting together a puzzle. A person comes to a clinician—who could be a psychologist, a psychiatrist, a school psychologist, a social worker, or another professional who specializes in mental and behavioral health conditions—with the puzzle pieces. The clinician's job is to put all of the pieces together to clarify the picture: to determine which if any diagnoses fit so that a good plan for treatment can be recommended. There are several ways to solve the puzzle, which vary based on the type of clinician you see and the concerns for which you are seeking care. For our purposes, we will focus on the assessment of anxiety and related disorders in adults and kids.

Psychodiagnostic evaluation

The most common assessment tool for identifying mental health conditions is a psychodiagnostic evaluation. This simply means having a conversation with a clinician about your symptoms. It can also be called a psychological interview, a clinical assessment, or an intake evaluation, but the process and goals are largely the same.

A psychodiagnostic evaluation often takes place during the first session or two of starting therapy, or as a onetime consultation. It's typically one to three hours long. It is a chance for the clinician to ask questions about you, about your life and the important people in it, about your identity and the things that you value, and about your symptoms and how they are messing things up for you. Importantly, the evaluation process gives you the chance to get to know the clinician and see if you feel comfortable working together. The process should feel conversational and ideally is the start of a meaningful therapeutic relationship.

Adults seeking assessment will most likely meet one-on-one with the clinician, perhaps in-person in their office, but increasingly clinicians are meeting via telehealth with patients of all ages. You may also be asked to complete some self-report questionnaires, which the clinician will review to learn more about your symptoms. The clinician may also ask your permission to connect with people in your life who know you well, like a spouse or—for young adults in particular—a parent. Or they may ask to connect with other providers who know you, like your primary care physician, your psychiatrist, or your past or current therapists. Contact with others helps the clinician clarify the diagnostic puzzle and establishes good continuity of care among your healthcare providers.

If you are seeking a diagnostic evaluation for your child, the clinician will likely want to meet with you and your child, either together or separately, to learn more. Clinicians who work with young people understand that speaking with a seven-year-old about their mental health is different from speaking with a seventeen-year-old. Clinicians typically rely more on the reports of parents and caregivers with younger children than with older children. But not always. I've met with some wildly articulate and insightful seven-year-olds, and I've met with seventeen-year-olds who struggle to communicate. A good clinician gets that it can be tough to talk about personal things with a stranger, no matter how old you are, and will help you and your child to feel comfortable and understood.

In addition to a clinical interview, you and your child may be asked to complete questionnaires about your child's symptoms. There may also be parent-specific questionnaires to help the clinician learn more about your stress level, your response to your child's symptoms, and the impact of your child's symptoms on family life. Clinicians may also give you questionnaires to pass along to your child's teachers to further round out your child's diagnostic picture. Clinicians may ask for parents' permission to contact other professionals who know your child to clarify diagnoses—their pediatrician, their school counselor, or past or current therapists—and may also ask to review records such as prior psychiatric or academic testing, school-based accommodation plans, or medical records.

Sometimes a clinician may recommend a structured behavioral observation, where you and your child are given specific tasks to complete while being observed. This type of assessment is more likely if a child has behavioral challenges or neurodevelopmental concerns, and less likely if the concern is anxiety-related. All of these pieces help the clinician put together a complete puzzle, which results in a diagnostic summary and recommendations for treatment.

Neuropsychological evaluation

A neuropsychological evaluation may sometimes be recommended, particularly if there is a question about a neurodevelopmental condition like ADHD or a learning difference like dyslexia, or to better understand difficulties with memory, information processing, attention, social skills, or executive functioning. A neuropsychological evaluation is much more extensive than a psychodiagnostic evaluation and often takes place over several multihour testing sessions. It's unlikely that a neuropsychological evaluation would be recommended to diagnose an anxiety disorder, unless there is a co-occurring concern. For example, a neuropsychological evaluation can help clarify whether difficulties with attention and organization are due to ADHD, other deficits in executive functioning, or anxiety—or all three. Or a neuropsychological evaluation could be recommended following a concussion, where shifts in mood and anxiety can pop up along with physical symptoms like nausea, fatigue, and headaches. In these cases, neuropsychological evaluations can help the clinician tease apart the relationship between symptoms and make recommendations to aid recovery.

Anxiety Disorders

Anxiety disorders tend to emerge in childhood, and the most common age of onset is eleven years old. Teenagers are more likely to meet criteria for an anxiety disorder than elementary-school-aged children, and females are more likely to meet criteria than males.

Generally speaking, anxiety disorders and their symptoms are pretty similar in adults and kids; there aren't different social anxiety disorder symptoms for kids versus adults, for example. Most of the differences we see are due to differences in developmental stage. So younger kids with any anxiety disorder may cling, cry, and tantrum when distressed, and older kids and adults may be more likely to snap at others or experience a panic attack when anxiety ramps up. Differences in how the symptoms interfere in life are also largely due to development. Kids are more likely to stop extracurricular activities because of anxiety, while adults are more likely to stop dating; young kids who seek nonstop reassurance are more likely to turn to their parents, while teens and adults are more likely to turn to their peers or partners.

One caveat is that kids may be more likely to complain of the physical symptoms that accompany anxiety, like stomachaches, headaches, or "I just don't feel good," as opposed to communicating about the source of their fears. This is because kids are undergoing massive changes in brain development and may not yet be able to accurately identify and talk about their fears. To be fair, this can be hard for adults, too.

The anxiety disorders of the DSM-5-TR are all characterized by fear or anxiety that is *excessive,* meaning the fear is out of proportion to what most people would be likely to experience given the same stressors. And the focus of the fear is what differentiates one anxiety disorder from another. Let's consider each of the anxiety disorders in turn.

Separation anxiety disorder

We expect to see separation anxiety in infancy, and it is a sign that the baby is forming a healthy attachment to primary caregivers. Beyond early childhood, however, persistent and interfering separation anxiety is an anxiety disorder. At its core, it's a fear of being separated from caregivers, usually due to a fear that something bad will happen—injury, kidnapping, abandonment, disasters, or death—to the child or the caregivers when they are apart. Scary stuff.

Given these overwhelming fears, kids may cry, tantrum, or panic when separating from caregivers. These are the kids who follow parents around from room to room, terrified of what might happen if parents leave their sight. Separation anxiety makes it difficult to go places that require being apart from caregivers—school, friends' houses, extracurricular activities—and also makes it tough for caregivers to leave the home. No date nights for the parents of these kids. For kids, this diagnosis will be assigned once the separation anxiety concerns have been getting in the way for at least four weeks.

Adults can meet criteria for separation anxiety disorder as well. This is more likely to look like fear of being away from a close family member, like a spouse, and may manifest as texting excessively, becoming dependent on tracking software, or limiting activities that would take you away from your "safety" person. In adults, symptoms need to be interfering for at least six months to warrant a diagnosis.

Selective mutism

Selective mutism is a condition in which people with the ability to speak do not do so in situations where they need to speak. It is much more prevalent in children than adults. Kids with selective mutism can speak—there are no speech, cognitive, developmental, or language-based delays that impair speech. Instead, kids with selective mutism speak in front of select people and in certain places—typically around family members and at home—but refuse to speak in front of others because of anxiety. Sometimes they do speak but briefly and at a nearly inaudible volume. These kids appear to freeze up in situations where speech is expected—at school, in restaurants, even with extended family members or close friends. Consequently, their difficulty speaking leads to a range of challenges with making friends, keeping up at school, or engaging in other developmentally appropriate activities.

If this pattern persists for at least one month—not counting the first month of school—a selective mutism diagnosis is warranted. Effective treatment for selective mutism involves the child and their caregivers, as it is crucial that caregivers change how they respond in order to break the cycle that drives the disorder.

Specific phobias

A phobia occurs when there is a rapid increase in fear around a specific object or situation. There are different categories of phobias, including the animal subtype (fear of dogs, insects, snakes, etc.) and the natural environment subtype (fear of heights, bodies of water, storms, etc.). There is the blood-injection-injury subtype, which includes fears of seeing blood, getting vaccinations, or having blood drawn, medical procedures, and injury. Situational-type phobias include fear of flying or fear of small spaces like elevators. Other common phobias include vomit phobia (emetophobia) and fears of costumed characters.

The most common phobia stimuli would have been adaptive for

our early ancestors to avoid. This is why modern humans are much more likely to develop phobias around situations that could have actually been dangerous for our early ancestors—like death from deadly snakes or contracting illness from blood or vomit—than we are to develop phobias of less lethal stimuli.

Kids with specific phobias are likely to demonstrate their distress by tantruming or crying. This can be the case with teenagers or adults, too, but because older kids and adults have more control over their lives, they are more likely to be able to restructure their routines in order to avoid the things they are afraid of.

You can hate snakes, get really uncomfortable around needles, or really dislike flying, but that may not be enough to warrant a disorder unless it's interfering in daily life. For example, a specific phobia of vomiting may lead you to restrict what you eat to a point that you become malnourished. Or it may lead you to stop going anywhere in public—to school, to work, to stores or restaurants—because you are afraid to contract germs that might lead to vomiting. Or it can lead to problems with other family members or siblings, like when a family member gets a stomach bug, and the child's fear of vomiting causes so much stress in the family that the sick family member is sent to a hotel. A specific phobia is only assigned when the fear causes significant interference in daily life for at least six months.

Social anxiety disorder

Most of us can feel a bit self-conscious around others, and we may be concerned that we might do or say something that will lead people around us to judge us harshly. Remember, this fear was adaptive—early humans who were rejected died alone in the wilderness. Social fears evolved because they motivated the "fitting in" that was necessary for survival in small groups in a dangerous world. No one wants to get voted off the island.

Social anxiety disorder is the extreme version of this concern, in which the fear of judgment by others is pervasive, excessive, and interfering. Out of all of the anxiety disorders, it is the most common. People coping with social anxiety feel constantly in the spotlight, worrying that they will say or do something that will be viewed as embarrassing or offensive. Common fears driving this disorder are that you will be seen as stupid, annoying, unlikable, or unwanted. This leads to avoidance of situations that open up the possibility of being judged by others—that is, most social situations.

People with social anxiety disorder avoid parties, playdates, extra-curriculars, school, or work, not because they don't want to do the activities, but because doing so means human interaction, leaving them vulnerable to being judged. Kids with social anxiety disorder may avoid drawing attention to themselves at school by never raising their hand in class, refusing to seek help from teachers, or avoiding participation in anything performance-related, like school musicals, even if they are Broadway aficionados. If you have social anxiety disorder, you may avoid eating or drinking in public because of concerns that others will think you are "gross." You may avoid getting haircuts because that would require small talk with the stylist. Dating or parties can feel out of the question without alcohol or drugs to take the edge off.

One of the painful consequences of social anxiety is that the fears can become self-fulfilling. If you are worried that the people at a party don't like you, you are likely to be more reserved, to keep to yourself. As a consequence, other people are more likely to view you as stand-offish, disinterested, maybe even kind of rude. They are then less likely to engage with you, which you will see as confirmation of your fear that no one likes you. So you leave the party early and are more likely to decline similar invitations in the future. As this pattern repeats, it's easy to see how, over time, people struggling with social anxiety can become more and more socially isolated, bolstering beliefs in their unlovability.

Social anxiety disorder captures fears that are *out of proportion* to the risk. But people can be terrible, and sometimes there is a valid reason that someone is afraid in social situations. Marginalized people may have very real concerns about judgment in situations where bias and prejudice are at work. Kids who have a history of bullying or are victims of harassment or discrimination have valid, learned fears of social situations. That does not mean that a social anxiety disorder is *never* an appropriate diagnosis for someone with a history of being discriminated against; rather, it highlights the importance of considering the environment in addition to the person when making a diagnosis.

Panic disorder

To understand panic disorder, you need to first understand panic attacks. *Panic attack* is the term for experiencing the physical and cognitive symptoms of anxiety intensely and all at once. It is the purest manifestation of the fight-or-flight response. You automatically jump into high gear when you perceive a threat, as your body shifts energy to the large muscle groups that need it most to fight or flee. This involves changes in your breathing patterns and heart rate to send more oxygen rapidly around your body. A panic attack is due to the consequences of this automatic shift: increased heart rate, hyperventilation, sweating, trembling, hot or cold flashes, dizzyness or lightheadedness, a feeling of choking, and nausea or stomach distress. These uncomfortable sensations can trick you into thinking that you are losing control, going crazy, or even dying.

Experiencing at least four of these symptoms at one time qualifies as a panic attack. Panic attacks typically peak within about ten minutes and then start to decrease in intensity. Sometimes panic attacks have a clear cause and occur in response to stressful situations. But panic attacks can also be unexpected or "uncued," meaning that there is no easily identifiable trigger or stressor. These attacks appear to come from out of the blue, sometimes showing up while people are "doing nothing," like reading a book or walking home from school. They can be even more disturbing because they feel so unpredictable. There can even be panic attacks that happen during sleep, where people are jolted awake by overwhelming symptoms.

Having panic attacks alone isn't enough for a diagnosis of panic disorder; in fact, many other mental and physical health conditions, including other anxiety disorders, can be accompanied by panic attacks. In contrast, people with panic disorder have repeated, unexpected panic attacks and become so afraid of having another one that they change their behavior to try to avoid future ones. This is why, at its core, panic disorder is *the fear of fear*: It is the fear of experiencing future panic.

For a diagnosis of panic disorder, there need to be repeated panic attacks and at least a month of changes in behavior to avoid future panic attacks. There may be places you won't go or things you won't do because you are afraid that you will have a panic attack. Kids and adults alike have a hard time returning to a place where they once had a panic attack—like school, work, or a certain restaurant or business. You may avoid doing anything that might bring up a panic-like sensation. Kids drop out of sports or dance and adults stop exercising, drinking caffeine, or pursuing sexual activity because of the panic-like symptoms that arise.

Agoraphobia

Agoraphobia is when people are afraid of certain situations because they are afraid that they will have a panic attack or otherwise lose control—embarrassing or endangering themselves or others. If you have agoraphobia, you may be afraid of crowded places like stadiums, malls, or standing in lines—not because these places themselves are scary, but because you fear that if you have a panic attack or a medical issue, escaping would be difficult or embarrassing. You might be terrified of taking public transportation like planes, subways, or buses, or you might be afraid of riding within enclosed spaces like elevators or cars because you are afraid to be "stuck" somewhere that you couldn't escape or get help. So it's not a specific phobia of flying or grocery stores that's at play, it's the fear of having an issue in these situations where escaping or getting help would be difficult, embarrassing, or both.

People with agoraphobia worry about developing panic-like symptoms, which is why panic attacks and/or panic disorder often show up alongside this condition. In addition to fears of having a panic attack in a situation where you can't escape, you may also be afraid of embarrassing or incapacitating consequences, like being unable to get to a bathroom in time or falling and becoming injured. As with many other anxiety disorders, agoraphobia is assigned if the fears and interference have been present for at least six months.

Think of all the ways you would be driven to restructure your life if you were overwhelmed by agoraphobia. You would do your best to avoid anywhere new where you might become distressed and feel "trapped." This could include any unknown places, like a classmate's home or a new gym, or even familiar places like school or work where it would be seen as odd to just get up and leave. It could also include places where it's nearly impossible to leave quickly—like an airplane midflight, a concert, or the middle of a bridge. If you couldn't avoid these places entirely, you would be anxiously mapping out exit routes, clocking the closest bathroom, or looking up the nearest hospital before you went. You would likely need to have "safety" people with you, meaning that you ultimately would be dependent on others to do anything outside the home. Over time, the things that you felt comfortable doing, the places you felt comfortable going, and the people around whom you felt safe would become more and more limited. Kids and adults can both become housebound in the face of agoraphobia.

Generalized anxiety disorder

People with generalized anxiety disorder worry most of the day, every day. The worry is out of proportion to actual stressors in their life, and it's hard to control. These are the folks whose answer to the question "Do you find yourself worrying, even when there isn't anything to worry about?" is emphatically "*Yes*, I will find something."

Worry puts your body on high alert, priming you to act if danger appears. Your body and mind are going to feel the effects of being in a constantly hypervigilant state, so generalized anxiety disorder is marked by uncomfortable physical and cognitive symptoms: feeling restless or on edge, being easily fatigued, and experiencing irritability, difficulty concentrating, muscle tension (backaches, shoulder aches, tension headaches, and stomach distress are common), and sleep disruption. In adults, a generalized anxiety diagnosis needs to include persistent worry for at least six months, along with at least three of these additional symptoms. For kids, only one additional symptom, in addition to persistent worry, is required for the diagnosis.

If you have generalized anxiety disorder, you are typically worried about the same sorts of normal stressful things that most people worry a bit about, but the worry is on overdrive. You worry about how you are performing in school or at work; being liked and accepted by others; your health and safety and the health and safety of those you love; and community and world events like crime, politics, climate change, and worries about the future. You struggle with the unexpected and uncertain, so changes in plans can send you reeling. You may be highly perfectionistic. To try to cope with this worry, you may rigidly adhere to routines, trying to exert control and predictability in an often uncontrollable and unpredictable world. Or you get sucked into rabbit holes of information-gathering, hoping to arm yourself with knowledge and plans to build security. Or you seek constant reassurance from others that you have said, done, or thought the "right" thing.

Many people do these behaviors to some extent, and some worry is of course normal. The difference between normal worry and generalized anxiety disorder is the over-the-top nature of the worries, the high level of distress caused by these worries, and the physical and cognitive symptoms that accompany the worry.

Kids may have a hard time talking about their worries, given that their brains are still developing, and so relying on a kid to be able to tell you why they are worried and about what may be a fool's errand.

Irritability is a more easily observable symptom in kids, as are physical complaints like having a headache or stomachache. Difficulty concentrating and academic struggles may also be red flags that a kid is struggling with unspoken worries.

Postpartum anxiety disorder

Our diagnostic system is always evolving to reflect updates in research and understanding of mental health conditions. To this effect, our understanding of perinatal mood and anxiety disorders—meaning clinically interfering anxiety or depression that begins somewhere between pregnancy and following childbirth—is a work in progress. While the *International Classification of Diseases,* 11th Revision (ICD-11) includes a category for "mental or behavioural disorders associated with pregnancy, childbirth, or the puerperium," these disorders aren't listed in the DSM-5-TR.

Symptoms of anxiety disorders related to pregnancy can include persistent and excessive worry, a perpetual feeling that something bad may be about to happen, panic-like symptoms, restlessness, irritability, and difficulties with eating or sleeping, on top of the expected sleep disturbances that come with having an infant. These experiences can get in the way of the ability to connect with or enjoy your new baby and make an already stressful period that much more difficult.

Sadly, perinatal mood and anxiety disorders are underrecognized and undertreated, and stigma around these conditions persists. Many parents struggling with anxiety and depression during this time feel deeply ashamed that they are "failing at joy." Misunderstandings about the safety and benefits of available treatments can deter women from seeking needed care.

But things are getting better. Providers are increasingly aware of the vulnerabilities that birthing parents face given the many physical, social, and emotional shifts of the period around pregnancy. And universal screening for mood and anxiety disorders related to pregnancy is now common practice at follow-up visits after giving birth. Organizations like Postpartum Support International (PSI) offer a ton of resources, from virtual peer support groups to provider referrals. As with all the anxiety disorders that we have discussed, there is help, and treatments are available.

Co-Occurring and Related Conditions

Anxiety disorders often co-occur with one another and with other mental health conditions. In fact, having multiple anxiety disorders is the norm, rather than the exception, even in kids.

A few conditions tend to go along with anxiety disorders, particularly in young people. I want to highlight diagnoses that commonly co-occur with—or are misidentified as—anxiety disorders in kids to give you a broader understanding. As with anxiety disorders, the presentation of these disorders in kids and adults is often pretty similar, once we account for developmental factors.

Obsessive-Compulsive Disorder (OCD)

There is a ton of overlap between OCD and anxiety disorders, and with good reason: OCD used to be classified as an anxiety disorder. However, brain-based research has shown that the neurobiology of OCD is distinct from anxiety disorders, and OCD is now housed in a separate "Obsessive-Compulsive and Related Disorders" section of the DSM-5 along with conditions like body dysmorphic disorder, excoriation (skin-picking) disorder, and trichotillomania (hair-pulling disorder).

As the name implies, obsessive-compulsive disorder includes obsessions and compulsions. An obsession is an intrusive and upsetting thought, image, or impulse that sort of pops into your mind and "sticks." This could range from a violent mental image of something terrible happening to your parents, the thought that your hands are contaminated with germs, or an inexplicable urge to push your friend into traffic. It could be an overwhelming drive to organize your belongings so that they are "just right," the thought that you didn't unplug your space heater, or a disturbing sexual image. These obsessions keep popping up, and people describe them as getting "stuck" in their minds. Obsessions cause a ton of emotional distress, often in the form of fear, but other negative emotions like shame or disgust are also common. In response, the person feels driven to *do something* to suppress or neutralize the obsession.

Enter compulsions, which are behaviors that the person feels that they must do to get rid of or neutralize the obsession. This includes behaviors you can see, like excessive handwashing to neutralize contamination fears, or checking outlets to be sure you unplugged the heater. It can also include unobservable mental acts, like praying to get rid of a violent image or counting in sets of threes to suppress an urge to push someone. Compulsions can have a superstitious quality to them, like avoiding the cracks in the sidewalk because you feel that otherwise your parents will die. Folks with OCD recognize that this behavior is irrational but still feel driven to complete compulsions.

While compulsions provide short-term relief from upsetting obsessions, they actually make things worse in the long term, and the obsessive-compulsive cycle snowballs. If you have OCD, you may find yourself spending hours a day in compulsive cleaning, checking, straightening, counting, stepping, or praying rituals in attempts to neutralize or suppress obsessions, until the cycle dominates your life.

OCD can be easily confused with generalized anxiety disorder, as obsessions can seem like excessive worry. By and large, the worries of generalized anxiety disorder tend to be excessive versions about realistic concerns, like worries about whether you will do well in school. In contrast, the obsessions in OCD tend to have more of a peculiar, unrealistic quality, like an intrusive thought that you might be a pedophile even though the idea of that is abhorrent to you, or the thought that your loved ones will get hurt unless you erase and rewrite a sentence until it looks "perfect."

There is a difference between "being obsessed" with something and the obsessions of OCD. For example, parents sometimes seek

OCD treatment for their child who they believe is "obsessed" with videogames. But the core feature of OCD-based obsessions is that they cause emotional distress—they are unwanted thoughts or urges that are upsetting—whereas being "obsessed" with videogames implies that the child really likes videogames. Thinking about videogames and playing videogames is enjoyable for the kid—even if it's disruptive. In contrast, the obsessions and the compulsions of OCD are unwanted, distressing experiences.

Post-Traumatic Stress Disorder (PTSD)

"I was totally traumatized" is now a common way to express that something was upsetting. Relatedly, people often look back on difficult events and stressors, like the death of a grandparent or a move to a new town, and call them traumas because they were an upsetting change. And there is the tendency in modern culture to characterize normal stressors as traumas, like getting rejected from a college or being excluded by classmates. However, the traumas associated with mental health disorders are distinctly different from the things that anxiety can tell us is scary or the regular, if not unhappy, stressors of life. Trauma-based disorders like PTSD are defined first and foremost by the experience of a distinct trauma.

A trauma, as defined in the DSM-5-TR, occurs when there is exposure to actual or threatened death, injury, or sexual violence. The event can be directly experienced by the person or witnessed as it happened to others. A trauma can also include learning that actual or threatened death, injury, or violence happened to a loved one, or it can involve repeated exposure to the traumas of others, as experienced by first responders. Notably, traumas do not apply to exposure to traumatic experiences as seen through electronic media, movies, TV, or pictures.

Sadly, traumas are not uncommon. An estimated 70 percent of the world's adult population has experienced at least one traumatic event, and over 30 percent of those folks reported experiencing four or more traumas. But not everyone who experiences a trauma will develop PTSD, which is characterized by the occurrence of a trauma *plus* a number of distressing emotional, cognitive, and behavioral changes in response to the trauma that cause distress and interference across the person's daily life and relationships, for at least a month.

There are certainly areas of symptom overlap between anxiety disorders and PTSD: sleep disturbances, irritability, hypervigilance, difficulty concentrating, and avoidance of certain people, places, or situations, to name a few. However, if there is no traumatic event, there is no PTSD. This is different from anxiety disorders, which don't need to have a defined, triggering event that kicked off the distress. People with PTSD may also meet criteria for other anxiety and mood disorders, but PTSD is distinct from anxiety disorders.

Attention Deficit/Hyperactivity Disorder (ADHD)

Imagine that your seven-year-old kid has been struggling in class. His teachers say he is constantly fidgeting. He is having difficulty staying on task, and teachers have to repeat directions multiple times. He has been requesting more bathroom breaks. He has been acting out uncharacteristically and has been sent out of the classroom several times for interrupting, often during more challenging academic tasks. His teachers suggest that he may have ADHD.

These symptoms certainly look like ADHD, and it would be totally understandable if you sought consultation with your child's pediatrician and asked about medication-based treatments. However, symptoms of ADHD overlap with many other conditions, and it is important to be thorough before jumping to diagnostic conclusions. For parents, knowing a bit about what to look for can be helpful.

ADHD is considered a neurodevelopmental disorder, which means it has to do with the way a person's brain grows and develops. ADHD and other neurodevelopmental disorders, like communication disorders or learning disorders, emerge in childhood. To receive a diagnosis of ADHD, symptoms have to have been present and interfering during childhood, no later than age twelve. Even if ADHD isn't diagnosed until adulthood, symptoms can't just emerge from out of the blue at age twenty-five. Diagnosis should involve considering the person's childhood history. It requires that the symptoms of inattention or hyperactivity were present and getting in the way in multiple settings—home, school, and in public—prior to age twelve.

Of course, boundless energy and minuscule attention spans are hallmarks of early childhood, but a four-year-old with ADHD is likely to be *even more* inattentive or *even more* hyperactive than their peers. It should stand out. In addition, the inattentive or hyperactive behaviors need to be present and interfering across situations—if a child only shows problematic hyperactivity at home but doesn't have any difficulty at school or in public, ADHD is probably not an accurate diagnosis. This means that in addition to learning about the child's developmental history, confirming an ADHD diagnosis typically involves getting information from multiple people who know the child well—caregivers and teachers.

Let's circle back to our seven-year-old. If this child's inattentive and disruptive behavior is new for this year's teachers but is pretty much his M.O. since preschool, then yes, ADHD may be at play. In contrast, if it's new—if this is a kid who doesn't have a history of significant restlessness, concentration difficulties, or acting out—there may be something else going on.

ADHD shares many symptoms with anxiety disorders, particularly with generalized anxiety disorder: difficulty with attention and concentration, avoidance of tasks that need sustained attention, and restlessness. So, both as a parent and as an assessing clinician, I would want to know: Is he struggling to concentrate because of a brain-based difficulty with attention, or because he is preoccupied with worries or hypervigilant to potential dangers? Is he taking bathroom breaks because he physically can't sit still, or because the bathroom breaks give him a breather when he feels overwhelmed by anxiety? Is he interrupting because he struggles with impulse control, or is acting out a coping strategy? Has he learned that when he faces a hard task, he can get sent out of class and escape the demand if he is disruptive? Many anxious kids "act out" as a way to avoid challenging or anxiety-provoking situations; going to the principal's office feels safer than feeling unable to do schoolwork.

Whenever possible, a neuropsychological evaluation is best for confirming a diagnosis of ADHD. This is because it can be difficult to disentangle ADHD from anxiety or other conditions when we are relying only on self- or parent report, but neuropsychological tests can do so with more confidence.

Can someone meet criteria for both ADHD and anxiety disorders? Of course, and this is frequently the case. Nearly one in four adults with generalized anxiety disorder also meet criteria for ADHD, and children with ADHD are four to six times as likely to also have generalized anxiety disorder compared to children without ADHD. While these disorders may co-occur, the brain-based mechanisms driving them differ, and so do the treatments. The main treatments for ADHD, which include psychiatric medications plus strategies to shape behavior, are way less helpful if ADHD isn't actually part of the picture and can even make things worse.

While they are distinct, treatments for anxiety and ADHD can be complementary; a combination of behavioral therapies and psychiatric medications is the gold-standard treatment for both. And while ADHD medications can have a side effect of increasing anxiety, the benefits of medication targeting ADHD can sometimes override any anxiety-related side effects. So effective treatment for one doesn't necessarily prohibit effective treatment for the other, but the more diagnostic clarity you have, the better targeted the treatment.

Autism spectrum disorders

Like ADHD, autism spectrum disorders—commonly referred to as autism—are lifelong neurodevelopmental disorders identifiable in early childhood. Autism represents a huge range of symptom presentation, ability level, and functioning but is characterized by differences in social communication and the presence of restricted interests or behaviors. Many folks with autism experience co-occurring behavioral health conditions. Anxiety disorders are among the most frequent comorbid diagnoses, and social anxiety disorder, specific phobias, and generalized anxiety disorder are common in individuals with autism.

Anxiety symptoms are often linked to autism features. Given sensory processing and social communication differences, autistic people often report high levels of anxiety associated with sensory overload (such as loud noises and crowds) and often experience elevated anxiety in response to uncertainty, changes in routine, or unstructured social situations. Sadly, differences in social communication and restricted interests and behaviors can mean that individuals with autism are more vulnerable to bullying and victimization, which exacerbates anxiety.

CBT remains the frontline treatment recommendation for autistic people with co-occurring anxiety disorders, with modifications to better address the intersection of autism features and anxiety. Group-based CBT may be particularly beneficial, as it provides opportunities for social anxiety exposures and social skills training.

School avoidance or refusal

School avoidance, or school refusal, is not actually a diagnosis. It's a *behavior* that refers to difficulty attending school or remaining in class for the entire day. It captures a range in attendance problems, from kids who go to school but with lots of distress and pleading to complete absence from school for an extended period of time.

School avoidance behavior has several different causes. We use the term "emotionally based school avoidance" to characterize school avoidance driven by disorders like anxiety and depression. This is distinct from school avoidance that is caused by other factors, like truancy, which is typically due to oppositional behavior or disengagement from school. It is crucial for parents and educators to recognize that avoidance fuels school refusal. The behavior itself—avoiding or refusing school—actually becomes the thing that keeps it going, because the more you avoid school, the more likely you are to avoid school in the future. You have to understand the function that school avoidance behavior serves for a given child in order to address it properly; in other words, what does refusing school *do* for the child that makes it likely to happen again in the future? If avoiding school decreases anxiety—meaning that anxiety is driving the school refusal behavior—you need to treat the anxiety to address the school refusal.

I am very serious when I say that school refusal is a crisis for the child's development. Because avoiding school is *so reinforcing,* this is a very hard cycle to break. Think about it. If your choice is to go to school where you feel distressed, or stay home in your comfort zone, you are *always* going to stay home if you can. But the more you stay home, the harder it is to go back to school. You miss out on class material, so when you do go back you feel behind. You also lose out on social interactions, so you feel out of the loop with your friends. As kids become more socially disconnected and more academically behind, anxiety about school quickly snowballs, and avoiding school becomes that much more reinforcing. Combating anxiety-based school refusal is most effective if the child, parent, treatment providers, and school personnel are all working together toward the same goal—to get the child back to school as quickly as possible to break the cycle of avoidance and anxiety.

Depression

Major depressive disorder, more commonly called "depression," is often the unwelcome buddy of anxiety disorders. As anxiety disorders are the extreme version of the normal emotions of fear and anxiety, depression is the extreme version of the normal emotion of sadness. Depression describes a sadness that is very different from what you could expect to feel if a pet died or a friend moved away; it means a distinct period of at least two weeks of constant depressed mood—feeling deeply sad, hopeless, empty, or irritable, or being unable to feel interest or pleasure from the things that used to bring enjoyment. In addition to one or both of these symptoms, a depressive episode includes changes in activity, appetite or weight, and sleep behaviors; fatigue; difficulty concentrating or making decisions; feelings of worthlessness or guilt; or thoughts about death and suicide.

There are a few ways in which depression can present differently in kids than in adults. One of the main symptoms required to meet criteria for major depressive disorder is depressed mood, for most of the day, every day, for at least two weeks. However, in kids, this criterion can be met if the mood is irritable, rather than depressed. And yes, teenagers are basically irritable by definition, but this is a different, almost universal irritability—these kids will seem angry at everyone and with everything, all the time.

Sadly, kids with depression who are primarily irritable often go undiagnosed and untreated, because they don't "seem sad," and irritability is too often dismissed. Or they get misdiagnosed. The adults in kids' lives may be subject to bias when they identify depression in kids. Compared to their white peers, Black youth with depression in the United States are much more likely to be diagnosed as having an impulse control disorder or behavioral problems, which will lead to the wrong treatment for kids who are already struggling with not only mental health concerns but the additive stressors that often accompany minority status. So persistent irritability is definitely a red flag for depression in children and adolescents.

There may also be differences in how we view the symptom of changes in appetite or weight. In adults, depression can come with noticeable changes in weight or appetite. In kids, however, we expect to see weight gain across development, and growth spurts are normal. So we are more concerned that changes in weight in kids may be a symptom of depression if there is failure to make expected weight gain, in addition to either rapid weight loss or gain.

Coping with Anxiety and Depression

What if you—or your child—are coping with both anxiety and depression? Should you prioritize treatment for one over the other? There is a fair amount of overlap between treatments for anxiety and depression, so you may not need to focus on one versus the other. That being said, it can be helpful when communicating with providers if you have a sense of which condition is "primary," meaning which is the more severe and interfering.

For example, sometimes the depression is so impairing that you don't regularly make it to treatment or can't practice the anxiety-fighting strategies learned in sessions. This may be because depression is impacting your ability to do the basic activities of daily living like getting out of bed, showering, or managing your time. Or, even more worryingly, sometimes depression is driving suicidal thoughts and behaviors. In these scenarios, depression would likely be considered primary and treatment goals would center on safety and stabilization.

In circumstances where depression isn't interfering in treatment, anxiety-based interventions can offer many benefits. As treatment prioritizing anxiety disorders progresses, depression often starts to naturally improve, even though it's not directly being targeted, as you start to feel more hopeful and more confident about your ability to manage your symptoms. And sometimes you just don't know until you try. Treatment is an opportunity for ongoing assessment, which sheds light on the most important areas to target as you go.

GLOSSARY

Active ignoring: a behavioral management technique where a caregiver deliberately removes their attention from a child's undesirable behaviors while remaining emotionally present and ready to reinforce positive behaviors

Amygdala hijack: an immediate and overwhelming response to negative emotions that bypasses rational thinking due to the activation of the amygdala, the brain's emotional processing center

Authoritative parenting: a parenting style defined by high responsiveness and high demandingness, in which parents set clear rules and expectations while also being warm, supportive, and responsive to their child's needs

Cognitive behavioral therapy (CBT): a structured, evidence-based approach to the psychological treatment of emotional disorders that emphasizes identifying and shifting negative thought patterns and behaviors that drive emotional distress and impairment. CBT is the gold-standard approach to treating anxiety disorders across the lifespan

Cognitive defusion: a cognitive coping concept that involves creating distance and detaching from unhelpful thoughts, rather than allowing them to drive behavior. The goal of cognitive defusion is to see thoughts as just words or mental events—not absolute truths or commands that must be followed

Cognitive fusion: a state of becoming overly entangled with thoughts, such that they are seen as absolute truths, commands, or direct reflections of reality. In this state, thoughts strongly influence emotions and behaviors, leading to distress and unhelpful actions. Also known as "getting hooked"

Cognitive restructuring: a cognitive coping technique that involves identifying, challenging, and modifying negative or distorted thought patterns to develop more balanced and helpful thinking. Also known as cognitive reappraisal

Concerted cultivation: a parenting style that involves actively and deliberately fostering a child's talents, skills, and abilities through a variety of structured activities and close parental involvement

Dialectic: a process of reasoning used to explore and resolve contradictions between opposing ideas. A dialectic occurs when two things that seem contradictory are actually true at the same time

Distress intolerance: the perceived inability to tolerate and manage emotional pain, discomfort, or distress without resorting to problematic coping strategies

Emotion socialization: the process through which children learn about emotions, how to express them, and how to regulate them, primarily through interactions with caregivers and family members

Emotionally based school avoidance: school avoidance or refusal behavior that is driven by emotional disorders like anxiety and depression; distinct from school avoidance that is caused by other factors, like truancy

Experiential avoidance: the tendency to avoid, control, or suppress unpleasant thoughts, emotions, memories, or physical sensations rather than confronting or accepting them

Exposure therapy: the cardinal component of cognitive behavioral treatment for anxiety and related disorders that helps individuals confront and reduce the fear or anxiety associated with specific objects, situations, or memories through controlled, gradual exposure to these stimuli. Also called exposure with response prevention (ERP)

Extinction burst: a temporary increase in the intensity or frequency of a behavior when it is no longer reinforced

Fear and avoidance hierarchy (FAH): a structured, individualized list that ranks anxiety-provoking or distressing situations from least to most anxiety-provoking. The goal is to provide a road map for helping individuals face their fears in a controlled, manageable way through graduated exposure practices

Habituation: the process through which an individual's emotional response to a stimulus gradually decreases over time as they are repeatedly exposed to it and "get used to it"

Inhibitory learning: the process through which individuals learn new, non-fearful associations to a previously feared stimulus, which reduces the intensity of their fear response. Inhibitory learning involves creating new learning that weakens or inhibits the old fear-based responses

Intensive Parenting: one of the most dominant and influential concepts in understanding the contemporary parenting ideals and practices of Western countries; a highly involved approach to parenting where parents place a strong emphasis on being constantly present, monitoring and managing almost every aspect of their child's life; it involves significant time, effort, and resources spent on optimizing a child's outcomes

Invalidation: the act of dismissing, belittling, or rejecting another person's feelings, thoughts, or experiences; can be intentional or unintentional, but it typically leads to feelings of shame, isolation, or confusion

Mindfulness: the practice of paying focused, nonjudgmental attention to one's experience in the present moment—including thoughts, feelings, bodily sensations, and the surrounding environment—and observing these experiences without attempting to change, avoid, or judge them

Negative reinforcement: occurs when a person engages in a behavior to avoid or eliminate something unpleasant, which leads to an increase in the likelihood of that behavior being repeated in the future

Parental accommodation: actions taken by parents to help alleviate or prevent their child's anxiety, distress, or compulsive behaviors, particularly in the context of anxiety and related disorders

Parental determinism: the belief that a child's behavior, emotional responses, or mental health outcomes are primarily determined by their parents' actions, decisions, or parenting style

Positive-opposite behavior: the active opposite of a harmful or unwanted behavior, framed in a positive, constructive way that promotes healthier or more functional responses

Positive reinforcement: occurs when a behavior is followed by something rewarding, which increases the likelihood of that behavior being repeated in the future

Psychological flexibility: the ability to be open to and aware of whatever is happening in the moment, while also being able to take effective, values-driven action, rather than being controlled by negative emotions, thoughts, or past experiences; a skill set that allows individuals to adapt to life's challenges and uncertainties in ways that align with their deeper values, instead of getting stuck in unhelpful patterns of behavior or thought

Safety behaviors: actions or strategies that individuals use to prevent or minimize perceived danger or discomfort during a feared situation, which provide temporary relief but reinforce the fear by preventing the person from learning that the feared event is unlikely to occur; also called safety signals

Subjective Units of Distress (SUDS): a scale from 0 to 10 used to rate how intensely a person is experiencing their anxiety/distress at any given moment

Supportive statement: an empathetic and confidence-building verbal response that acknowledges the child's emotional experience while providing validation and encouragement, based on the equation that support = acceptance + confidence

Validation: the act of acknowledging and accepting another person's experience, thoughts, or feelings as understandable and acceptable. Validation involves recognizing and respecting the emotional experience of the other person and helping them feel heard, accepted, and supported

White-knuckling: the process of going through the motions of an exposure while at the same time trying to control or suppress the uncomfortable feelings that arise; enduring a feared situation by trying to push through discomfort without actually engaging in the process of confronting or processing fear in a healthy way

NOTES

Introduction

3   **rates of pediatric anxiety disorders:** Bitsko, R. H., Holbrook, J. R., et al. (2018). Epidemiology and impact of health care provider–diagnosed anxiety and depression among US children. *Journal of Developmental and Behavioral Pediatrics, 39*(5), 395–403. https://doi.org.10.1097/DBP.0000000000000571.

3   **Anxiety disorders are:** Kessler, R. C., Berglund, P., et al. (2005). Lifetime prevalence and age-of-onset distributions of DSM-IV disorders in the National Comorbidity Survey Replication. *Archives of General Psychiatry, 62*(6), 593–602. https://doi.org/10.1001/archpsyc.62.6.593; Merikangas, K. R., He, J.-P., et al. (2010). Lifetime prevalence of mental disorders in U.S. Adolescents: Results from the National Comorbidity Survey Replication–Adolescent Supplement (NCS-A). *Journal of the American Academy of Child and Adolescent Psychiatry, 49*(10), 980–89. https://doi.org/10.1016/j.jaac .2010.05.017.

3   **identification of anxiety disorders has certainly improved:** Pediatric anxiety disorders have been increasing over the past twenty years. Data from the National Survey of Children's Health (NSCH), an annual parent-report survey of U.S. families, found that in 2003, 5.4 percent of parents of kids ages six to seventeen reported that they had been told by a healthcare provider that their child had an anxiety disorder. By 2011–2012, this percentage increased to 8.4 percent. This rate increased between 2016 and 2019 to 9.4 percent, meaning that on the threshold of the pandemic, nearly one in ten school-aged kids were diagnosed with an anxiety disorder by a healthcare provider. Then along came COVID, and child anxiety doubled: In 2021, nearly one in five kids globally were experiencing elevated anxiety symptoms. See Bitsko, R. H., Holbrook, J. R., et al. (2018). Epidemiology and impact of health care provider–diagnosed anxiety and depression among US children. *Journal of Developmental and Behavioral Pediatrics, 39*(5), 395–403. https://doi.org.10 .1097/DBP.0000000000000571; Bitsko, R. H., Clauseen, A. J., et al. (2022). Mental health surveillance among children—United States, 2013–2019.

Mortality and Morbidity Weekly Report (MMWR) Supplement, 71(2), 1–42. https://doi.org.10.15585/mmwr.su7102a1; Racine, N., McArthur, B. A., et al. (2021). Global prevalence of depressive and anxiety symptoms in children and adolescents during COVID-19: A meta-analysis. *JAMA Pediatrics,* 175(11), 1142–50. https://doi.org.10.1001/jamapediatrics.2021.2482.

4   **the dominance of smartphones:** Haidt, J. (2024). *The anxious generation: How the great rewiring of childhood is causing an epidemic of mental illness.* Penguin Press.

4   **the decrease in childhood independence:** Skenazy, L. (2021). *Free-range kids: How parents and teachers can let go and let grow.* Wiley.

4   **pressures to achieve:** Wallace, J. B. (2023). *Never enough: When achievement culture becomes toxic—and what we can do about it.* Portfolio/Penguin.

4   **mental health experts themselves:** Shrier, A. (2024). *Bad therapy: Why the kids aren't growing up.* Sentinel.

4   **in 2021, the U.S. Surgeon General:** Office of the Surgeon General (OSG). (2021). *Protecting youth mental health: The U.S. Surgeon General's advisory.* U.S. Department of Health and Human Services.

4   **kids with unmet healthcare needs:** Lebrun-Harris, L. A., Ghandour, R. M., et al. (2022). Five-year trends in US children's health. *JAMA Pediatrics,* 176(7), e220056. https://doi.org.10.1001/jamapediatrics.2022.0056.

4   **Less than two-thirds:** Ghandour, R. M., Sherman, L. J., et al. (2019). Prevalence and treatment of depression, anxiety, and conduct problems in US children. *Journal of Pediatrics,* 206, 256–67. https://doi.org.10.1016/j.jpeds .2018.09.021.

4   **kids from racial or ethnic minority populations:** Fante-Coleman, T., & Jackson-Best, F. (2020). Barriers and facilitators to accessing mental healthcare in Canada for Black youth: A scoping review. *Adolescent Research Review,* 5(2), 115–36. https://doi.org.10.1007/s40894-020-00133-2; Bitsko, R. H., Claussen, A. H., et al. (2022). Mental health surveillance among children—United States, 2013–2019. *Mortality and Morbidity Weekly Report (MMWR) Supplement,* 71(2), 1–42. https://doi.org/10.15585/mmwr.su7102a1.

4   **up to *twenty-one times* as much:** Bodden D. H. M., Dirksen, C. D., & Bögels, S. M. (2008). Societal burden of clinically anxious youth referred for treatment: A cost-of-illness study. *Journal of Abnormal Child Psychology,* 36(4), 487–97. https://doi.org/10.1007/s10802-007-9194-4.

4   **untreated anxiety disorders:** Pine, D. S., Cohen, P., et al. (1998). The risk for early-adulthood anxiety and depressive disorders in adolescents with anxiety and depressive disorders. *Archives of General Psychiatry,* 55(1) 56–64. https:// doi.org/10.1001/archpsyc.55.1.56; Roza, S. J., Hofstra, M. B., et al. (2003). Stable prediction of mood and anxiety disorders based on behavioral and emotional problems in childhood: A 14-year follow-up during childhood, adolescence, and young adulthood. *American Journal of Psychiatry,* 160(12), 2116–21. https://doi.org/10.1176/appi.ajp.160.12.2116.

4   **odds of suicidal thinking:** Boden, J. M., Fergusson, D. M., & Horwood, J. L.

(2007). Anxiety disorders and suicidal behaviours in adolescence and young adulthood: Findings from a longitudinal study. *Psychological Medicine, 37*(3), 431–40. https://doi.org/10.1017/S0033291706009147.

5   **Between 2016 and 2020:** Lebrun-Harris, L. A., Ghandour, R. M., et al. (2022). Five-year trends in US children's health. *JAMA Pediatrics, 176*(7), e220056. https://10.1001/jamapediatrics.2022.0056.

5   **over two-thirds of parents believe:** Auxier, B., Anderson, M., et al. (2020, July 28). *Parenting children in the age of screens.* Pew Research Center: Internet, Science & Tech. https://www.pewresearch.org/internet/2020/07/28/parenting-children-in-the-age-of-screens/.

5   **in 2024, the U.S. Surgeon General:** Murthy, V. (2024, August 28). *Parents under pressure: The U.S. Surgeon General's advisory on the mental health & well-being of parents.* United States. Public Health Service. Office of the Surgeon General.

5   **And new research reinforces:** Daw, J. R., MacCallum-Bridges, C. L., & Admon, L. K. (2025). Trends and disparities in maternal self-reported mental and physical health. *JAMA Internal Medicine.* Advance online publication. https://doi.org/10.1001/jamainternmed.2025.1260.

5   **declining parent mental health:** Bennett, A. C., Brewer, K. C., & Rankin, K. M. (2007). The association of child mental health conditions and parent mental health status among U.S. children. *Maternal and Child Health, 16*(6) 1266–75. https://doi.org.10.1007/s10995-011-0888-4.

8   **how to deal with their negative emotions:** O'Neil Rodriguez, K. A., & Kendall, P. C. (2014). Suicidal ideation in anxiety-disordered youth: Identifying predictors of risk. *Journal of Clinical Child and Adolescent Psychology, 43*(1), 51–62. https://doi.org/10.1080/15374416.2013.843463.

8   **On the extreme end of this:** Brewer, A. G., Doss, W., et al. (2022). Trends in suicidal ideation-related emergency department visits for youth in Illinois: 2016–2021. *Pediatrics, 150*(6), e2022056793. https://doi.org/10.1542/peds.2022-056793.

11   **By developing psychological flexibility:** Harris, R. (2019). *ACT made simple* (2nd ed., p. 8). New Harbinger.

Chapter 1: In My Feelings

17   **a set of universal human emotions:** Izard, C. E. (2007). Basic emotions, natural kinds, emotion schemas, and a new paradigm. *Perspectives on Psychological Science: A Journal of the Association for Psychological Science,* 2(3), 260–80. https://doi.org/10.1111/j.1745-6916.2007.00044.x.

18   **In contrast, negative emotions:** Nesse, R. M. (2004). Natural selection and the elusiveness of happiness. *Philosophical transactions of the Royal Society of London. Series B, Biological sciences,* 359 (1449), 1333–47. https://doi.org/10.1098/rstb.2004.1511.

Chapter 2: We're *All* Freaking Out (and That's Okay!)

33 **Evolutionary psychiatrist Randolph Nesse:** Nesse, R. M. (2004). Natural selection and the elusiveness of happiness. *Philosophical transactions of the Royal Society of London. Series B, Biological sciences, 359*(1449), 1333–47. https://doi.org/10.1098/rstb.2004.1511.

40 *amygdala hijack:* Siegel, D. J., & Payne Bryson, T. (2011). *The whole-brain child: 12 revolutionary strategies to nurture your child's developing mind* (p. 42). Bantam Books.

Chapter 3: Is This Normal?

50 **some improvements to their sleep:** Crowe, K., & Spiro-Levitt, C. (2024). Sleep-related problems and pediatric anxiety disorders. *Psychiatric Clinics of North America, 47*(1), 213–28. https://doi.org/10.1016/j.psc.2023.06.014.

50 **The American Academy of Sleep Medicine:** Paruthi, S., Brooks, L. J., et al. (2016). Consensus statement of the American Academy of Sleep Medicine on the recommended amount of sleep for healthy children: Methodology and discussion. *Journal of Clinical Sleep Medicine, 12*(11), 1549–61. https://doi.org/10.5664/jcsm.6288.

Chapter 4: How Avoidance Fuels Anxiety

70 **leaning into rather than away from anxiety:** Kazdin, A. E. (2009). Understanding how and why psychotherapy leads to change. *Psychotherapy Research, 19*(4–5), 418–28. https://doi.org/10.1080/10503300802448899; Kazdin, A. E., & Kendall, P. C. (1998). Current progress and future plans for developing effective treatments: Comments and perspectives. *Journal of Clinical Child Psychology, 27*(2), 217–26. https://doi.org/10.1207/s15374424jccp2702_8.

70 **Kids get a ton of information:** Nimphy, C. A., Venetikidi, M., et al. (2023). Parent to offspring fear transmission via modeling in early life: A systematic review and meta analysis. *Clinical Child and Family Psychology Review, 26*(3), 751–72. https://doi.org/10.1007/s10567-023-00448-1.

74 **Supportive statements are a tool:** The developer of an evidence-based parent-based treatment for anxiety disorders, Dr. Eli Lebowitz, notes that supportive statements are a two-ingredient recipe, like macaroni and cheese; you can't have one without the other and still call it a meal. We need both. See Lebowitz, E. R. (2021). *Breaking free of child anxiety and OCD: A scientifically proven program for parents* (pp. 108–15). Oxford University Press.

Chapter 5: The Intensive Parenting Paradox

84 **more engagement with "InstaMum" accounts:** Moujaes, M., & Verrier, D. (2021). Instagram use, InstaMums, and anxiety in mothers of young children.

Journal of Media Psychology: Theories, Methods, and Applications, 33(2), 72–81. https://doi.org/10.1027/1864-1105/a000282.

86 **U.S. sociologist Sharon Hays:** Hays, S. (1996). *The cultural contradictions of motherhood.* Yale University Press.

86 **In her book *The Cultural Contradictions of Motherhood:*** Hays, S. (1996). *The cultural contradictions of motherhood* (p. 9). Yale University Press.

87 **primarily mothers:** Men are increasingly involved in parenting and can be influenced by the Intensive Parenting norms as well. However, by and large mothers continue to be more likely to internalize the messages of Intensive Parenting while fathers are more likely to reject or dismiss them. See Faircloth, C. (2014). Intensive fatherhood? The (un)involved dad. In E. Lee, J. Bristow, C. Faircloth, & J. Macvarish (Eds.), *Parenting culture studies* (pp. 184–99). Palgrave Macmillan.

88 **modern parents dedicate way more time:** Gauthier, A. H., Smeeding, T. M., & Furstenberg, F. F., Jr. (2004). Are parents investing less time in children? Trends in selected industrialized countries. *Population and Development Review,* 30(4), 647–72. https://doi.org/10.1111/j.1728-4457.2004.00036.x.

88 **particularly parents with higher levels of education:** Dotti Sani, G. M., & Treas, J. (2016). Educational gradients in parents' child-care time across countries, 1965–2012. *Journal of Marriage and Family,* 78(4), 1083–96. https://doi.org/10.1111/jomf.12305.

88 **the Intensive Parent should be knowledgeable:** Cucchiara and Steinbugler articulate this well when they write, "Contemporary models of motherhood expect more than nurture and sacrifice; modern mothers must also be highly skilled and well-informed." Cucchiara, M., & Steinbugler, A. C. (2021). "The books make you feel bad": Expert advice and maternal anxiety in the early 21st century. *Sociological Forum,* 36(4), 939–61. https://doi.org/10.1111/socf.12748.

89 **Though identified in the 1990s:** Scholars note the intensification of intensive parenting following advances in brain development studies. Wall, G. (2010). Mothers' experiences with intensive parenting and brain development discourse. *Women's Studies International Forum,* 33(3), 253–63. https://doi.org/10.1016/j.wsif.2010.02.019.

89 **an article in *The Atlantic:*** Pinsker, J. (2019, January). Intensive parenting is now the norm in America. *The Atlantic.* https://www.theatlantic.com/family/archive/2019/01/intensive-helicopter-parenting-inequality/580528/.

89 **even more vulnerable:** Faircloth, C. (2014). Intensive parenting and the expansion of parenting. In E. J. Lee, J. Bristow, et al. (Eds.), *Parenting culture studies* (pp. 25–51). Palgrave Macmillan.

89 *concerted cultivation:* Lareau, A. (2011). *Unequal childhoods: Class, race, and family life* (2nd ed., pp. 1–13). University of California Press.

90 **Seventy-one percent of parents of young adults:** This is known as parental determinism, a principle that emphasizes parents' childrearing practices as crucial determinants of child outcomes. See Pew Research Center. (2023, January 24). *Parenting in America today.* https://www.pewresearch.org/social-trends/2023/01/24/parenting-in-america-today.

90   **how Intensive Parenting pressures and beliefs play out:** Minnotte, K. L. (2023). Decentering intensive mothering: More fully accounting for race and class in motherhood norms. *Sociology Compass,* 17(8), https://doi.org/10.1111/soc4.13095; Verduzco-Baker, L. (2017). I don't want them to be a statistic: Mothering practices of low-income mothers. *Journal of Family Issues,* 38(7), 1010–38. https://doi.org/10.1177/0192513X15610616.

90   **parents from across social classes show similar, positive attitudes:** Ishizuka, P. (2019). Social class, gender, and contemporary parenting standards in the United States: Evidence from a national survey experiment. *Social Forces,* 98(1), 31–58. https://doi.org/10.1093/sf/soy107.

90   **This naturally disadvantages:** Minnotte, K. L. (2023). Decentering intensive mothering: More fully accounting for race and class in motherhood norms. *Sociology Compass,* 17(8), Article e13095. https://doi.org/10.1111/soc4.13095.

90   **can become a vehicle for judging:** Minnotte writes, "Yet, mothers operating from other racialized and classed locations have at once both been informed by their own motherhood norms and judged by intensive mothering norms, despite historical and structural circumstances that necessitate other forms of mothering." Minnotte, K. L. (2023). Decentering intensive mothering: More fully accounting for race and class in motherhood norms. *Sociology Compass,* 17(8), Article e13095. https://doi.org/10.1111/soc4.13095.

91   **a form of "status safeguarding":** Milkie, M. A., & Warner, C. H. (2014). Status safeguarding: Mothers' work to secure children's place in the social hierarchy. In L. R. Ennis (ed.), *Intensive mothering: The cultural contradictions of modern motherhood* (pp. 66–85). Demeter Press.

91   **Nate G. Higler argues:** Higler, N. G. (2022, October 20). Stop pretending that intensive parenting doesn't work: It's expensive and time-consuming. But the data proves that kids benefit. *The Atlantic.* https://www.theatlantic.com/ideas/archive/2022/10/intensive-parenting-kids-happiness-health/671782/.

91   **A 2021 study:** Yerkes, M. A., Hopman, M., et al. (2021). In the best interests of children? The paradox of intensive parenting and children's health. *Critical Public Health,* 31(3), 349–60. https://doi.org/10.1080/09581596.2019.1690632.

92   **"The focus on probable risks for children's health . . .":** Yerkes, M. A., Hopman, M., et al. (2021). In the best interests of children? The paradox of intensive parenting and children's health. *Critical Public Health,* 31(3), 357. https://doi.org/10.1080/09581596.2019.1690632.

92   **mothers who identify more strongly:** Rizzo, K. M., Schiffrin, H. H., & Liss, M. (2013). Insight into the parenthood paradox: Mental health outcomes of intensive mothering. *Journal of Child and Family Studies,* 22(5), 614–20. https://doi.org/10.1007/s10826-012-9615-z.

92   **Intensive Parenting was cited by the U.S. Surgeon General:** Murthy, V. (2024, August 28). *Parents under pressure: The U.S. Surgeon General's advisory on the mental health & well-being of parents.* United States. Public Health Service. Office of the Surgeon General.

Chapter 6: Overparenting

96   **The Pew Research Center's 2023 survey:** Pew Research Center. (2023, January 24). Parenting in America today. https://www.pewresearch.org/social-trends/2023/01/24/parenting-in-america-today.

96   **studies of child development:** Krohne, H. W., & Hock, M. (1991). Relationships between restrictive mother-child interactions and anxiety of the child. *Anxiety Research,* 4, 109–24; Budinger, M. C., Drazdowski, T. K., & Ginsburg, G. S. (2013). Anxiety-promoting parenting behaviors: A comparison of anxious parents with and without social anxiety disorder. *Child Psychiatry and Human Development,* 44(3), 412–18. https://doi.org/10.1007/s10578-012-0335-9.

96   **factors that can protect against child anxiety:** Remmes, C. S., & Ehrenreich-May, J. (2014). Parental emotion regulation strategy use and responses to youth negative affect. *Journal of Cognitive Psychotherapy,* 28(1), 34–47. https://doi.org/10.1891/0889-8391.28.1.34.

97   **Any way you slice it:** Bögels, S. M., & Brechman-Toussaint, M. L. (2006). Family issues in child anxiety: Attachment, family functioning, parental rearing and beliefs. *Clinical Psychology Review,* 26(7), 834–56. https://doi.org/10.1016/j.cpr.2005.08.001.

97   **Additionally, parental warmth:** Butterfield, R. D., Silk, J. S., et al. (2021). Parents still matter! Parental warmth predicts adolescent brain function and anxiety and depressive symptoms 2 years later. *Development and Psychopathology,* 33(1), 226–39. https://doi.org/10.1017/S0954579419001718.

97   **The other side of this coin:** Donovan, C. L., & Spence, S. H. (2000). Prevention of childhood anxiety disorders. *Clinical Psychology Review,* 20(4), 509–31. https://doi.org/10.1016/S0272-7358(99)00040-9; Kidd, K. N., Prasad, D., et al. (2022). The relationship between parental bonding and mood, anxiety and related disorders in adulthood: A systematic review and meta-analysis. *Journal of Affective Disorders,* 307, 221–36. https://doi.org/10.1016/j.jad.2022.03.069.

97   **positive social support:** Donovan, C. L., & Spence, S. H. (2000). Prevention of childhood anxiety disorders. *Clinical Psychology Review,* 20(4), 509–31. https://doi.org/10.1016/s0272-7358(99)00040-9.

97   **"emotion coaching philosophy":** Gottman, J. M., Katz, L. F., & Hooven, C. (1996). Parental meta-emotion philosophy and the emotional life of families: Theoretical models and preliminary data. *Journal of Family Psychology,* 10(3), 243–68. https://doi.org/10.1037/0893-3200.10.3.243.

98   **Approaches that fall:** Pezalla, A. E., Davidson, A. J., & Clark, M. D. (2024). "Trying to remain calm . . . but I do reach my limit sometimes": An exploration of the meaning of gentle parenting. *PloS One,* 19(7), e0307492. https://doi.org/10.1371/journal.pone.0307492.

98   **parents with better emotion regulation skills:** Zimmer-Gembeck, M. J., Rudolph, J., et al. (2022). Parent emotional regulation: A meta-analytic review of its association with parenting and child adjustment. *International*

Journal of Behavioral Development, 46(1), 63–82. https://doi.org/10.1177/01650254211051086.

98 **Tutoring can help kids academically:** Guryan, J., Ludwig, J., et al. (2023). Not too late: Improving academic outcomes among adolescents. *American Economic Review,* 113(3), 738–65. https://doi.org/10.1257/aer.20210434.

98 **Participation in structured extracurricular activities:** Makles, A., & Schneider, K. (2017). Extracurricular educational programs and school readiness: Evidence from a quasi-experiment with preschool children. *Empirical Economics,* 52(4), 1181–1204. https://doi.org/10.1007/s00181-016 -1119-z; Felfe, C., Lechner, M., et al. (2016). Sports and child development. *PloS One,* 11(5), e0151729. https://doi.org/10.1371/journal.pone.0151729.

98 **more financial resources:** Killingsworth, M. A. (2021). Experienced well-being rises with income, even above $75,000 per year. *Proceedings of the National Academy of Sciences—PNAS,* 118(4), 1–6. https://doi.org/10.1073/pnas.2016976118.

99 **particularly ones that include physical activity:** Zhu, X., Haegele, J. A., & Healy, S. (2019). Movement and mental health: Behavioral correlates of anxiety and depression among children of 6–17 years old in the US. *Mental Health and Physical Activity,* 16, 60–65. https://doi.org/10.1016/j.mhpa.2019.04.002.

99 **A degree of parental monitoring:** Rothon, C., Goodwin, L., & Stansfeld, S. (2012). Family social support, community "social capital" and adolescents' mental health and educational outcomes: A longitudinal study in England. *Social Psychiatry and Psychiatric Epidemiology,* 47(5), 697–709. https://doi.org/10.1007/s00127-011-0391-7.

99 **This is what Judith Warner refers to:** Warner, J. (2005). *Perfect madness: Motherhood in the age of anxiety* (p. 3). Riverhead Books.

100 **parenting styles and behaviors:** Chorpita, B. F., & Barlow, D. H. (1998). The development of anxiety: The role of control in the early environment. *Psychological Bulletin,* 124(1), 3–21. https://doi.org/10.1037/0033-2909.124.1.3.

100 **This breeds more dependence:** Hudson, J. L., Comer, J. S., & Kendall, P. C. (2008). Parental responses to positive and negative emotions in anxious and nonanxious children. *Journal of Clinical Child and Adolescent Psychology,* 37(2), 303–13. https://doi.org/10.1080/15374410801955839.

100 **mothers of anxious children:** Hudson, J. L., & Rapee, R. M. (2001). Parent–child interactions and anxiety disorders: An observational study. *Behaviour Research and Therapy,* 39(12), 1411–27. https://doi.org/10.1016/S0005 -7967(00)00107-8.

102 **independence-focused therapy has increasing support:** Independence-focused therapy is an emerging treatment for child anxiety that specifically targets increasing the child's independent activities while simultaneously decreasing parental overinvolvement. See Ortiz, C., & Fastman, M. (2024). A novel independence intervention to treat child anxiety: A nonconcurrent

multiple baseline evaluation. *Journal of Anxiety Disorders, 105,* 102893. https://doi.org/10.1016/j.janxdis.2024.102893.

102   **A recent survey on parenting:** Pew Research Center. (2023, January 24). Parenting in America today. https://www.pewresearch.org/social-trends/2023/01/24/parenting-in-america-today/.

102   **a 2021 study:** Casillas, L. M., Elkins, S. R., et al. (2021). Helicopter parenting style and parental accommodations: The moderating role of internalizing and externalizing symptomatology. *Family Journal, 29*(2), 245–55. https://doi.org/10.1177/1066480720961496.

103   **college-aged kids:** LeMoyne, T., & Buchanan, T. (2011). Does "hovering" matter? Helicopter parenting and its effect on well-being. *Sociological Spectrum, 31*(4), 399–418. https://doi.org/10.1080/02732173.2011.574038.

103   **helicopter parenting and "tiger parenting":** See Tam, H., Kwok, S. Y. C. L., et al. (2018). The moderating effects of positive psychological strengths on the relationship between tiger parenting and child anxiety. *Children and Youth Services Review, 94,* 207–15. https://doi.org/10.1016/j.childyouth.2018.10.012; Zhang, R., & Wang, Z. (2024). Effects of helicopter parenting, tiger parenting and inhibitory control on the development of children's anxiety and depressive symptoms. *Child Psychiatry and Human Development.* https://doi.org./10.1007/s10578-024-01685-3.

103   **Tiger parenting is a bit of a double whammy:** Kim, S. Y., Wang, Y., Orozco-Lapray, D., Shen, Y., & Murtuza, M. (2013). Does "Tiger Parenting" exist? Parenting profiles of Chinese Americans and adolescent developmental outcomes. *Asian American Journal of Psychology, 4*(1), 7–18. http://doi.org/10.037.a0030612.

103   **children at high-achieving schools:** Wallace, J. B. (2019, September 26). Students in high-achieving schools now named an "at-risk" group, study says. *Washington Post.* https://www.washingtonpost.com/lifestyle/2019/09/26/students-high-achieving-schools-are-now-named-an-at-risk-group/.

103   **But the data is clear:** Luthar, S. S., Kumar, N. L., & Zillmer, N. (2020). High-achieving schools connote risks for adolescents: Problems documented, processes implicated, and directions for interventions. *American Psychologist, 75*(7), 983–95. https://doi.org/10.1037/amp0000556.

104   **define the Gentle Parenting construct:** Pezalla, A. E., Davidson, A. J., & Clark, M. D. (2024). "Trying to remain calm . . . but I do reach my limit sometimes": An exploration of the meaning of gentle parenting. *PloS One, 19*(7), e0307492. https://doi.org/10.1371/journal.pone.0307492.

105   **parent with an anxiety disorder:** Bögels, S. M., & Brechman-Toussaint, M. L. (2006). Family issues in child anxiety: Attachment, family functioning, parental rearing and beliefs. *Clinical Psychology Review, 26*(7), 834–56. https://doi.org/10.1016/j.cpr.2005.08.001.

105   **estimated heredity of anxiety disorders:** Kendler, K. S., Neale, M. C., et al. (1992). The genetic epidemiology of phobias in women. *Archives of General Psychiatry, 49,* 273–81.; Gottschalk, M. G., & Domschke, K. (2017). Genetics

of generalized anxiety disorder and related traits. *Dialogues in Clinical Neuroscience,* 19(2), 159–68. https://doi.org/10.31887/DCNS.2017.19.2/kdomschke.

106 **potential dangers in a child's environment:** Lebowitz, E. R., Leckman, J. F., et al. (2016). Cross-generational influences on childhood anxiety disorders: Pathways and mechanisms. *Journal of Neural Transmission,* 123(9), 1053–67. https://doi.org/10.1007/s00702-016-1565-y.

106 **kids then internalize these messages:** Krohne, H. W., & Hock, M. (1991). Relationships between restrictive mother-child interactions and anxiety of the child. *Anxiety Research,* 4(2), 109–24. https://doi.org/10.1080/08917779108248768.

106 **decrease in the freedom we are giving kids:** Gray, P., Lancy, D. F., & Bjorklund, D. F. (2023). Decline in independent activity as a cause of decline in children's mental well-being: Summary of the evidence. *Journal of Pediatrics,* 260, 113352. https://doi.org/10.1016/j.jpeds.2023.02.004.

106 **Anxious parents are more likely:** Settipani, C. A., & Kendall, P. C. (2017). The effect of child distress on accommodation of anxiety: Relations with maternal beliefs, empathy, and anxiety. *Journal of Clinical Child and Adolescent Psychology,* 46, 810–23. https://doi.org/10.1080/15374416.2015.1094741.

106 **They are more likely to believe:** Francis, S. E., & Chorpita, B. F. (2011). Parental beliefs about child anxiety as a mediator of parent and child anxiety. *Cognitive Therapy and Research,* 35(1), 21–29. https://doi.org/10.1007/s10608-009-9255-9.

107 **anxious mothers are more likely to expect:** Cobham, V. E., Dadds, M. R., & Spence, S. H. (1999). Anxious children and their parents: What do they expect? *Journal of Clinical Child Psychology,* 28(2), 220–31. https://doi.org/10.1207/s15374424jccp2802_9.

107 **Anxious parents tend to feel an outsized responsibility:** Apetroaia, A., Hill, C., & Creswell, C. (2015). Parental responsibility beliefs: Associations with parental anxiety and behaviours in the context of childhood anxiety disorders. *Journal of Affective Disorders,* 188, 127–33. https://doi.org/10.1016/j.jad.2015.08.059.

108 *distress intolerance:* Casline, E., Patel, Z. S., et al. (2021). Exploring the link between transdiagnostic cognitive risk factors, anxiogenic parenting behaviors, and child anxiety. *Child Psychiatry and Human Development,* 52(6), 1032–43. https://doi.org/10.1007/s10578-020-01078-2.

108 **Naturally, parents with this tendency:** Cheron, D. M., Ehrenreich, J. T., & Pincus, D. B. (2009). Assessment of parental experiential avoidance in a clinical sample of children with anxiety disorders. *Child Psychiatry and Human Development,* 40(3), 383–403. https://doi.org/10.1007/s10578-009-0135-z.

108 **distress intolerance and experiential avoidance:** McHugh, R. K., Reynolds, E. K., et al. (2013). An examination of the association of distress intolerance and emotion regulation with avoidance. *Cognitive Therapy and Research,* 37(2), 363–67. https://doi.org/10.1007/s10608-012-9463-6.

Chapter 7: The Flexibility Factor

114 **This is the essence of psychological flexibility:** Hayes, S. C., Luoma, J. B., et al. (2006). Acceptance and commitment therapy: Model, processes and outcomes. *Behaviour Research and Therapy*, 44(1), 1–25. https://doi.org/10.1016/j.brat.2005.06.006.

116 **psychological flexibility within parenting:** Brassell, A. A., Rosenberg, E., et al. (2016). Parent's psychological flexibility: Associations with parenting and child psychosocial well-being. *Journal of Contextual Behavioral Science*, 5(2), 111–20. https://doi.org/10.1016/j.jcbs.2016.03.001; Burke, K., & Moore, S. (2015). Development of the Parental Psychological Flexibility Questionnaire. *Child Psychiatry & Human Development*, 46(4), 548–57. https://doi.org/10.1007/s10578-014-0495-x.

116 **Parents with more psychological flexibility:** These positive parenting practices are consistent with the authoritative parenting style first identified by Diana Baumrind. Baumrind, D. (1971). Current patterns of parental authority. *Developmental Psychology Monograph*, 4, 1–103. http://dx.doi.org/10.1037/h0030372.

117 **Unsurprisingly, greater parenting psychological flexibility:** Brassell, A. A., Rosenberg, E., et al. (2016). Parent's psychological flexibility: Associations with parenting and child psychosocial well-being. *Journal of Contextual Behavioral Science*, 5(2), 111–20. https://doi.org/10.1016/j.jcbs.2016.03.001.

122 **A Portuguese study:** Fonseca, A., Moreira, H., & Canavarro, M. C. (2020). Uncovering the links between parenting stress and parenting styles: The role of psychological flexibility within parenting and global psychological flexibility. *Journal of Contextual Behavioral Science*, 18, 59–67. https://doi.org/10.1016/j.jcbs.2020.08.004.

122 **when emotions are high:** Cheron, D. M., Ehrenreich, J. T., & Pincus, D. B. (2009). Assessment of parental experiential avoidance in a clinical sample of children with anxiety disorders. *Child Psychiatry and Human Development*, 40(3), 383–403. https://doi.org/10.1007/s10578-009-0135-z.

127 **Dr. Russ Harris defines values:** Harris, R. (2019). *ACT made simple: An easy-to-read primer on acceptance and commitment therapy* (2nd ed., p. 7). New Harbinger.

127 **in her book *The Family Firm*:** Oster, E. (2021). *The family firm: A data-driven guide to better decision making in the early school years* (pp. 39–45). Penguin Press.

Chapter 8: The Gold Standard

135 **Child and Adolescent Multimodal Treatment Study:** Walkup, J. T., Albano, A. M., et al. (2008). Cognitive behavioral therapy, sertraline, or a combination in childhood anxiety. *New England Journal of Medicine*, 359(26), 2753–66.

135 **But the kids who had a combination:** Piacentini, J., Bennett, S., et al. (2014). 24- and 36-week outcomes for the Child/Adolescent Anxiety Multimodal

Study (CAMS). *Journal of the American Academy of Child and Adolescent Psychiatry*, 53(3), 297–310. https://doi.org/10.1016/j.jaac.2013.11.010.

135 **And when researchers followed up:** Swan, A. J., Kendall, P. C., et al. (2018). Results from the Child/Adolescent Anxiety Multimodal Longitudinal Study (CAMELS): Functional outcomes. *Journal of Consulting and Clinical Psychology*, 86(9), 738–50. https://doi.org/10.1037/ccp0000334.

135 **the "best" approach to treating adult anxiety:** Szuhany, K. L., & Simon, N. M. (2022). Anxiety disorders: A review. *Journal of the American Medical Association*, 328(24), 2431–45. https://doi.org/10.1001/jama.2022.22744.

140 **take steps to slow your breathing:** Jhang, J., Park, S., et al. (2024). A top-down slow breathing circuit that alleviates negative affect in mice. *Nature Neuroscience*, 27(12), 2455–65. https://doi.org/10.1038/s41593-024-01799-w.

148 **Exposure therapy is the key ingredient:** Gosch, E. A., Flannery-Schroeder, E., et al. (2006). Principles of cognitive-behavioral therapy for anxiety disorders in children. *Journal of Cognitive Psychotherapy*, 20(3), 247–62. https://doi.org/10.1891/jcop.20.3.247; Kazdin, A. E. (2009). Understanding how and why psychotherapy leads to change. *Psychotherapy Research*, 19(4–5), 418–28. https://doi.org:10.1080/10503300802448899; Szuhany, K. L., & Simon, N. M. (2022). Anxiety disorders: A review. *Journal of the American Medical Association*, 328(24), 2431–45. https://doi.org/10.1001/jama.2022.22744.

149 **at least half of their sessions:** Kendall, P. C., Hudson, J., et al. (2005). Cognitive-behavioral treatment for childhood anxiety disorders. In E. D. Hibbs & P. S. Jensen (Eds.), *Psychosocial treatments for child and adolescent disorders: Empirically based strategies for private practice* (pp. 47–73). American Psychological Association.

Chapter 9: Unpacking Exposure Therapy

158 **the painstaking process of *habituation*:** Foa, E. B., & McNally, R. J. (1996). Mechanisms of change in exposure therapy. In M. Rapee (Ed.), *Current controversies in the anxiety disorders* (pp. 329–43). Guilford Press.

160 **This principle is called *inhibitory learning*:** Craske, M. (2015). Optimizing exposure therapy for anxiety disorders: An inhibitory learning and inhibitory regulation approach. *Verhaltenstherapie*, 25(2), 134–43. https://doi.org/10.1159/000381574.

Chapter 10: The Comfort Trap

176 ***Parental accommodation* specifically refers to changes:** Lebowitz, E. R., Woolston, J., et al. (2013). Family accommodation in pediatric anxiety disorders. *Depression and Anxiety*, 30(1), 47–54. http://doi.org.10.1002/da.21998.

177 **The vast majority (95 to 98 percent):** Lebowitz, E. R., Woolston, J., et al. (2013). Family accommodation in pediatric anxiety disorders. *Depression and Anxiety*, 30(1), 47–54. https://doi.org.10.1002/da.21998.

177 **and 61 percent of mothers:** Benito, K. G., Caporino, N. E., et al. (2015). Development of the pediatric accommodation scale: Reliability and validity of clinician- and parent-report measures. *Journal of Anxiety Disorders, 29,* 14–24. https://doi.org.10.1016/j.janxdis.2014.10.004.

177 **children with more severe and debilitating anxiety:** See Benito, K. G., Caporino, N. E., et al. (2015). Development of the pediatric accommodation scale: Reliability and validity of clinician- and parent-report measures. *Journal of Anxiety Disorders, 29,* 14–24. https://doi.org.10.1016/j.janxdis.2014.10.004; Kagan, E. R., Frank, H. E., & Kendall, P. C. (2017). Accommodation in youth with OCD and anxiety. *Clinical Psychology Science and Practice, 24*(1), 78–98. https://doi.org./10.1111/cpsp.12186; and Lebowitz, E. R., Woolston, J., et al. (2013). Family accommodation in pediatric anxiety disorders. *Depression and Anxiety, 30*(1), 47–54. https://doi.org.10.1002/da.21998.

177 **these parents end up more anxious:** Most parents report experiencing distress while accommodating, and there is a strong correlation between accommodation and stress and anxiety in moms. See Lebowitz, E. R., Woolston, J., et al. (2013). Family accommodation in pediatric anxiety disorders. *Depression and Anxiety, 30*(1), 47–54. https://doi.org.10.1002/da .21998; Thompson-Hollands, J., Kerns, C. E., et al. (2014). Parental accommodation of child anxiety and related symptoms: Range, impact, and correlates. *Journal of Anxiety, 28,* 765–73. https://doi.org.10.1016/ j.j.anxdis.2014.09.007.

179 **However, one study found:** Twenty-three percent of mothers of children without anxiety disorders reported engaging in at least one daily accommodation behavior. Lebowitz, E. R., Scharfstein, L. A., & Jones, J. (2014). Comparing family accommodation in pediatric obsessive-compulsive disorder, anxiety disorders, and nonanxious children. *Depression and Anxiety, 31,* 1018–25. https://doi.org/10.1002/da.22251.

180 **When determining whether a given parent behavior:** Lebowitz, E. R. (2021). *Breaking free of child anxiety and OCD: A scientifically proven program for parents* (pp. 67–87). Oxford University Press.

181 **studies show how parents' heart rates skyrocket:** Kerns, C. E., Pincus, D. B., et al. (2017). Maternal emotion regulation during child distress, child anxiety accommodation, and links between maternal and child anxiety. *Journal of Anxiety Disorders, 50,* 52–59. https://doi.org.10.1016/j.janxdis .2017.05.002.

191 **Over the last decade:** Lebowitz, E. R., Omer, H., et al. (2014). Parent training for childhood anxiety disorders: The SPACE program. *Cognitive and Behavioral Practice, 21,* 459–69. https://doi.org.10.1016/j.cbpra.2013.10.004.

191 **And this parent-based treatment:** Lebowitz, E. R., Marin, C., et al. (2020). Parent-based treatment as efficacious as cognitive-behavioral therapy for childhood anxiety: A randomized noninferiority study of supportive parenting for anxious childhood emotions. *Journal of the American Academy of Child and Adolescent Psychiatry, 59*(3), 362–72. https://doi.org.10.1016/j .jaac.2019.02.014.

Chapter 11: Ripping Off the Band-Aid

203   **Rewards can be problematic:** Eisenberger, R., & Cameron, J. (1996). Detrimental effects of reward: Reality or myth? *American Psychologist*, 51, 1153–66. https://doi.org/10.1037/0003-066X.51.11.1153.

205   **Dr. Eli Lebowitz:** Lebowitz, E. R. (2021). *Breaking free of child anxiety and OCD: A scientifically proven program for parents.* Oxford University Press.

Chapter 13: When the Sh*t Hits the Fan

233   **This is particularly likely:** Fulton, J. J., Kiel, E. J., et al. (2014). Associations between perceived parental overprotection, experiential avoidance, and anxiety. *Journal of Experimental Psychopathology*, 5(2), 200–211. https://doi .org/10.5127/jep.034813.

237   **In her book *Real Self-Care*:** Lakshmin, P. (2023). *Real self-care: A transformative program for redefining wellness (crystals, cleanses, and bubble baths not included)* (pp. 81–125). Penguin Life.

Chapter 14: Finding Your Way

250   **These approaches are self-paced:** Some self-paced and independently administered online CBT programs for anxiety have seen good effects. See Andrews, G., Basu, A., et al. (2018). Computer therapy for the anxiety and depression disorders is effective, acceptable and practical health care: An updated meta-analysis. *Journal of Anxiety Disorders*, 55, 70–78. https://doi .org/10.1016/j.janxdis.2018.01.001. However, the software for these programs is typically proprietary, developed for a given study, and given the rapid improvement in computer graphics these programs very quickly appear dated.

251   **By and large, research does *not* find:** See Carpenter, A. L., Pincus, D. B., et al. (2018). Working from home: An initial pilot examination of videoconferencing-based cognitive behavioral therapy for anxious youth delivered to the home setting. *Behavior Therapy*, 49(6), 917–30. https://doi .org/10.1016/j.beth.2018.01.007; Comer, J. S., Furr, J. M., et al. (2017). Internet-delivered, family-based treatment for early-onset OCD: A pilot randomized trial. *Journal of Consulting and Clinical Psychology*, 85(2), 178–86. https://doi.org/10.1037/ccp0000155; Gittins Stone, D. I., Elkins, R. M., et al. (2024). Examining the effectiveness of an intensive telemental health treatment for pediatric anxiety and OCD during the COVID-19 pandemic and pediatric mental health crisis. *Child Psychiatry and Human Development*, 55(5), 1398–1412. https://doi.org/10.1007/s10578-023-01500-5.

254   **We know that for kids with anxiety:** Walkup, J. T., Albano, A. M., et al. (2008). Cognitive behavioral therapy, sertraline, or a combination in childhood anxiety. *New England Journal of Medicine*, 359(26), 2753–66. https://doi.org/10.1056/nejmoa0804633.

257 **They can also interfere:** Szuhany, K. L., & Simon, N. M. (2022). Anxiety disorders: A review. *Journal of the American Medical Association, 328*(24), 2431–45. https://doi.org/10.1001/jama.2022.22744.

257 **ACT works about as well as traditional CBT:** Haller, H., Breilmann, P., et al. (2021). A systematic review and meta-analysis of acceptance- and mindfulness-based interventions for DSM-5 anxiety disorders. *Scientific Reports, 11*(1), 20385. https://doi.org/10.1038/s41598-021-99882-w.

257 **many of the strategies in DBT:** Stark, A. M., Tirpak, J. W., et al. (2024). Intensive exposure therapy for an individual with history of self-harm and suicidality. *Cognitive and Behavioral Practice.* https://doi.org/10.1016/j.cbpra.2023.12.005.

259 **A 2009 study showed:** Thomas, K. C., Ellis, A. R., et al. (2009). County-level estimates of mental health professional shortage in the United States. *Psychiatric Services, 60*(10), 1323–28. https://doi.org/10.1176/ps.2009.60.10.1323.

259 **and a 2023 study showed:** Ramesh, T., McBain, R. K., et al. (2023). Mental health outcomes among patients living in US counties lacking broadband access and psychiatrists. *JAMA Network Open, 6*(9), e2333781. https://doi.org/10.1001/jamanetworkopen.2023.33781.

259 **For adults, finding a provider:** Szuhany, K. L., & Simon, N. M. (2022). Anxiety disorders: A review. *Journal of the American Medical Association, 328*(24), 2431–45. https://doi.org/10.1001/jama.2022.22744.

259 **Out-of-network usage:** A study showed that the average reimbursement for all medical healthcare clinician office visits was 21.7 percent higher in 2021 than for all behavioral healthcare clinician office visits. See Mark, T. L., & Parish, W. J. (2024). *Behavioral health parity—pervasive disparities in access to in-network care continue.* RTI International. https://www.rti.org/publication/behavioral-health-parity-pervasive-disparities-access-network-care-continue.

260 **This system massively disincentivizes:** National Public Radio (NPR). (2024, August 25). Finding a therapist who takes your insurance can be nearly impossible. Here is why. NPR. https://www.npr.org/sections/shots-health-news/2024/08/24/nx-s1-5028551/insurance-therapy-therapist-mental-health-coverage.

260 **children from low-income households:** Santiago, C. D., Kaltman, S., & Miranda, J. (2013). Poverty and mental health: How do low-income adults and children fare in psychotherapy? *Journal of Clinical Psychology, 69*(2), 115–26. https://doi.org/10.1002/jclp.21951.

260 **white children are more likely:** Bitsko, R. H., Claussen, A. H., et al. (2022). Mental health surveillance among children—United States, 2013–2019. *Mortality and Morbidity Weekly Report (MMWR) Supplement, 71*(2), 1–42. https://doi.org/10.15585/mmwr.su7102a1.

260 **Latinx youth with anxiety:** In a national study, Latinx children had the highest level of unmet need, with 88 percent of Latinx children in need of mental healthcare not receiving that care. See Kataoka, S. H., Zhang, L., & Wells, K. B. (2002). Unmet need for mental health care among U.S. children:

Variation by ethnicity and insurance status. *American Journal of Psychiatry,* 159(9), 1548–55. https://doi.org/10.1176/appi.ajp.159.9.1548. See also Daskalska, L., Tarima, S., et al. (2024). Child anxiety and depression during the COVID-19 pandemic and unmet mental health care needs. *Child Psychiatry and Human Development.* https://doi.org/10.1007/s10578-024 -01668-4.

264   **one of the very best protections:** Garner, A., & Yogman, M. (2021). Preventing childhood toxic stress: Partnering with families and communities to promote relational health. *Pediatrics,* 148(2), 1. https://doi.org/10.1542/ peds.2021-052582.

Appendix: Decoding Diagnoses

277   **DSM-5-TR:** American Psychiatric Association. (2022). *Diagnostic and statistical manual of mental disorders* (5th ed., text rev.). American Psychiatric Publishing.

290   ***International Classification of Diseases,* 11th Revision (ICD-11):** World Health Organization. (2019). *International classification of diseases for mortality and morbidity statistics* (11th ed.). https://icd.who.int/.

293   **70 percent of the world's adult population:** Benjet, C., Bromet, E., et al. (2016). The epidemiology of traumatic event exposure worldwide: Results from the World Mental Health Survey Consortium. *Psychological Medicine,* 46(2), 327–43. https://doi.org/10.1017/S0033291715001981.

296   **Nearly one in four adults:** Van Ameringen, M., Mancini, C., et al. (2011). Adult attention deficit hyperactivity disorder in an anxiety disorders population: ADHD in anxiety disorders. *CNS Neuroscience & Therapeutics,* 17(4), 221–26. https://doi.org/10.1111/j.1755-5949.2010.00148.x.

296   **children with ADHD are four to six times:** Willcutt, E. G., Nigg, J. T., et al. (2012). Validity of DSM-IV attention deficit/hyperactivity disorder symptom dimensions and subtypes. *Journal of Abnormal Psychology,* 121(4), 991–1010. https://doi.org/10.1037/a0027347.

296   **autism spectrum disorders:** Schiltz, H. K., McVey, A. J., & Lord, C. (2024). Anxiety disorders in autistic people: A narrative review. *Psychiatric Clinics of North America,* 47(4), 753–73. https://doi.org/10.1016/j.psc.2024.04.016.

299   **Black youth with depression:** Martin, R., Banaag, A., et al. (2022). Minority adolescent mental health diagnosis differences in a national sample. *Military Medicine,* 187(7–8), e969–e977. https://doi.org/10.1093/milmed/usab326.

RESOURCES

Blank Three-Component Model (TCM)

Directions: First, identify a recent situation that you'd like to unpack—for example, "my first day of school" or "my son refused to attend his grandmother's birthday party." Next, think back to what you experienced during that situation and identify the feelings, thoughts, and behaviors that you noticed. Recall that the "feelings" section can include both physical sensations (heart pounding, nausea, muscle tension) and emotions (anxiety, stress, anger).

You can also do this exercise in real time—for a current situation. Notice your feelings, thoughts, and behaviors, and pay particular attention to the *urges* that you have to behave a certain way (for example, to yell or to avoid) but that you may or may not give in to.

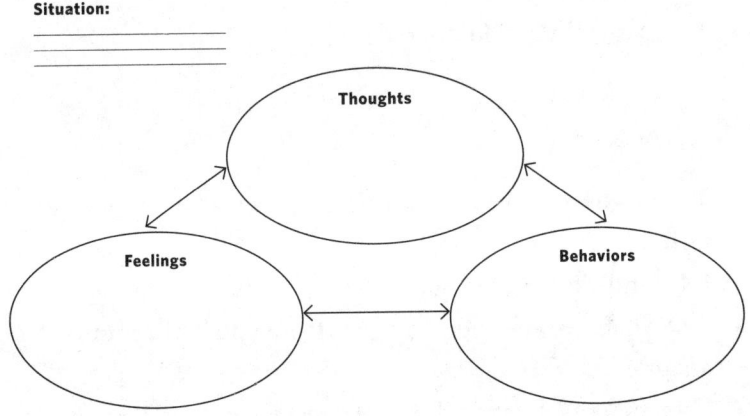

Blank Three-Component Model (TCM)

Validation Cheat Sheet

How to Validate

- Pause, pay attention, and actively listen.
- Get curious.
- Reflect.
- Look for the grain of truth.

Phrases to Get You Started

- "You seem [emotion]."
- "I wonder if you are feeling [emotion]."
- "It makes sense that you would feel [emotion]."
- "I believe you that you are [emotion]."

What to Avoid During Validation

- Less is often more. Sometimes just actively listening, without speaking, is enough.
- Resist the urge to fill the space with lots of talking.
- Resist the urge to jump into problem-solving mode.
- Be mindful of your own reactions.
- Avoid the phrase "I understand how you feel."

Pro Tips

- Take a guess or ask if you aren't sure what the other person is feeling.
- Use "and" instead of "but."
- Ask what the other person needs from you in the moment; don't assume.
- Remember: Validation does not equal agreement. You can validate the emotion without agreeing with or condoning the behavior.

List of Common Parenting Values

Your parenting values describe how you want to parent, now and on an ongoing basis. They describe your heart's deepest desires for your children and your family life, what you want your family to stand for, the aspects of your family life that you prioritize the most, and the personal qualities that you hope your children will prioritize as they grow.

The following chart contains a list of common parenting values. Note that these are common parenting values—not the "right" parenting values. Read through the list below and rate them on a scale of 1 to 3, based on how important they are to you in your role as a parent, where 1 indicates "very important to me," 2 indicates "somewhat important to me," and 3 indicates "not that important to me." Try to reserve 1 for no more than five to ten values.

	Accountability		Flexibility		Open communication
	Achievement		Forgiveness		Perseverance
	Ambition		Friendliness		Physical affection
	Artistry		Friendship		Positive attitude
	Assertiveness		Fun		Realism
	Authenticity		Generosity		Religious faith
	Authority		Gratitude		Resilience
	Caring		Growth/striving		Respect for others
	Civic involvement		Health		Responsibility
	Commitment		Helpfulness		Risk-taking
	Compassion		Honesty		Safety and protection
	Contribution		Humility		Self-acceptance
	Cooperation		Humor		Self-control
	Courage		Independence		Self-reflection
	Courtesy		Industry / hard work		Self-respect

	Creativity		Intimacy		Service
	Critical thinking		Justice/fairness		Simplicity
	Curiosity		Leisure		Spirituality
	Dependability		Love		Supportiveness
	Determination		Love of learning		Tolerance
	Discipline		Loyalty		Tradition
	Engagement		Manners/ politeness		Virtue
	Family		Mastery/ skillfulness		Wealth
	Fitness		Obedience		Other value:

List of Common Personal Values

Your values describe how you want to behave, now and on an ongoing basis. They describe your chosen direction in life; what you want to stand for as a person; how you want to treat yourself, others, and the world around you; and the kind of person you want to be.

The following chart contains a list of common personal values. There is considerable overlap with parenting values. Read through the list and rate each value on a scale of 1 to 3, based on how important they are to you as an individual, where 1 indicates "very important to me," 2 indicates "somewhat important to me," and 3 indicates "not that important to me." Try to reserve 1 for no more than five to ten values.

	Accountability		Friendliness		Pleasure
	Achievement		Friendship		Popularity
	Adventure		Fun		Positive attitude
	Ambition		Generosity		Power
	Artistry		Genuineness		Purpose
	Authenticity		Gratitude		Realism
	Autonomy/ independence		Growth/striving		Religious faith

Beauty	Health	Resilience
Caring	Helpfulness	Respect for others
Civic involvement	Honesty	Responsibility
Comfort	Humility	Risk-taking
Commitment	Humor	Safety and protection
Compassion/ empathy	Industry / hard work	Self-acceptance
Connection	Intimacy	Self-care
Cooperation	Justice/fairness	Self-control
Courage	Kindness	Self-reflection
Courtesy	Leisure	Self-respect
Creativity	Logic	Service
Critical thinking	Love	Sexuality
Curiosity	Loyalty	Simplicity
Dependability	Mastery / skillfulness	Spirituality
Determination	Moderation	Stability
Family	Musicality	Supportiveness
Fitness	Order	Tolerance
Flexibility	Perseverance	Tradition
Forgiveness	Physical affection	Wealth
Other value:	Other value:	Other value:

Common Thinking Traps

- Catastrophizing: Assuming that the "worst ever" outcome is going to happen.
- Jumping to conclusions: Rushing to judgment about a person/ situation/thing without considering all the facts.
- Mind reading: Assuming you know what other people are thinking.

- *Should* statements: Thinking I *should* always be perfect; I shouldn't make mistakes.
- Perfectionistic thoughts: Setting expectations that are too high or saying things to yourself like "I am going to fail" or "I am not good enough unless I do everything perfectly."
- Labeling: Applying broad labels or judgments that ignore nuance and complexity, like "I'm a loser," "I'm bad at my job," or "Life is miserable."
- Ignoring the positive: Not considering the possible good things that could happen, focusing instead on the unwanted outcomes.
- Overgeneralizing: Assuming that because something happened once, it will always happen that way in the future.

Challenge the Thinking Trap

Ask yourself the following questions:
- What do your past experiences tell you about the likelihood that your thought is accurate?
- What do the experiences of other people tell you about the likelihood that your thought is accurate?
- Have there been times when you expected your thoughts to be true, but something else happened instead?
- What might you tell a friend who had the same thoughts?
- How might someone else see your situation?
- Is this thought based on how you *feel* or on actual circumstances?
- Even if this thought were true, how helpful or unhelpful is it for you to act on this thought?

Blank Fear and Avoidance Hierarchy (FAH)

SUDS	Exposure Situation
10	
9	
8	
7	
6	
5	
4	
3	
2	
1	

Recommended Resources

Books

Albano, A. M. (2013). *You and your anxious child: Free your child from fear and worries and create a joyful family life.* Penguin.

Damour, L. (2023). *The emotional lives of teenagers: Raising connected, capable, and compassionate adolescents.* Ballantine Books.

Galanti, R. (2020). *Anxiety relief for teens: Essential CBT skills and mindfulness practices to overcome anxiety and stress.* Zeitgeist.

Harris, R. (2022). *The happiness trap: How to stop struggling and start living* (2nd ed.). Shambhala.

Khanna, M. S., & Kendall, P. C. (2021). *The resilience recipe: A parent's guide to raising fearless kids in the age of anxiety.* New Harbinger.

Kissen, D., Ioffe, M., & Romain, H. (2022). *Overcoming parental anxiety: Rewire your brain to worry less and enjoy parenting more.* New Harbinger.

Lakshmin, P. (2023). *Real self-care: a transformative program for redefining wellness (crystals, cleanses, and bubble baths not included).* Penguin Life.

Lebowitz, E. R. (2021). *Breaking free of child anxiety and OCD: A scientifically proven program for parents.* Oxford University Press.

Oster, E. (2021). *The family firm: A data-driven guide to better decision making in the early school years.* Penguin Press Spark.

Pincus, D. B. (2012). *Growing up brave: Expert strategies for helping your child overcome fear, stress, and anxiety.* Little, Brown Spark.

Sperling, J. (2021). *Find your fierce: How to put social anxiety in its place.* Magination Press.

Online Resources

The American Psychological Association's Therapist Locator: www.locator.apa.org

Anxiety and Depressive Disorders Association of America (ADAA): www.adaa.org

Association for Behavioral and Cognitive Therapies (ABCT): www.abct.org

The National Register of Health Service Psychologists: www.findapsychologist.org

Overcoming Perfectionism: www.overcomingperfectionism.com

Postpartum Support International (PSI): www.postpartum.net

Psychology Today: www.psychologytoday.com

The Society of Clinical Child and Adolescent Psychology: www.effectivechildtherapy.org

Supportive Parenting for Anxious Childhood Emotions (SPACE) Treatment: www.spacetreatment.net

The Unified Protocol Institute: www.unifiedprotocol.com

INDEX

ABC categories, 241
acceptance and commitment therapy
    (ACT), 257
accommodation/parental
    accommodation
  anxiety intensity and, 187–90
  comfort trap and, 185–91
  consequences of, 177
  context for, 180
  cycle of, 185–91
  defined, 103, 303
  examples of, 178, 179
  fear and avoidance hierarchy (FAH)
    for reduction in, 200–202
  flexibility factor regarding, 192–93,
    205–6
  in generalized anxiety disorder, 222,
    234
  overview of, 176–79
  parental values and, 192–93
  parent-based treatment for, 191–92
  positive reinforcement in reducing,
    202–4, 207
  reduction in, 191–92, 198–206
  as reinforcing, 181–82
  setting realistic expectations in,
    198–99
  statistics regarding, 177, 179,
    317n181
  takeaways regarding, 193–94, 206–7
active ignoring, 217–18, 223–24, 301

agoraphobia, 3, 134, 287–88
amygdala hijack, 40, 225, 228, 301
anger, 18, 19, 21, 42
antidepressant medications, 135, 254
anxiety/anxiety disorders
  avoidance as fueling, 7, 60–76, 180
  as beyond normal, 52–58
  characterization of, 3, 37–38
  clinical, 46, 53–57
  cycle of, 66–67
  defined, 34, 52
  expectations of, 36, 106
  experiencing, 22–26
  fear as compared to, 33–34
  as normal, 51–52, 58–59
  overview of, 281–82
  pediatric, 3, 4–5, 205, 305n3
  physical symptoms of, 23, 24, 34–37,
    252
  See also specific disorders
attention deficit/hyperactivity disorder
    (ADHD), 278, 280–81, 294–96
authoritative parenting, 116, 301
autism spectrum disorders, 296–97
avoidance, 7, 8, 21–22, 27, 60–76, 106,
    121–22, 168, 180, 302

battery, internal, 208–25, 226
behavioral/mental healthcare, 247–48,
    251–52, 254–57, 259–66, 319n262.
    See also therapy

ABOUT THE AUTHOR

DR. MEREDITH ELKINS is a clinical psychologist specializing in the research and treatment of anxiety disorders in children, adolescents, and parents. She is a faculty member at Harvard Medical School and the co-program director at the McLean Anxiety Mastery Program (MAMP) at McLean Hospital, an intensive outpatient program for youth with anxiety disorders. She also has a private practice dedicated to addressing anxiety in new and expectant mothers and in parents. Dr. Elkins earned her doctoral degree in clinical psychology at Boston University and completed her postdoctoral fellowship at Columbia University Medical Center. She has contributed to more than sixty academic publications and has been featured in media outlets, including *The Boston Globe, The Wall Street Journal, Parents* magazine, and *The Harvard Gazette.* A native of Baltimore, Dr. Elkins lives on the South Shore of Massachusetts with her husband, their daughter, and their golden retriever, Bromley— who is never anxious about anything.